The
Australian Labor Party
and Federal Politics

The Australian Labor Party and Federal Politics

A Documentary Survey

Edited and introduced by
BRON STEVENS
and
PAT WELLER

MELBOURNE UNIVERSITY PRESS

1976

First published 1976
Printed in Australia by
Wilke and Co. Ltd., Clayton, Victoria 3186, for
Melbourne University Press, Carlton, Victoria 3053
U.S.A. and Canada: International Scholarly Book Services, Inc.,
Box 555, Forest Grove, Oregon 97116
Great Britain, Europe, the Middle East, Africa and the Caribbean:
International Book Distributors Ltd (Prentice-Hall International),
66 Wood Lane End, Hemel Hempstead, Hertfordshire HP2 4RG, England

329.994
A 938

National Library of Australia Cataloguing in Publication data

The Australian Labor Party and federal politics.

Index.
Bibliography.
ISBN 0 522 84094 9.

1. Australian Labor Party—History.
2. Australia—Politics and government—1891–1976.
I. Stevens, Bronwyn Elizabeth, ed. II. Weller, Patrick
Moray, joint ed.   *79-1401*
329.994

Contents

Preface

The Labor party has a long and proud tradition in Australia. This book of documents about its history has been designed to explain how the party works and what part it has played in our country's history. No set of documents could do justice to the wide variety of interests that the party has. We have deliberately taken as many documents as possible from the Labor party's own records as these would be the most difficult for students themselves to find. Where necessary we have supplemented them by the use of newspapers and the occasional private paper. We hope that this selection will be useful for students in secondary schools and tertiary institutions. Occasionally we have used more than one account of the single events; sometimes they are contradictory. These may be useful for historiographical purposes.

We have reproduced all documents as accurately as possible, given the need to commit the original documents to print here. Spellings and typing errors have been corrected. Where sections of a document have been omitted, an ellipsis is inserted. In reproducing sections of the caucus minutes, we have included them as they would have appeared in a final version. Crossings out, additions, etc. are not indicated separately; if readers want to see where they have occurred, they should consult the relevant pages of *Caucus Minutes 1901–1949* (M.U.P., 1975).

We would like to thank the federal parliamentary Labor party for permission to publish excerpts from the caucus minutes, and the various newspapers for permission to reproduce excerpts from their columns. We would also thank Kath Bourke and her fellow-workers in the Political Science department, Research School of Social Sciences, Australian National University, for patiently typing the manuscript, Beverley Lloyd for helping locate some documents, and all those others who have offered advice, gratuitous or otherwise.

We would like to point out that chapter 5 is not a printer's error.

B. E. S.
P. M. W.

Canberra, March 1976

Abbreviations

A.C.T.	Australian Capital Territory
ACTU	
A.C.T.U.	Australian Council of Trade Unions
A.L.P.	Australian Labor Party
AWU	Australian Workers' Union
DLP	Democratic Labor Party
F.P.L.P.	Federal Parliamentary Labor Party
Ind.	Independent
I.W.W.	Industrial Workers of the World
MHR	
M.H.R.	member of the House of Representatives (federal)
M.L.A.	member of the Legislative Assembly (New South Wales, Queensland, Victoria and Western Australia)
M.L.C.	member of the Legislative Council (upper House, all states)
MP	member of parliament
NSW	
N.S.W.	New South Wales
P.L.C.	Political Labor Council
Q.	
Qld	Queensland
S.A.	South Australia
T	
T.	
Tas.	Tasmania
TUDC	Trade Union Defence Committee
V.	
Vic.	Victoria
WA	
W.A.	Western Australia
W.P.O.	Workers Political Organization

Introduction

The Australian Labor Party is the oldest party in Australia. It was first founded in New South Wales and Queensland in 1891 and has been continuously in existence since then. The 1890s were important formative years. The Labor parties were originally founded by trade unions which had previously been the most effective instrument of organization for working men against the wealthier classes. Intent on extending their influence and further persuaded of the need for political action by the failure of the maritime strike in 1890, the unions decided to promote candidates in the elections and founded the Labor parties for that purpose. Many of the attitudes of the unions, and particularly their egalitarian ethos, were carried over into the Labor party. As a result the most striking methods of the party—the caucus, the pledge and the supremacy of the conference over parliamentarians—were irrevocably forged in the 1890s. By 1900 the Labor parties and their organizations were well established in two states and set a precedent which the federal party was to follow.

But in other colonies the Labor party developed more slowly. In Victoria, where the forces of liberalism were well established, its growth was slow, erratic and limited only to Melbourne. In Western Australia no Labor party was formed until 1900 or in Tasmania until 1903. Further, there was little communication between the branches of the party in different colonies, even though some of the larger unions, and particularly the Australian Workers' Union, had union branches in each colony. The colonial Labor parties developed in response to the particular problems and needs of their area and they were shaped partly by the personalities and ambitions of the leading party members. In 1900 delegates from the parties in the four eastern mainland colonies met in a conference in Sydney to discuss a common platform for the first federal election, but they found they had little common ground. Rather than try to reach an agreement on the more divisive issues, they accepted a basic platform of four main planks. Each state party then ran its own electoral campaign. In the 1901 election sixteen Labor members of the House of Representatives and eight senators were elected. They met on 8 May 1901 and decided to form a federal Labor party. Since then the federal Labor party has been in continuous existence.

The party's history has been tinged with disaster. After a highly successful first fifteen years, the party has promised much but achieved comparatively little. Of the first seventy-five years of this century the party has been in office for only nineteen. At first the future looked more hopeful. Although the smallest of the three parties in the first federal parliament, the Labor party gradually increased its strength and twice, in 1904 and 1908, formed a ministry, although in both cases the party was in a minority in the House of Representatives and was soon defeated. In 1910 the party won a clear majority in both Houses and was able to govern comfortably for three years. In 1913 it narrowly lost its majority in the House; but since its Senate majority remained intact, it quickly created the conditions for a double dissolution by rejecting one major piece of legislation twice. A motion in caucus that would have meant the rejecting of supply was defeated out of hand. In the 1914 election, which was contested as war began in Europe, the Labor party won easily in both Houses. Since the party was also by that time in power in four of the states it appeared likely that the Labor party would become the dominant party in the commonwealth. But the triumph of 1914 and Labor control of both Houses have been repeated only once since then, in the six-year period 1943−9.

Labor's assumption of power in 1914 coincided with the beginning of World War I. During the election campaign the party's leader, Andrew Fisher, had promised to support Britain 'to the last man and the last shilling'. The government had to choose between measures which would help to promote the war effort and those which would forward the economic and social objectives of the party. The ministry concentrated on the war effort and introduced among other legislation the War Precautions Act which gave the government wide powers of censorship and the capacity to restrict further civil liberties. Its priorities led to severe criticism from within the party and from the unions. In particular the ministers were attacked for failing to keep prices down and to stamp out black marketeers. The unity of the party was already strained when the new prime minister, W. M. (Billy) Hughes, returned from a trip to Britain determined to introduce conscription for overseas service. The proposal split the party in two. As a concession to the opponents of the proposal in the party Hughes agreed to hold a referendum to seek the approval of the people, but many members of the party and most of the state branches campaigned against the government. The proposal was defeated. When the caucus met on 14 November 1916, Hughes was faced by a vote of censure; rather than wait for his inevitable defeat, he and his followers walked out and formed a national government, uniting his small band of ex-Labor men with the Liberal opposition. The Labor party went into opposition for the next twelve years.

Dissatisfaction with the opportunism of parliamentarians and dismay at the disastrous defeat of the party at the 1917 elections led many to look elsewhere for means of changing society. For a time the trade unions and the Communist party seemed more likely vehicles for success and the Labor party was regarded with disdain. But the Communist party soon proved to be no more effective and the attempt to create a single large union to combat the bosses failed. Gradually support and talent returned to the Labor party and in 1929 it finally regained power. But the time was unfortunate. The worst effects of the great depression were beginning to become obvious and the government was faced by major problems of unemployment, industrial unrest and pressure to reduce government expenditure. The party once again split as members supported different solutions. One small group joined the opposition; another group from New South Wales formed a 'Lang Labor' party. They supported the solutions to the depression's problems that had been proposed by J. T. Lang, the premier of New South Wales. For eight months the government of J. H. Scullin depended on the support of the Lang group to maintain its majority in the House. In November 1931 that support was withdrawn; the Scullin government was defeated on the floor of the House and later annihilated at the polls.

From 1932 to 1941 the party remained in opposition. But after the 1940 election R. G. Menzies' government depended on two independents for its majority and Labor co-operation was needed to ensure that the parliament did not become unworkable and that the war effort remained effective. After some months of ineffective government the two independents became disillusioned with the Menzies—Fadden cabinet and agreed to support a Labor motion of censure. The government was defeated and resigned and John Curtin was sworn in as prime minister. A month later the problems of the new government were immeasurably increased when Japan entered the war.

The Labor governments led by Curtin and his successor, Ben Chifley, represent the high watermark of Labor's fortunes. Even while the war was being fought, new social reforms were planned and gradually implemented. The federal government became more involved in economic management and social services and tried to take over the banking system by nationalization. Although a bill to nationalize the banks passed both Houses of parliament with their safe Labor majorities, it was later declared unconstitutional by the High Court. As the election of 1949 approached, problems mounted for the government. A wave of strikes, the need to reintroduce petrol rationing to preserve foreign currency reserves and the unscrupulous anti-communist propaganda of the opposition helped to undermine the popularity of the government and it was defeated at the polls.

In 1949 no one realized how long the party's stay in the wilderness would be. Its lack of success may have partly been due to the political ability of Menzies, but it was also due to the internal splits and divisions of the Labor party itself. Between 1949 and 1955 the party gradually disintegrated, primarily over the question of communist influence in the party and the trade unions. In 1951 Menzies held a referendum, seeking power to ban the Communist party. Led by its new leader, Dr. H. V. Evatt, most of the Labor party campaigned vigorously and successfully against this attempt to infringe civil liberties. But some sections of the party were as concerned about communist influence as the Liberals and finally in 1955 the party, and particularly the state branches in Victoria and Queensland, split. The sections that were expelled later formed the Democratic Labor party which was largely Catholic in its membership and was virulently anti-communist (and anti-just about everything else). The Labor party itself remained divided and factious and appeared more concerned with its internal fights than with gaining office. In 1961 it came within one seat of victory, but in 1966 was again badly defeated. In that election the party leader, Arthur Calwell, campaigned primarily on a platform of opposition to conscription and the country's military involvement in Vietnam. But support for that undeclared war and irrational fears of communist expansion were still strong in the Australian electorate.

From 1967 to 1972 the party gradually pulled itself from the abyss of despair to electoral victory. This recovery started with the election of Gough Whitlam as leader and with his development of new federal issues such as greater federal involvement in urban renewal and education. It was assisted by the growing antipathy towards conscription and the Vietnam commitment that was epitomized by the mass 'moratorium' demonstrations which brought thousands of protesting citizens onto the streets of Australia's capital cities. After the Labor party gained seats at the 1969 election, the Liberal party also began to disintegrate, and in 1972, amid widespread enthusiasm, the Labor party returned to power. Its aspirations and promise led to high hopes of social change among the electorate.

These hopes did not survive for long. In many areas the Whitlam government was a great success. It revitalized the country's foreign policy, increased expenditure on education and social welfare and supported the causes of many underprivileged groups, like Aborigines, women and migrants. But in other respects it was a disaster. It failed to control inflation and unemployment; the number of people out of work reached the highest level since the great depression. Its ministers became involved in a series of public scandals, particularly over attempts to raise money from Arab sources via shady 'funny money' middlemen. The cabinet often appeared divided, muddled and incapable of finding solutions to the pressing problems of the time.

Yet the Whitlam government was hindered by the fact that it never had a majority in the Senate. Not only was it unable to get its legislation accepted, but it was also at the mercy of an opposition which used the forms of the constitution with unprecedented ruthlessness. In April 1974 they used their numbers in the Senate to block supply and forced a double dissolution. This move challenged the conventional assumption that, as long as a government retained its majority in the House of Representatives, it should retain office. The Labor party narrowly regained office in May 1974. Then, a mere eighteen months later, when the Labor government's reputation had slumped even more, the Senate once again used its numbers and delayed the budget. This time Whitlam refused to call an election, the opposition refused to pass the budget, a stalemate developed and lasted for a month. The government was gradually running out of money and the solidarity of the Liberals was under great strain when the governor-general intervened. He sacked Whitlam and instated Fraser as caretaker prime minister while an election was held. His action brought the office of governor-general into the arena of partisan politics; it effectively endorsed the view that the Senate could, by convention as well as by law, stop the budget and that in future a majority in the lower house was not enough to maintain a government. It also ensured that in future only reliable party hacks would be appointed governor-general.

In the election that followed the dismissal of Whitlam, the Labor party was annihilated. Although it tried to make the constitutional crisis the key issue of the campaign, the levels of inflation and unemployment were so high that the party had little chance of diverting the voters from the economic situation. At the beginning of 1976, as in 1917 and 1932, it was obvious that the party had to face a long hard road back to office.

Two particularly important lessons can be drawn from this brief survey. Firstly, the Labor party was after 1917 only in office at infrequent periods. Few of its incoming ministers had experience in running departments. In 1931 none of Scullin's colleagues had been federal ministers before, although two had been state premiers. In 1941 four ministers only had held junior office under Scullin, while in 1972 none of the incoming cabinet had any ministerial experience at all. This lack of experience could often lead to difficulties and mistakes in their early days of office. Secondly, because of their short periods in office, Labor parties have tended to initiate changes at a phrenetic pace, hoping that when they are defeated the opposition will consolidate these changes. Because the Labor party is the major force for change, it has been called the 'party of initiative' and contrasted with the 'parties of resistance' that are concerned mainly with the preservation of the *status quo*.

To understand how the Labor party works it is necessary to know far more than an outline of its history. It is necessary to know where power lies in the party, who can exercise it and on what principles the party is based. Too often comment on the Labor party is inaccurate because it does not take into account these fundamental factors or assumes that the Labor party works on the same principle as other parties.

The Labor party is based on the assumption that political action should be taken only after the fullest and most democratic discussion of an issue has taken place between all those entitled to participate. Then the decision should be accepted and actively supported by all the participants in the discussion. The most fundamental assumptions of the Labor party are the demands for democracy and solidarity. The party believes that all members of the party should be regarded as equal. Theoretically each member of a branch or affiliated union has an equal voice with every other party member in the formulation of policy or determination of strategy. But since in a party with a large membership the participation of all members on equal terms is obviously impossible, the party accepts a series of basic procedures which are compatible with that fundamental assumption and allow it to be put into some sort of practice. All officials, whether branch delegates, members of the state executive, parliamentary candidates or party leaders, are elected by those they represent and are answerable to them; they have to face regular re-election and can be removed if their performance is unsatisfactory. All officials are regarded as delegates. They are supposed to represent the views of those who elect them and to express those views regardless of their personal opinion. Decisions are reached by taking a vote of all present, with each person having only one vote. Whatever decision receives the support of a majority, all members are bound to accept it, whether it deals with a pre-selection, a question of policy or a matter of tactics. At various times many of these procedures may have been thwarted and ignored, or manipulated to somebody's advantage; but they still lie at the basis of the Labor party's actions and they must be remembered whenever the actions of the Labor party are being discussed.

The federal Labor party consists of four major parts: the six state branches, the federal conference, the federal executive and the parliamentary party (which is generally referred to as the caucus). The power to influence decisions, policies and people is distributed between these bodies and may vary from time to time. Each in turn requires some examination.

The state branches are each run like minor fiefdoms. They control all the internal affairs of the party within the state. Conferences usually meet annually to discuss the state platform and the state executives make all relevant decisions between conferences. Both unions and party branches send delegates to the conference and the conference elects the executive.

Each state branch has its own rules, procedures and membership qualifications. The proportion of unionists who attend the state conferences as official union delegates varies, and so do the voting methods by which the state executive is elected. In some states the members of the local branches pre-select parliamentary candidates; in others the state executive plays a major role. It would therefore be a mistake to assume that all state branches are alike or that the federal party consists of six similar branches, even though the state branches in theory are subordinate to the federal conference or the federal executive on any matters that touch on the commonwealth government.

In fact the state branches still wield the main power on the day-to-day matters of party business. Further they can exert considerable pressure on the federal organs of the party and on the federal parliamentary party. State branches may bind their delegates to the federal executive and conference to support particular positions. More importantly they can threaten the pre-selection of federal members. Without party pre-selection no parliamentarian has any real chance of securing re-election; senators in particular rely on their place on the party ticket for re-election. The power to challenge or change the pre-selection of a member can be a powerful threat, although like most threats it can not be used too often. But one result is that federal members must always be involved in the faction fighting and problems of the local branches; they must attend the meetings of local branches and ensure that their power base in the party is secure if they are to retain their seats. Even though state branches may not be allowed to issue instructions directly to federal members (although they have done so at times), informal pressure on members can be considerable.

There is an even more important reason why the federal Labor party has to maintain harmony with the states. If the state branches are divided or weak, if there are seen to be divisions between the state branches and the federal machine, then the electoral chances of the Labor party at both levels are diminished. This is particularly true where a state Labor government finds that it has marked differences of opinion with a federal Labor government, although it may be able to exert considerable pressure on federal members to persuade the cabinet to change its views. It is important to realize that the federal party is made up of these six state branches and that their influence and their differences of opinion are important factors in determining what action a federal Labor government might take.

The federal conference is the supreme policy-making body of the federal Labor party. It consists of six delegates from each state branch. Recently the four leaders of the federal parliamentary party, the six state parliamentary leaders and delegates from the A.C.T. and the Northern Territory were added. The conference is responsible for drawing up the party platform and for issuing statements of official policy on a wide variety of issues. It also serves as the final court of appeal for any disputes within the party. All decisions of the conference are binding on all members of the party. At first, in 1902, the party platform was simple, limited and direct, consisting of four fighting planks and a few more general objectives. Since then the platform has become far more complex, covering all aspects of the social and economic life of the country. It now covers some forty pages and spells out in detail the measures that the party intends to introduce.

Yet, as so often happens in large organizations, the body that has the formal power is not best suited to use it. With up to forty-eight delegates present and eligible to speak, the process of debate is a cumbersome and not particularly competent way of determining priorities or policies. Often it is more important for a delegate to ensure that he has the support necessary to get a policy accepted in general terms than it is to take care that the actual proposals can be implemented easily. Numbers are more important than brains. Further all conferences are made up of a wide range of delegates who represent a variety of interests; most policies are the result of compromise between these interests.

The power of the conference is also limited by the fact that it meets only once every two or three years, and then only for four or five days. Many decisions have to be made between conferences by the federal executive or the parliamentary party and on these occasions the conference usually can do little but endorse the decision. It has few real sanctions short of expulsion which it can use to coerce disobedient members. The development of a detailed policy does make it difficult for a Labor government to act decisively against the platform; it may act as a means of preventing government action. But it is difficult for conference to force a government to take positive action. The cabinet can argue fairly easily that other priorities are more important or that the time is not yet opportune to implement that particular policy. In these circumstances the conference is usually left without means of enforcing its decisions.

Between conferences its powers are vested in the federal executive which consisted before 1967 of two delegates from each state branch. Since then the four federal leaders and delegates from the A.C.T. and Northern Territory have been included. Decisions of the federal executive are binding on all members and all state branches. Its responsibility is to interpret where necessary the party platform—and considering the ambiguity of some of the planks, this is an important power—and to intervene in the internal affairs of the state branches if it considers action necessary for the good of the party as a whole. The executive can expel any member or any state branch. But the executive's powers have only gradually become established. When it first proposed to become involved in the internal affairs of the New South Wales branch in 1922, the state branch denied that it had any right to interfere; but its objections were overruled. By 1969−70 no one denied that the executive had the right to intervene in Victoria and New South Wales, although there was a question of whether those wanting to intervene had sufficient numbers to do it.

The federal executive is the only body which between conferences has the right to direct caucus, but it itself has often been dominated by parliamentarians, particularly since 1967 when the federal leaders were added to it. Indeed sometimes parliamentary leaders have persuaded the executive to accept proposals as a means of binding dissident members of caucus. It would be wrong to argue that power is ever clearly defined in the Labor party, because one section can often use its personalities, skills and political resources to persuade a different section to adopt views. The system is generally flexible, although when disputes arise, reference is then made to the rules and formal powers.

The most important body of the federal Labor party is undoubtedly the federal parliamentary Labor party, the caucus. It consists of the Labor senators and members of the House of Representatives; no one else is allowed to attend, and this includes all other officials of the party. Caucus is the most important section not because it formally has the supreme power but because it is the body which meets most frequently and is the only group that has the opportunity, through a Labor cabinet, to put the party's policy into effect. Caucus has considerable power. It elects the leader of the party. When the party gains power, the caucus also elects ministers, although the leader retains the right to distribute portfolios. Before 1975 it was always assumed that a Labor prime minister could not dismiss Labor ministers. Then Whitlam's actions proved that he could, as long as he could maintain sufficient support in caucus to endorse his decisions.

In theory all decisions of caucus are binding on caucus and the cabinet, whether those decisions relate to tactics or a piece of legislation. Caucus can reject cabinet decisions, force changes in government policy and instruct the government to introduce particular measures. Sometimes it has done so, and the press has been quick to talk about 'caucus rule'.

But in fact the capacity of caucus to exercise its powers is limited. Cabinet ministers meet regularly throughout the year and can draw on the public service for advice and information. Sometimes the ministers even adopt the policy of voting solidly in caucus in favour of decisions of cabinet. By contrast, caucus meets only when parliament is sitting and then usually only once a week for two or three hours. Even when caucus established a set of committees to consider the new legislation that was to be introduced, these committees seldom had the time to consider the bills in any detail and were able only to react to the rush of the government's business. The backbench members usually have to collect information themselves and they are occupied with such a wide variety of duties that detailed research invariably takes a low priority. In almost every respect cabinet members have advantages over their backbench colleagues in caucus, and not surprisingly most of the cabinet's proposals are accepted. Occasionally one or two cabinet decisions are rejected by caucus, sometimes because it considers that it has not been consulted enough. These actions are a reassertion of its power. But the picture, so commonly portrayed by journalists, of caucus regularly overturning cabinet decisions is inaccurate because backbench members of caucus have neither the time nor the information to scrutinize all the cabinet's administrative and legislative decisions. Like many theoretical proposals that demand wide participation the theory that caucus should make the final decision in all cases is simply not practicable.

The leader's position in the Labor party is also affected by the party's basic ideas. In theory he is no more than the first among equals; he has only one vote in caucus or on the federal executive and he is bound to accept and obey majority decisions of caucus, even when prime minister, whether he agrees with them or not. He is meant to be the spokesman of the party. In practice his power is far greater. As leader of the party and sometimes as prime minister his views and actions receive far more attention than those of the normal backbencher. He must speak regularly in reaction to events and obviously cannot consult with caucus before making every statement. Besides, a leader must have had a wide range of support in the first place to have been elected and as leader he is likely to retain that support, if only because it would be embarrassing for the party if its leader was frequently forced to change his publicly stated view. In fact no leader has ever stood for re-election and been defeated, although Hughes walked out before a vote could be taken on a motion of censure and two other leaders were persuaded to retire. The actual independence that a leader enjoys depends very much on his personality and on the way that he chooses to act. Some, like F. G. Tudor, have chosen to be no more than the spokesman of caucus; others, like Chifley and Andrew Fisher, have carefully manipulated the members of caucus, ensuring that they have had the support they require and usually avoiding any confrontation. A further group of leaders, notably Hughes, Curtin and Whitlam, have preferred to demand support, leading the party from in front and attempting to 'crash through' problems. Depending on the personality of the leader, this tactic can lead to disaster or success. In each case the actual influence of each leader has been dependent on his personality; but it has always been far greater than the theory of the party suggests.

During its chequered history the Labor party has espoused many causes, some successfully, others with disastrous results for the party. There is no space here to discuss all those issues. Rather we will discuss four factors that have been relevant to the party since it was founded and that are crucial to explain its approach to politics. These themes will be the centralism of the party, its opposition to war and conscription, the conflict within its ranks between reformism and socialism, and finally the total male domination.

Any government that wants to change society by democratic means needs the power to implement its reforms. The Australian constitution was drawn up by a group of conservative politicians who were interested in preserving the power of the states; not a single Labor member participated in the constitutional convention. The constitution is designed to limit the power of the federal government to particular areas. The Labor party has frequently, and usually unsuccessfully, sought to increase the power of the federal government by means of referenda designed to change the constitution. Labor members have argued that uniformity of industrial conditions, economic management and other broad policies require that full power in these areas should reside with the federal government; but the electors have seldom agreed.

However the Labor party has succeeded in increasing central power by more indirect means, particularly making use of wartime conditions where it could justify extended government involvement under its defence powers. Most importantly in 1944 the Labor government gained a virtual monopoly of the income-tax powers by agreeing to make grants to the states in exchange for their vacating that tax field. This change has given the federal government control of the purse-strings and allowed it to increase its influence. It has used tied grants, permissable under section 96 of the constitution, by which it gives money to the states provided that the states spend it on specific purposes which are spelt out by the federal government. More recently the federal government has attempted to undermine the states by developing forms of regional government. The Labor ministries are not the only federal governments to increase the power of the central government; Liberal cabinets have also succeeded in this direction, despite their protestations of belief in states' rights. But despite the occasional denial that the party is centralist, the Labor party has been more open and direct in its attempts to increase the federal government's power. Indeed, as long as the government wants to act across a wide range of social problems, many of which are constitutionally the responsibility of the states, and as long as it holds the purse-strings, it is almost inevitable that a Labor government will be centralist in its attempts to solve problems.

Any active and reformist government has to determine what it wants and how quickly it wants to achieve those ends. In the Labor party, as in any other party of reform, there is considerable dispute about the objective of the party and the desirable speed of reform. Some members want the formal objective of the party, 'the democratic socialization of the means of production, distribution and exchange', achieved as soon as possible and they seriously look forward to the time when their brand of socialism will be implemented. Others are more sceptical about the possibilities and more reformist in their approach. They accept the objective but argue that change must be gradual, that reforms must tinker with the system and that a complete change of direction is not possible, given the federal structure of the country. Besides, they argue with some sense, however desirable nationalization may be, it would be electorally suicidal. Although it is clearly wrong to divide the Labor party distinctly into groups, at some times in opposition the more radical fringe appears to dominate; but usually when the party has been in office the administrative difficulties appear far too great and changes have been fairly gradual. It is quite simply not possible to argue that the Labor party is socialist, or that any Labor government has ever had a majority of ministers who were socialist in the sense that they seriously and consistently tried to extend state control. Instead they have usually been reformist in outlook, tinkering with the social and economic system of the country, but not altering its basic structure.

Defence, and particularly the issue of conscription for overseas service, has always been an issue of importance and significance to the Labor party. Its members have always had less sympathy for appeals of Empire unity than their conservative opponents. Before 1914 the Labor party advocated a system of compulsory military training for everyone, but only for home defence. In 1914 Fisher, the leader of the Labor party, promised full support for Britain, and Labor members consistently aided recruiting drives. But all those who joined the army in Europe were volunteers. When in 1916 Hughes advocated the introduction of conscription for overseas service, the movement split and the ensuing referendum campaign was unparalleled in Australian history for its vitriolic bitterness. The referenda of 1916 and 1917 were defeated, and those vicious campaigns served as a furnace in which to temper the steel of the next generations of the party.

In the inter-war years the Labor party became isolationist in its outlook, to the extent that when Italy invaded Abyssinia in 1935, the party attacked the idea of involvement in European wars and declared strongly that its policy was one of non-intervention. But in 1942, when the party was back in power, the war was closer to home, in New Guinea and Timor. The proposal then was to introduce conscription for the south-west Pacific region, and it was finally accepted by a federal conference after a long and bitter struggle within the party.

Then again in 1966—72 the Labor party fought a long battle against conscription for the Vietnam war, although some elements of the party were more outspoken than others. Its leader in the 1966 campaign, Calwell, had received his political apprenticeship during the 1916—17 campaigns and had led the party opposition to conscription in 1942. Indeed opposition to the Vietnam war and conscription became a unifying symbol for the Labor party, for the latter has been one of the persistent themes within the history of the party.

Finally it is worth commenting that the Labor party has been dominated by men. Before 1974 not one woman had been elected as a Labor member to the House of Representatives, and there had only been one woman senator. Partly this paucity of women was due to their comparative lack of involvement in party affairs; partly it was due to the fact that the trade unions, which are a power base for many members, are also bastions of male privilege and disinclined to support women as either union officials or party candidates. Caucus started with good intentions. In 1901 it supported a motion accepting equal pay for equal work; but there was no attempt to implement that until 1973. Generally until recently the Labor party has been more concerned with industrial and economic issues and, as befits a party that depends heavily on Catholic votes, has often been conservative on issues of social conscience, although to some extent that has changed over the last decade. Whether women will in future play a larger role remains a major question for the party.

PART I

The Federal Labor Party

1

The Origins and Early Development of the Party

In 1900 Labor parties existed in four of the Australian colonies, but the parties had reached very different stages of development. In New South Wales the party had been firmly extablished for six years and had worked out some of the problems of determining what type of political action should be followed. In Queensland the party had even formed a government for a week in 1899. In other states it was weaker. Further each state party had been formed to solve local problems and on an Australia-wide basis it had little unity or cohesion. In 1900 delegates from four states met and settled on a four-point platform which was later endorsed by the state parties (1.1). The first interstate conference which included delegates from all states was held in 1902 (1.2) and it adopted a slightly larger programme (1.3).

When the federal parliament met for the first time in 1901, there was no federal organization. The members elected on a Labor ticket met and decided to form their own party (1.4); they adopted a constitution and platform (1.5). One of the most immediate and pressing problems was the need to decide on what issues the party would vote solidly and what pledge should be signed by Labor candidates. Caucus made its own decision at an early stage (1.6) and the 1902 conference later adopted a specific pledge for all states (1.7). The system of the pledge, and the idea that all members had to subordinate their views to the majority view of caucus, was often attacked by the party's political opponents on the grounds that it led to an abuse of the system of parliamentary government (1.8). These charges were denied by Labor members who defended the pledge as a means of ensuring that members remained true to their electoral promises (1.9, 1.10).

During the first ten years of its existence, the federal caucus made several important decisions. If motions of caucus were to be binding on all members of the party, a quorum was important to ensure that the party could not be manipulated by a small minority. Only Labor members of parliament were allowed to attend caucus (1.11). Committees were also formed so that members of the party could get through all their varied demands on their time (1.12).

The selection of Labor candidates always remained the responsibility of the state branches (1.13), a decision that was to be important in the future when state branches tried to put pressure on members to obey their instructions.

The Labor party was usually proud of its procedures and argued that it carried out its responsibilities efficiently and well (1.14). But others, including some members of the Labor party, were more sceptical and believed that the Labor caucus did not control the actions of the party as fully as it should (1.15).

The Labor party was essentially a reforming party in its early days, committed to piecemeal parliamentary reform and not to intellectual views of political action. Fisher's speech (1.16) catches the essential spirit of Labor members in the early years of the party.

1.1 New South Wales conference accepts decisions of 1900 interstate conference
Worker, 3 February 1900

THE FEDERAL PLATFORM

Labor-Member Brown presented the report of the Committee re Federal Labor Platform. The Committee strongly recommended the adoption of the Federal Labor Platform adopted by the Interstate Labor Conference, namely—
"1. —General legislation: (1) Electoral reform, providing for one adult one vote; (2) total exclusion of colored and other undesirable races; (3) old age pensions.
"2. —Amendment of Federal Constitution. The Federal Constitution to be amended to provide for the initiative and national referendum.
(a) For the alteration of Constitution; (b) substitution of the national referendum for the double dissolution for the settlement of deadlocks between the two Houses."
They also endorsed the decision of the Interstate Conference—"That the question of customs taxation be not made the subject of a plank of the Labor Platform, but that the matter be left an open question for determination of the candidates."
Labor-Member Brown moved the adption of the Committee's report. He did not feel called upon to explain the planks of the suggested platform or to urge its adoption by the Conference. The platform had been agreed upon at the first—but he hoped not the last—Interstate Labor Conference, and he felt it would be the desire of the Conference to accept it without alteration or addition on the part of the Labor Parties of Australia.
Mr. E. Riley seconded the motion. The delegates from the other States were prepared to advocate the adoption of the platform agreed upon. It was a short programme, but the shorter the programme the more likely were they to secure united action. The fiscal question had been found to be a vexed one, and it had therefore been decided to leave it to the discretion of the candidates.

1.2 Welcome to delegates to 1902 interstate conference
Conference report, 1902, p. 3

OPENING OF CONFERENCE

Mr. H. Lamond, president of the New South Wales Political Labor League, in declaring the Conference open, extended a welcome on behalf of the P.L.L. to the delegates. This was the second conference of the kind that had been held since the passing of the Federal Constitution Bill, and in some respects would be even more important than the previous gathering. It was then feared the Federal Parliament would be conservative in character and that the constitution placed almost insuperable barriers in the path of reform. But the elections had brought into being the most democratic Parliament that had existed in Australia and one in which Labor representation had been most effective. They now had their second Conference, at which delegates would be required to frame a platform on which Labor would stand solidly throughout the Commonwealth. They had for the first time a representative from Tasmania, which completed the chain of unity around the Commonwealth. In that respect the Conference was unique. The results of the deliberations would be awaited by Labor bodies throughout Australia with the keenest interest, and he felt sure he was expressing the opinion of the vast majority of Trades Unionists and Laborists when he said they had every confidence the Conference would frame a platform that would be for the advantage, not of a section of the community only, but for humanity as a whole.

1.3 Federal platform adopted by 1902 interstate conference
Conference Report, 1902, pp. 13-14

ADOPTION OF A FEDERAL PLATFORM
The committee appointed to submit a report respecting the platform to be adopted by the Labor Party recommended the following planks for the consideration by the Conference:—

Fighting Platform
1. Maintenance of a White Australia.
2. Compulsory Arbitration.
3. Old Age Pensions.
4. Nationalization of Monopolies.
5. Citizen Defence Force
6. Restriction of Public Borrowing.
7. Navigation Laws.

On the motion of Mr. Hinchcliffe, seconded by Mr. Colborne, the platform was adopted.

General Platform
The general platform was considered and adopted in the following form:—
1. Maintenance of a White Australia.
2. Compulsory Arbitration to settle industrial disputes, with provision for the exclusion of the legal profession.
3. Old Age Pensions.
4. Nationalization of Monopolies.
5. Citizen Military Force and Australian owned Navy.
6. Restriction of Public Borrowing.
7. Navigation Laws to provide
    (a) for the protection of Australian shipping against unfair competition
    (b) registration of all vessels engaged in the coastal trade
    (c) the efficient manning of vessels
    (d) the proper supply of life-saving and other equipment
    (e) the regulations of hours and conditions of work
    (f) proper accommodation for passengers and seamen
    (g) proper loading gear and inspection of same.
8. Commonwealth Bank of Deposit and Issue and Life and Fire Insurance Department, the management of each to be free from political influence.
9. Federal Patent Law, providing for simplifying and cheapening the registration of patents.
10. Uniform industrial legislation: alteration of Constitution to provide for same.

1.4 First meeting of caucus
Caucus minutes, 7, 8 May 1901

A preliminary meeting of members of the Federal Parliament favourable to the formation of a Commonwealth Labor Party was held at Parliament House on Tuesday the 7th May 1901.

The following members were present:

Senators		House of Representatives	
Mr. Dawson	Q.	Mr. Fisher	Q.
Higgs	"	McDonald	"
Stewart	"	Page	"
		Thomas	N.S.W.
		Watson	"
		Watkins	"

Mr. Dawson was voted to the Chair, and Mr. Watson was requested to take the Minutes of the meeting.

A general conversation took place, the result of which was that a meeting was fixed for the next day (Tuesday the 8th) at 11 a.m., Mr. Watson being requested to intimate the same to certain members who were not present.

A meeting of members of the Federal Parliament favourable to the formation of a Commonwealth Labor Party was held at Parliament House on the 8th May 1901.

The following members were present:

Senators		House of Representatives	
Mr. De Largie	W.A.	Mr. Fowler	W.A.
Pearce	"	Batchelor	S.A.
McGregor	S.A.	Thomas	N.S.W.
Barrett	V.	Brown	"
Higgs	Q.	Spence	"
Dawson	"	Watson	"
Stewart	"	Watkins	"
O'Keefe	T.	Tudor	V.
		Ronald	"
		McDonald	Q.
		Fisher	"
		Page	"
		Bamford	"
		O'Malley	T.

Mr. Dawson was voted to the chair.

It was moved by Mr. McDonald 'That we form ourselves into a Federal Labor Party.'

Seconded by Mr. Ronald and carried.

On the motion of Mr. Higgs, seconded by Mr. Thomas, Mr. Stewart was chosen Secretary pro tem.

Mr. Thomas moved that the members of each House select one man to speak for the party temporarily. Seconded by Mr. Fisher and carried.

Mr. McGregor was chosen to represent the party in the Senate, and Mr. Watson in the House of Representatives.

.   .   .

It was agreed to remit the drafting of a Constitution for the Party with rules of debate etc. to a committee, and the following members were appointed to act on that Committee, viz: Messrs. Ronald (V.), Batchelor (S.A.), De Largie (W.A.), O'Keefe (Tas.), McDonald (Q.) and Watson (N.S.W.), the Committee to present its report on Monday the 13th inst. Mr. McDonald moved that the next meeting of the party be held on Monday the 13th inst. at 10 a.m. Carried.

1.5   Rules and platform of caucus, 1901
Caucus minutes, 20 May 1901

The report of the committee appointed to frame the Constitution, Rules, etc., was read as follows:

REPORT OF COMMITTEE APPOINTED TO FRAME CONSTITUTION, RULES, etc.
The Committee recommend
1. That the Party be named 'The Commonwealth Labor Party'.
2. That the Party sit in each House on the cross benches.
3. That the Executive of the Party be elected annually and that it consist of a Chairman, a Vice Chairman, a Secretary, an Assistant Secretary, and three members. The Secretary and Assistant Secretary to act as Whips in their respective Houses.
4. That members of the Federal Parliament not elected on the Labor ticket be admitted on a two thirds vote of the party & on signing the Federal Labor platform.
5. That current politics take precedence at all caucus meetings of the party.
6. That the Commonwealth Parliamentary or fighting Labor Platform consist of the following planks, viz:
    1. A White Australia.
    2. Adult Suffrage.
    3. Old Age pensions.
    4. A citizen army.
    5. Compulsory arbitration.
The Committee consider that as some of the members from the smaller States are opposed to the National Referendum, and as the question is not likely to come up in an acute form for some time, it would be unwise to insist upon its inclusion in our platform at present. Members, however, who have pledged themselves to that plank should be quite free to advocate it.

It was moved that the report of the Committee be received. Carried.

Mr. Hughes moved and Mr. Ronald seconded 'That consideration of the report be remitted to a special meeting.' Carried.

1.6   Decisions of caucus on pledge
Caucus minutes, 6 June 1901

MAJORITY OF CAUCUS ON PLATFORM
Watkins moved that McDonald's motion be amended to read as follows: 'That the members of the Party have a free hand on the Tariff bill, or on any motion directly affecting the fiscal issue, but on all questions affecting the platform shall be bound by the majority vote of the caucus.'

After debate the amendment was carried by 10 votes to 3.

1.7   Pledge adopted by 1902 conference
Conference report, 1902, p. 4

THE FEDERAL PLEDGE

After considering the proposal by the Executive of the Political Labor League
(N.S.W.) respecting the pledge to be signed by all Labor candidates for the
Federal Parliament, the Conference adopted the following pledge:

"I hereby pledge myself not to oppose the candidate selected by the
recognized political organization, and if elected to do my utmost to carry out
the principles embodied in the Federal Labor Platform and on all questions
affecting that Platform to vote as a majority of the Parliamentary Party may
decide at a duly constituted caucus meeting."

1.8   George Reid attacks caucus system
Argus, 30 July 1904

MR. REID AT WARRAGUL

"Ever since the Labor Party came into power we have been living under a state
of politics which is absolutely an outrage upon every principle of responsible
and of pure government. Those who have studied the British Constitution know
that the responsibility of Ministers to the people through the representatives of
the people was the greatest victory that free man ever won from tyranny.
(Cheers). The true principle of responsible government is that the Ministry hold
their positions as possessing the confidence of the representatives of the people,
but the present Government is not responsible to the people at all. It is
responsible to an assemblage of members known as the labour caucus, which
meets somewhere down in the vaults once a week. Your ministers of Australia
have to go to the vault, or room, whatever it is, as members of the caucus which
has absolute control and supremacy over them, and your affairs are being dealt
with in a Secret Session, week after week, away from the light of Parliamentary
scrutiny and discussion. It is going back to the dark days, when the power of the
people was exercised in Star Chambers by cliques and nominees. You are giving
up the grandeur of your Parliamentary system, which looks upon Ministers, not
as the minions of a caucus, but as the trustees of a nation. (Cheers). There is
another power behind the caucus, for the caucus itself is a bond slave . . .

The Ministry has got a Master inside the House, and they have got a Master
outside. There is not one member who has not to go to the Political League,
with his national policy if he wants to submit it to the people, and he must begin
in the office of that league by signing a pledge not to oppose the selected
candidate of the league."

1.9   Watson defends caucus and pledge
Argus, 1 August 1904

MR. WATSON REPLIES

Ministers and the Caucus

"There does not seem to be anything particularly new in it," the Prime
Minister remarked on Saturday morning, as he read the report of Mr. Reid's
Warragul speech in "The Argus". But it is to be hoped that there is something
behind it on this occasion. For weeks past I have heard about the Ministry
going to be challenged, but the threat never seems to materialise, so it is rather
to be wished that, for this once, business is meant. I am rather tired of the

continued assertion that the Cabinet has only a minority behind it in the House without any attempt being made to prove the statement. I notice that Mr. Reid accuses the Ministry of not being responsible to the people, but only to an assemblage of members known as the labour caucus. I rather imagine that, in view of the frequent meetings in caucus of the members of the other two parties during the last month or two, the people are alive to the fact that the labour party is not peculiar, so far as the caucus is concerned. It shares that method of the party discipline with the followers of Mr. Reid and Mr. Deakin. So it is hypocrisy for men belonging to those two groups to talk about the caucus as if it were a thing to be avoided, for we know that in all important matters the opinion of members of the party is taken whether it be the labour, protectionist, or free-trade party.

"There is no truth in the suggestion by Mr. Reid that the Ministry has to submit matters to the caucus, though on several occasions, as a matter of courtesy, after something has been decided upon, it has been reported to the caucus. And while the platform, as fixed by the central conference, is not departed from, a Labor Cabinet has just the same freedom of action as is possessed by any other Ministry. Even if the present Ministry had consulted its supporters upon a matter of importance, it would not have been unprecedented, as I think Mr. Reid is quite aware. He will understand that."

The Prime Minister chuckled when he made that point.

"Then Mr. Reid states that the political Labor League controls the Cabinet; that we have a master outside Parliament, and that if a member wants to submit a policy to the people he must first begin by signing a pledge not to oppose the selected candidate of the League. That is—I will put it mildly—an inaccurate assertion on Mr. Reid's part. The platform of the political Labor League of Australia is agreed to at a conference, at which all the Labor Leagues and affiliated organizations are represented, and after it has been agreed upon, it affects only candidates at the next ensuing election. The man who does not subscribe to that platform cannot stand as a League candidate. If he assents to it—personally I have never been asked to sign a pledge—he is bound by it for the life of the Parliament which is subsequently elected. In other words, the programme is only compulsory for the Parliament. If any changes are made during the currency of the Parliament, the Labor member is not under any obligation to adopt them. They only come into force at the next election."

1.10   Hughes defends pledge
'Case for Labor', *Daily Telegraph,* 24 July 1908

Will our critics who accuse us of not being free men tell us by what we are bound save our own word, freely given? If we believe in certain principles, ought we not to do what we can to give effect to them? And if we are not ashamed but rather glory in our cause, why should we not openly testify to its virtues and solemnly pledge ourselves to stand by it? Do we cease to be free men because we earnestly advocate certain principles which we believe are essential to the social and industrial salvation of mankind? Or because we pledge ourselves to do that which we declare above all other things ought to be done and must be done if the people are to be economically saved?

Freedom and Honor
We are not free to break our word, abandon our principles, desert our party, betray our constituents. But the pledge cannot prevent us doing any one or all of

these things if our inclination lies in that direction. Some people talk as though the Labor Party resorted to methods unfamiliar, barbarous, and terrible to compel obedience in its members. Such talk is mere idle babble. There is nothing to prevent a Labor man voting against his party on party matters if he chooses to disregard his promises not to do so. And no consequence will follow from his act, other than those which attend such an act by a member of any other party.

If we are not free men—free to act dishonorably—then it is only because we chose to regard our promise, voluntarily given, as binding. But at any time we choose to disregard this promise we can be free.

The Caucus and the Pledge

Now, as to the charge that the Labor Party are, by reason of their pledge, slaves of the Caucus. For an exposition of the nature and scope and purpose of the caucus the curious may be referred to some previous articles of mine in this column, where the matter is dealt with in detail. It is unnecessary here to do more than emphasise two points—one, that only the platform can be dealt with by the caucus; the other that jurisdiction of the caucus is severally limited in another direction. It cannot add to or take from the platform, nor can it modify or amend existing planks.

Its functions are rigidly confined to determining the most effective way of placing the planks of the platform upon the Statute Book. It cannot make any member vote against a plank of the platform—save in those rare cases when two planks clash, when it may determine which of the two shall be supported. The caucus mainly concerns itself with details and tactics, and, where there is ambiguity of language in matters subsidiary and contingent to the platform, decides its correct meaning.

1.11 Rules and procedures of caucus
Caucus minutes, 3 July 1901, 26 February 1902

QUORUM CAUCUS
On the motion of Batchelor, seconded by McGregor, it was determined that one third of members be a quorum of caucus.

ATTENDANCE AT CAUCUS
Mr. Thomas moved the following motion of which he had previously given notice, viz: 'That in future no one be permitted to attend a caucus meeting except duly qualified members of the Federal Labor Party.' After debate the following words were added with Mr. Thomas' consent, viz: 'Unless by special resolution of the caucus', & with this addition the motion was carried.

1.12 Establishment of committees
Caucus minutes, 9 July 1917

PARTY COMMITTEES
The Committee appointed by the previous meeting reported as follows:
1. The Executive of the Federal Parliamentary Labor Party shall consist of Leader, Deputy Leader, and Secretary, together with the Chairman of each of the Committees hereinafter mentioned.
2. The Party shall be divided into five Committees, and may, if found necessary, be further divided.

3. Each Committee to have a Chairman, who shall be elected by the Party, and Secretary, and as far as possible, be so arranged as to have one or the other of these officers in the Senate or House of Representatives.
4. The Leader, Deputy Leader, and Secretary shall be ex-officio members of all Committees.
5. The work of the Party shall be allotted to the Committees as follows:
   (a) Prime Minister's and Attorney General's Department;
   (b) Treasury and Finance;
   (c) Defence, Naval and Military Departments;
   (d) Home and Territory, and Works;
   (e) Customs and Postal Departments.
6. The duties of each Committee shall be to watch all Bills, Regulations, administration and Departmental work.
7. The Committees shall report to the Executive who shall consider them and place the reports with their recommendations before the Party meeting each week.

1.13 Members joining the party
Conference report, 1902, pp. 4, 14

SELECTION OF PARLIAMENTARY CANDIDATES
Senator Higgs moved—"That subject to the acceptance of the Federal platform and pledge, each State shall control its selection of candidates for the Federal elections."

Mr. Spence seconded the motion.

Mr. Phillips urged the necessity under the present circumstances of each State being unencumbered at the next elections. In Melbourne next month there would be a plebiscite taken to determine the three candidates for the Senate, and it would be unwise for the Conference to interfere.

Mr. Guthrie said it would be within the scope of the State Party to have additional planks so long as they did not alter the spirit of the Federal platform.

The president stated that the position of the various States would be that if they were desirous of appointing men to contest an election such men would be required to adopt the platform carried by the Conference. Matters of local interest and importance could be added to the platform, and on the return of the candidates they would form part of the Federal Parliamentary Labor Party.

The motion was carried.

Conditions of Candidature
The conditions of candidature were adopted as follows:
1. That all candidates for the Federal Parliament shall sign the following pledge: I hereby pledge myself not to oppose the candidate selected by the recognized political labor organization and, if elected, to do my utmost to carry out the principles embodied in the Federal Labor platform and on all questions affecting the platform and vote as a majority of the Parliamentary Party may decide at a duly constituted caucus meeting.
2. That subject to the acceptance of the Federal platform and pledge, each State shall control the selection of its candidates for the Federal Parliament.
3. That all Labor candidates shall have a free hand on the fiscal question.

4. That no member of the Federal Labor Party shall accept office in the Federal Government except with the consent of a duly constituted caucus of the Party.

1.14 W. G. Spence's description of how caucus works
Australia's Awakening, Sydney, 1909, p. 380

The party meets every Wednesday morning. On measures affecting the Platform the party votes are solidly together. On all other questions each member is absolutely free to vote as he likes. All important bills, whether affecting the Platform or not, are discussed and in most cases remitted to a committee of the party, who go through the measure and recommend amendments. The Leader would then take these amendments, if approved by caucus of the party, to the Minister in charge of the Bill. Many would be accepted, others would be left to the House to decide. This method helped to improve legislation and justified the claim that the party wielded an influence far greater than its members warranted. No other party worked so hard or so efficiently; hence the good done. The relations with the Government were open and above-board; the Cabinet readily considered any suggestions made by the party.

1.15 V. G. Childe's view of shortcomings of caucus
How Labour Governs, pp. 25—6

The Minister faced with the actual responsibilities of governing, administering the details of his department, surrounded by outwardly obsequious Civil Servants, courted by men of wealth and influence, an honoured guest at public functions, riding in his own State motor car, is prone to undergo a mental transformation. He inevitably looks at administrative questions from a different angle to that in which they appear to the private member. The latter wants a lot of things—mostly apparently small and simple—done for himself, his constituents, his friends, or his union; the Minister seems to possess the power to grant most of such requests. But the Minister is painfully aware of the limitations placed upon his power by considerations of finance, by constitutional usage, by the traditional procedure of his department, and by the very multiplicity of conflicting claims upon his favour. He is more fully seized of the implications of each question than a private member can be. He must beware of creating precedents rashly, confidential information in his possession cannot be revealed, lest it should slip out if too many persons are privy to it. The members of the Cabinet become bound together by sharing such difficulties, by the mutual recognition of the more intimate and secret problems of Government and a common desire to maintain their positions in the House and the Party, and to ensure both their return by the country and their re-election by Caucus. For that reason they tend to preserve a solid front to Caucus. They resent its criticism both because they can see ways of retaining the Party in office and dangers to themselves and the State, which it would be unsafe or useless to explain to their followers, and because the latter's criticism is often inspired by personal jealousy and ventilated by possible rivals. They can generally secure the support of a majority at any meeting by judicious concessions to the demands preferred by individual members on behalf of their constituencies, and thus buy over a sufficient number of waverers to secure their supremacy.

And then the decisions of Caucus can very often be ignored. It is hard to imagine that a majority of members would be prepared to vote against the Government on the floor of the House and thus jeopardise the Labor Ministry if Ministers took the bit in their teeth. In any Parliament composed of professional politicians the anti-dissolution party is always in a majority, and this is especially so in the case of a Labor Party where the members are not only professional politicians, but are practically kept off the labour market by the possession of seats. Hence the threat of a dissolution is always a powerful weapon in the hands of the Ministry.

1.16   Fisher discusses Labor party's approach to politics
Conference report, 1908, p. 14

Now, as to Socialism. I say with pleasure that in my 20 years of public life I have seen this question, from being tabooed, sneered at and scouted, brought to a first place in public discussion. We find it is the question in the Church, Parliament, in the streets and newspapers, and all over the civilised world. No more sneers and scorn for Socialism! Everyone has this one great question to consider. We are all Socialists now, and indeed the only qualification you hear from anybody is probably that he is "not an extreme Socialist". I do not think that the ideas of the originators have altered one jot. I do not say either, that the fundamental principles are better understood by a number of the people, but many have discovered the fact that it pays them to be Socialists. It is wonderful the influence a movement has on some people—trading people, too—when they find they can make profit by another name!

There are two distinct bodies in our Movement—the propaganda teacher and the practical politician. The very name of politician, of course, puts the politician outside the sphere of the teacher. The propagandist does not care whether he has two, three or more with him; the politician does his best for the mass of the people he is serving. Otherwise he should not have his place in Parliament. Under Socialism, now, we find the very men who were against us are coming to us. I refer to the clerical workers, who find that their skill does not protect them. In fact, no toiler is assured of a decent living under the present system of competition. As an individual I am in favour of proceeding by the way of law to help the workers. There are two ways open—the universal strike, and the other way of providing the necessary courts to see that the worker gets his just remuneration. I am for the latter. I believe we have reached the stage in Australia, where, with universal suffrage and an educated democracy, we can do in Parliament for the workers what we could not accomplish by the universal strike. There is no need for us to give up principles for expediency. If we cannot defend our position we have no right to succeed. If our opponents can show us by argument that we are wrong we should retrace our footsteps and admit our error. But we have yet to meet the opponents who can do so. We have been twenty years blazing the track, and whilst our opponents have condemned us for the path we have taken they have ended by trying to follow in our footsteps.

2

Caucus, Cabinet and Labor Governments

The Labor party, like almost every other political party, is concerned with office. Without getting into power, it can never put into effect its programme or shape the future of the country. It may not want power at any price, but once in office there may be differences of opinion about what should be done. And all members of the party usually want to be involved in making the decisions.

The first role that caucus always plays when the party gains office is to elect ministers. At the time of the party's first period in office in 1904, the leader was given the right to choose his own ministers (2.1). But in 1905 a conference motion stated that ministers should be elected by caucus. J. C. Watson objected to this resolution and offered his resignation to caucus because of it (2.2). In 1908 after debate the recommendation was reasserted (2.3) and in the same year, despite an attempt by Watson to prevent it, the caucus elected its ministers for the first time (2.4) and a clear procedure for electing ministers was established (2.5).

Thereafter Labor ministers have always been elected by caucus. Sometimes the elections were hotly contested, with rival tickets competing for advantage, at other times the elections have been held without any major divisions within the party becoming evident (2.6—2.9). Accounts often vary and the results can usually be interpreted in several ways.

One of the major changes that the involvement of caucus in decision-making brings to the parliamentary style of government is that it challenges, and even undermines, the convention of cabinet solidarity. According to this convention, once a cabinet has made a decision all members of cabinet support it in public whether or not they had supported it in cabinet. When Labor is in office, some ministers have argued that, as caucus is supposed to be the final court of appeal, they should be able to fight again in caucus the battles they have lost in cabinet. Within the Labor Party opinions have varied. In 1916 one member was not sure if he had the right to dissent (2.10); at other times different members of the same cabinet held varying views (2.11). At one stage conference even attempted to extend the system of cabinet government by giving each minister a group of backbenchers to assist him; but this motion was defeated, mainly at the instigation of federal and state parliamentarians who might have been directly affected by the change (2.12).

Caucus has the right to overrule cabinet. For instance, in 1941 it forced the cabinet to reconsider its budget (2.13) and in 1974 forced Whitlam to reconsider a proposal for a referendum (2.14) even though in the latter case Whitlam later persuaded caucus to reverse its decision. Assessments of caucus influence are common (2.15) and often misguided because they do not understand how limited caucus control can actually be.

2.1   Watson given free hand to choose his cabinet
Caucus minutes, 23 April 1904

SPECIAL CAUCUS

All members present except Stewart & O'Malley.

Minutes of the previous meeting read and confirmed.

Watson explained the present position and informed the Party that he expected to be sent for today by the Governor-General to form an administration.

LEADER TO ACCEPT COMMISSION

Dawson moved, McGregor seconded, that the Leader be authorized to accept the commission of his Excellency to form an administration. At 11.20 Caucus adjourned until 3 o'clock this afternoon.

Adjourned Caucus meeting continued at 3 p.m. All members present except Stewart.

WATSON ACCEPTS COMMISSION

Watson reported having waited on the Governor General & had accepted the Commission to form an administration.

Higgs moved, Fowler seconded (pro forma), that Mr. Watson approach Mr. Deakin with a view to the formation of a Ministry in which there must be at least four paid Labor Ministers.

On being put to a vote the motion was defeated.

McGregor moved, Brown seconded, that the Chairman have a free hand in the formation of his Ministry. Carried unanimously.

2.2   J. C. Watson objects to conference resolution requiring that caucus elect members
Watson to caucus members, 27 July 1905, Watson papers, National Library, Canberra

The second resolution to which I take exception reads as follows:— 'That this Conference recommends, in the event of the Labor Party obtaining the Ministerial benches, that the Labor Ministry be recommended by the Party in caucus.' This at least implies a censure upon myself in regard to the selection of the Federal Labor Ministry, and it was particularly hard to find it supported by several delegates who are members of the Federal Labor Party. Concerning my selection of colleagues on the recent occasion, I desire to say only that, so far as I have been since informed, it was one that would have received the endorsement of the great majority of the Party if it had been submitted to the members. Be that as it may, I chose those men who would, in my judgment, do most credit to our movement, though I admit there were others with nearly equal claims. But leaving aside the personnel of the last Labor Government, I most decidedly could not continue to lead the Party and be bound by such a condition as that contained in the resolution. The substitution of the word 'recommended' for 'selected' as contained in the original resolution, effects no real alteration in the position, and it therefore would bind the next Labor Prime Minister to accept at the hands of the caucus any colleagues it may choose for him. The Leader is usually supposed to have, or should have, the most matured judgment amongst the members of the Party; yet according to the Conference decision he is to be given no greater voice in the selection of his colleagues than the rawest recruit in the Party. While Party Government obtains, the responsibility for the Administration rests upon the Prime Minister, yet it is seriously proposed to foist upon him as colleagues men upon whose judgment and discretion he, possibly, could not rely. I admit that any Leader will make mistakes, but for the credit of the Party and himself he is naturally anxious to get a good Ministry together, and will therefore weigh carefully each man's qualifications before arriving at a decision. For the reasons mentioned, it would be impossible for me to accept the conditions sought to be imposed in this connection.

2.3   Conference supports moves for caucus to elect ministers
Conference report, 1908, pp. 31−2

SELECTION OF LABOUR MINISTRIES

Senator Findley moved: 'That it be a recommendation from this Conference that future Labour Ministries be selected by the Parliamentary party in caucus'. There was no member of the Party who would say that any leader of theirs was necessarily the embodiment of all wisdom. Somebody of course, had to shoulder the responsibility of leadership. In the ordinary way the leader would himself select his team, but he ventured to say that the Federal Labour party, if it were entrusted with this work, would put aside all personal elements and view the formation of a Ministry in the light of trying to do the best for the Movement. Members of the Party having had every opportunity of judging each other's capabilities and qualifications were best fitted, in his opinion, to exercise the choice of the men who should form the Labour Cabinet. Every member was anxious for the advance of his Party, and in spirit would co-operate to get whom they considered the best men. The carrying of this resolution would affirm a sound democratic principle, and it would be a fitting thing for a Labour Ministry to come in on these lines.

Mr. Catts seconded. The proposal followed a well-known principle adopted in this Conference and in their industrial organisations. The same party that elected its leader should surely be able to select his colleagues for the Cabinet.

Mrs. Dwyer urged that the present proposal would rob a leader of his strength and power. It would be the most suave men — the ones skilled in the art of "engineering" — who would be chosen under such a system.

Senator Henderson asked conference not to be blinded by any platitude with regard to a recommendation of this kind. Were they going to ask the leader of the Labour party, after he has been called upon by the representative of the King to form a Ministry, to come down and relegate the powers conferred on him to the caucus?

Mr. Foster, as a democrat, clung to the ideal of administration by the competent, and he would like to see the best men on the Treasury benches. He favoured the counsels of the many as against the wisdom of one man; and he had sufficient confidence in his colleagues to know that the leader would not have foisted on him a man unworthy of the position, nor one with whom he could not work.

Mr. Hutchison wanted to know if Senator Henderson believed in Labour following old world methods for ever in the mode of selecting a Ministry. A strong man might, conceivably, pick the weakest men so that he could dominate the Cabinet. The only way in which a Labour leader would have the fullest confidence in his Cabinet would be to leave its selection in the hands of members of the caucus.

Senator Needham contended that whilst it was right that they should elect their executive officers, he could not quite see the analogy in applying the same principle to the choice of a Cabinet.

Mr. Hurst stated that the same caucus that had selected Mr. Watson and then Mr. Fisher to lead them would surely be competent enough to select the Treasurer and other members of the Cabinet. The appointment by the caucus of a Ministry would remove any jealousy or heart-burning that might arise through exercise of an individual choice.

Mr. Spence looked upon it as a pleasant augury that they were deliberating upon the method of choosing a Labour Ministry. He did not think there would be very much difference in the personnel of a Cabinet picked by the leader or that chosen by the caucus.

Mr. King O'Malley felt that if a prospective candidate for office were rejected he would be quite satisfied that he had not been subject to the caprice or whim of merely one man, but had the verdict, from the whole Labour party.

Mr. Lamond had as high a regard for the men who were leaders in the Labour movement as anyone, and these men had certainly shown ability. So had other members. Whilst it was natural that the leader of a Labour party should desire to do as leaders of other parties had done, still Labour was always breaking fresh ground and seeking better methods. He agreed with the principle in the resolution, feeling that the caucus knew the best men just as well as the leader did. The ambitious man, instead of merely having to display his special virtues to his leader would have to make them apparent to the caucus before he was selected, and thus a choice would be arrived at which would bring good results for Labour.

The motion was carried by 20 votes to 4.

2.4   Fisher ministry selected in November 1908
Caucus minutes, 12, 17 November 1908

The Chairman reported that the Governor General had sent for him & had asked him to form an administration.

Watson moved, Needham seconded, That the Party, having every confidence in its Leader, leaves the selection of his colleagues in his hands.

Findley moved, Frazer seconded as an amendment, That we give effect to the resolution carried at the interstate conference at Melbourne 'That future Labor Ministers be Recommended by the parliamentary party in Caucus.' Amendment carried 24 to 17.

The Executives Report on the Question of procedure was read by Mr. Fisher. And adopted. Agreed that Mr. Fisher be recommended without Ballot.

Mr. O'Malley moved 'that Senator McGregor be recommended without Ballot.' Carried.

Mr. Watson moved & Senator Givens seconded, 'that the recommendations be made by open Ballot.' Lost.

Mr. Watson moved & Senator seconded, 'That candidates be nominated.' Lost.

Senator Givens moved & Senator Henderson seconded 'that there shall be three Ministerial positions allotted to the senate and six to the House of Representatives.' Lost.

The Meeting adjourned until 2 p.m. at which time the meeting resumed and the following Members were recommended as Ministers: Senator Pearce, Messrs. Hughes, Tudor, Batchelor, Thomas, Mahon & Hutchinson.

Mr. Fisher made a brief statement as to allotment of portfolios and said that He proposed to make a short statement to the House and ask for an adjournment until the 25th instant.

Moved by Senator Givens and seconded by Senator Finlay 'That the fact that Ministers were recommended by the party need no longer be denied.' Carried.

2.5   Procedure for electing ministers

Document entered in caucus minute book. The additional clauses were written on it by Fisher.

PROCEDURE FOR RECOMMENDING MEMBERS FOR MINISTERS

Recommendations of Members for Ministers

1. Recommendations to be made by exhaustive ballot.
2. Recommendation of Senators to be first taken.
3. Members shall vote for a candidate by placing a X opposite his name on the ballot paper.
4. If more or less than the required number be voted for the R.O. shall reject the ballot paper as informal.
5. Candidates receiving an absolute majority of the votes cast shall be recommended and their names shall be announced to the meeting by the R.O. and struck off the subsequent ballot papers.
6. If less than the required number receive an absolute majority of the votes cast in the first ballot, further ballots shall be taken after the names of all candidates who received less than *five** votes have been struck out. **amendment made at party meeting held 27/4/10. A.F.*
7. In all subsequent ballots the name of the candidate receiving the fewest votes shall be omitted until the required number have been recommended.
8. In the case of a tie, where only one is to be selected, the two names shall again be submitted to a ballot, if there is a further tie the Chairman shall give a casting vote.
9. Only the number of the votes received by members who have been recommended shall be announced to the meeting by the returning officer. *This clause was adopted at a party meeting held 27/4/10 A.F.*

Melbourne 1905 Conference.

2. That this Conference recommends that in the event of the Labor Party obtaining the Ministerial benches the Labor Ministry shall be recommended by the party in Caucus.

Andrew Fisher.

2.6   Fisher resigns and new ministry elected

Caucus minutes, 30 October 1915

Mr Fisher stated that he regretted to inform them that owing to the strain upon his health during the last two years he had decided to be an applicant for a position in the public service, namely the position of High Commissioner. He had been unanimously selected by his colleagues. It was with feelings of sorrow that he felt compelled to take this step as it would mean resigning the leadership of a party with whom he had so long been associated. He thanked the members for the loyal support they had also accorded him. He would ask them to appoint a successor and hoped they would give that gentleman the same consideration they had shown him.

Senator Givens moved and Mr. Thomas seconded 'That this party place on record its very high appreciation of the long and valuable service of Mr. Fisher to the Labour cause, and while heartily congratulating him upon his appointment as High Commissioner we express the utmost regret at his retirement as Leader of this party.'

The Resolution was supported by members and was then put and carried by acclamation.

Senator De Largie moved and Mr. Mathews seconded 'That Mr. W. M. Hughes be elected Leader of this party.'

The Resolution was carried unanimously.

Mr. Hughes then took the Chair and, in thanking the party for selecting him as their Leader and the high honor thus conferred upon him, ask them to consider that, no matter what he may do as their chief, without he had the same loyal support as they had accorded to Mr. Fisher he could not fill the position with satisfaction to himself or the party. We had a great deal to do. Not only were we in the midst of a protracted and ghastly war but had the Referenda fight in front of us which if carried would entail still more work on the party. They all knew him to be a man of strong opinions and he felt sure they would prefer him to express those opinions to the party. He would strive to do honor to the high position they had placed him in and in again thanking them felt sure of their cordial and loyal support in the fights they had before them.

Mr. Hughes asked them to decide whether they would proceed with the business arising out of the situation which arose owing to Mr. Fisher's resignation.

Mr. Webster moved and Mr. Burns seconded 'That we proceed to decide the course of action at once.' Carried.

Mr. Hughes stated that, as to the new position created, the resignation of Mr. Fisher did affect the position of other Ministers and without the party decided there was no need to elect more than one Minister.

Senator Long moved and Mr. Webster seconded 'That this party is of opinion that a reconstruction of the cabinet should follow the selection of a new Leader and that such be made in the usual way by exhaustive ballot.'

Debate ensued after which Senator Long's motion was put to the meeting and carried. Voting Ayes 39, Noes 24.

Mr. P. Moloney moved and Senator Grant seconded 'That the meeting adjourn until 7 p.m.' The meeting resumed at 7 p.m.

Senator Lynch moved and Mr. Thomas seconded 'That inasmuch as it is admitted that certain ministers have given unqualified satisfaction and are still required to go to the ballot after thirteen months, this Caucus is of opinion that all appointments made thirteen months ago should be now filled by ballot in the same manner.' Lost.

Senator Givens, Mr. McDonald & Mr. Chanter were appointed scrutineers for the Ballot for Ministers which was then proceeded with.

After several Ballots had been taken Mr. Thomas moved and Mr. P. J. Moloney seconded 'That all those receiving ten and under retire from the ballot.' Carried.

The voting resulted in the following Gentlemen being chosen as Ministers:

Senate		House of Representatives	
Senator Pearce	48	Mr. Jenson	64
Senator Gardiner	45	Mr. Mahon	51
Senator Russell	41	Mr. Tudor	46
		Mr. Higgs	37
		Mr. Webster	35
		Mr. O'Malley	34

Senator Newland moved and Mr. Thomas seconded that Senator G. H. Pearce be elected Deputy Leader of this party. Carried.

2.7 Curtin government elected, October 1941
Caucus minutes, 4 October 1941

Mr. Curtin made a statement to the Party regarding his visit to the Governor General and receiving a commission to form a Government. He suggested that there should be 19 Ministers, the same number as in the last Government. The allocation between the two Houses should be Senate 5 Ministers, 3 Senior and 2 non senior; House of Representatives including the Prime Minister and Deputy Prime Minister should be 14 Ministers, 9 Senior and 5 non senior.

Senator the Hon. J. Cunningham was elected Returning Officer. Messrs. Conelan, Baker and Brown were chosen as scrutineers.

Moved Mr. Scullin, seconded Mr. Barnard, The allocation of Ministers be as suggested by Mr. Curtin and that the Prime Minister be empowered to remove a Minister if at any time it was deemed desirable or/and necessary. Carried.

Curtin Ministry

Moved Mr. Makin, seconded Mr. Lawson, Mr. John Curtin be appointed Leader and Prime Minister. Carried unanimously.

Moved Dr. Evatt, seconded Mr. Makin, Mr. F. M. Forde be elected the Deputy Leader and Deputy Prime Minister. Carried unanimously.

The following members were elected for the Ministry: Messrs. Beasley, Chifley, Dedman, Drakeford, Evatt, Frost, Holloway, Makin, Scully, Ward, Senators Ashley, Collings, Keane.

Later ballots elected Senators Cameron, Fraser and Mr. Lazzarini. A further ballot elected Mr. G. Lawson.

2.8 First Whitlam government elected
Financial Review, 19 December 1972

PLUS—MINUS VOTE
A SLIGHT CASE OF WINNING TOO WELL
By Maximilian Walsh

Yesterday's Caucus election and the requirement that the Ministry consist of 27 elected members is going to mean that the application of real power within the political system is going to depend a great deal on the committee strength of those elected.

Interpersonal relations, not who was elected with the most votes, is what will count.

Prime Minister E. G. Whitlam enjoyed a superficial victory in that most of the people he said should be in the Ministry—his ticket—actually made it.

The Prime Minister will have the opportunity to consolidate this electoral advantage today when he announces the allocation of portfolios.

But even last night it was apparent that Mr Whitlam's desire to assert himself was running into uncomfortable political shoals.

The high vote, for example, given to Dr Rex Patterson in the first ballot after the leadership makes it very difficult for Mr Whitlam not to give the Department of Primary Industry to Dr Patterson.

Mr Whitlam has said that Dr Patterson would make an ideal Minister for Northern Development.

In point of fact this is an over-inflated department.

It is not and will never be a policy department.

Dr Patterson, a former senior public servant, knows this.

Had he polled poorly on the executive ticket he would be without a great deal of backup for arguing his entitlement to the Primary Industry portfolio.

He would have had to quietly go along with Mr Whitlam's intention of giving the portfolio to Senator Wriedt from Tasmania—an unexpected winner of one of the six ministerial positions allocated in the Labor Party to the Senate.

Dr Patterson has no institutional comeback at Mr Whitlam if the Prime Minister elects to give the Primary Industry portfolio to somebody else.

But it will be a very tough decision for Mr Whitlam to give it to anybody other than Dr Patterson.

Outside of the policy area of Primary Industry the most interesting aspect of yesterday's ministerial election was the success of the outgoing "shadow" Cabinet.

All succeeded in the first ballot.

Some, for example Mr Stewart and Mr Beazley, made it by the skin of their teeth.

Surprisingly, in one respect, it was Dr Cairns, the putative Minister for Trade, who topped the first ballot—after the unanimous election of the four leaders.

Dr Cairns enjoyed the top position on the ballot paper, but in a poll of 93 professional politicians you should not expect a donkey vote.

Getting 80 votes in an election where there were 93 voters (even allowing for the voting system) was no mean feat.

Second to Dr Cairns was the shadow Treasurer, Mr F. Crean, with 72; Mr W. Hayden (72); Dr Patterson (62); Mr F. Daly (58); Mr C. Cameron (55); Mr T. Uren (55); Mr C. Jones (54); Mr F. Stewart (51).

The Senate:—

In the Senate election—where there were four seats available—the successful men were Senators Doug McClelland (NSW), J. Cavanagh (SA), K. Wriedt (Tas.)

This was one of Mr Whitlam's more successful interventions in the ballot.

He supported Senator McClelland who had organised well himself anyway, Senator Bishop who had the support of the formidable Mr Cameron, and Senator Wriedt who had little more than his ability and Mr Whitlam's backing running for him.

. It was not surprising in view of the voting system, but the most formidable Labor men in the Senate, in parliamentary terms, missed out completely.

Senator Cavanagh owes his election to the support of the party's Left wing and Senator Bishop to the persuasive powers of Mr Cameron and Mr Whitlam—neither owes it to his performance as a Parliamentarian.

The tail-end of the Ministry—the final nine—provided, as expected, most surprises.

The last positions were won by Messrs G. Bryant (65 votes), R. F. Connor (58), A. Grassby (56), L. Johnson (54), K. Enderby (53), L. Bowen (43), D. Everingham (42), M. Cass (39), W. Morrison (38).

Mr Bryant, who missed out by one vote on the first ballot, was underrated as a chance for the Ministry.

Doctors Everingham and Cass were not regarded as being members of the second Whitlam Ministry.

Of the Labor sixty-niners, Mr Morrison, and Dr Cass were the only two successful newcomers to politics.

Mr K. Enderby should be included with them because he entered politics even later.

Mr Bowen and Mr Grassby—both in different ways not altogether expected in the Ministry—had previous political experience in the NSW Government.

Prime Minister Whitlam announced to the Caucus that he proposed to establish 35 departments in the Labor Government. He did not indicate whom he favoured to hold the portfolio for each department.

2.9   Whitlam's old team re-elected
Canberra Times, 11 June 1974

LABOR STICKS TO OLD TEAM
By David Solomon, Political Correspondent

The Labor Party turned conservative yesterday and re-elected its old Ministry, and most of its old office-bearers.

The one major change it determined was that Dr Jim Cairns should be Deputy Prime Minister in place of Mr Lance Barnard.

It also elected Senator John Wheeldon to replace Mr Al Grassby, the former Minister for Immigration, who was defeated in the general election.

The replacement lowered the average age of the Cabinet by a full month.

The lack of change in the personnel of the Ministry is likely to be reflected in the assignments given to ministers by the Prime Minister, Mr Whitlam.

He will change a few ministers but generally the Government is likely to be much the same as it was before the last elections.

He will probably announce his new Ministry tonight, and the ministers will be sworn in tomorrow.

.   .   .

Tactical Victory

The left wing scored a tactical victory when it persuaded the Returning Officer, Mr Ray Thorborn, that the ballots for Deputy Leadership and Senate Leadership should be held simultaneously.

While Senator Ron McAuliffe (Qld) expressed some protest, he was howled down by the caucus and the joint ballots were conducted. This meant that caucus members could not be concerned about providing "balance" in the leadership. (The four leaders in the Parliamentary ALP are members of the party's Federal Conference and Federal Executive.)

The result was that the two left-wing candidates, Dr Cairns and Senator Murphy, were elected.

Dr Cairns defeated Mr Barnard by 54 votes to 42 and Senator Murphy defeated Senator Wriedt by 55 to 41.

In each case, caucus members insisted they were voting more on the merits of the candidates than on their political leanings.

2.10   Higgs's view of ministerial responsibility
W. G. Higgs to A. Fisher, 28 August 1916

Ere this reaches you, you will know whether we are permanently out of office, for I take it that is what conscription means for the Labor party.

We have a caucus meeting tomorrow, and everyone seems to think that the Prime Minister will ask for conscription. Certainly his public speeches would indicate that he will do this. I am interested in what you say on this most contentious subject.

So far as I can learn the unions and the Labor political organisations are against conscription and the Political Labor Leagues have threatened to refuse endorsement to any sitting member voting in favour of conscription.

.   .   .

The atmosphere is electrical and a storm appears which is calculated to rend us in twain. I shall vote against conscription in the cabinet and in the caucus if allowed by Cabinet practice or decision to do so.

I cannot bring myself to vote for compelling any man to go abroad to fight against his will, though I am in favour of compulsion for service in Australia in time of invasion or threatened invasion.

2.11   John Dedman explains how cabinet responsibility worked under Curtin and Chifley
'The Practical Application of Collective Responsibility', *Politics,* vol. 3, no. 2, pp. 148–9, 159

Before caucus selected those who would comprise the first Curtin ministry (on 7 October 1941), Mr Scullin moved that power to dismiss a Minister be vested in the Prime Minister. As far as I remember, the resolution was carried without discussion; the power was never exercised by Mr Curtin or by his successors in Labor Governments. Mr Curtin took the first opportunity, at a cabinet meeting, to impress upon his Ministers the very heavy responsibilities which they had now assumed and expressed his hopes that cabinet solidarity would be maintained and that Ministers would accept collective responsibility for cabinet decisions. Whether it was because of the impression this made on me, or because of my respect for British tradition, or because I thought the principle to be a *sine-qua-non* of good government, I there and then decided that, no matter what my personal views might be, *outside cabinet* I would always stand up for its decisions. Never once, during my nine-year ministerial career did I diverge from this self-made rule of conduct. Some of my colleagues, whom I held and still hold in high esteem, did not accept this as a binding rule; and in retrospect I admit that there were a few occasions when I ought to have fought in the party room for the acceptance of views which I had been unable to prevail upon my colleagues to accept in cabinet. However, even if I had done so, it is improbable that the course of events would have been changed.

The British tradition is that a Minister who is not prepared to defend a cabinet decision must resign; but even in Great Britain this rule is not absolute.

In the National Government of 1931, the Prime Minister devised a formula whereby four cabinet ministers were freed to vote against tariff proposals which their colleagues supported.

This situation was more or less duplicated in Australia soon after I entered Parliament in 1940, when Mr Menzies was Prime Minister. The division list on the second reading of the Motor Vehicles Agreement Bill records the names of a number of Country Party Ministers among the "Noes" while the Prime Minister and his non-Country Party colleagues were included in the "Ayes". In this same division, my name is listed in the "Noes" while all other Labor members are included in the "Ayes". Because I felt that the Bill was inimical to the interests of the Ford Motor Company in my electorate, I was given permission by the party to record a vote against it; a futile gesture for, without Labor support, the Bill would not have been passed. The proposals were never implemented and some years later, as Minister for Post-War Reconstruction, I piloted through the House a Bill to repeal the 1940 act.

.   .   .

On 3 December, the day before the caucus debate on Bretton Woods was due to be resumed, there was a lengthy discussion in cabinet on whether Ministers had the right to dissent from cabinet decisions. I think it was Mr Holloway who asserted that Ministers should be entitled to put their views to the members of caucus which had the right to decide what action should be taken in the Parliament: Mr Ward went further and argued that a Minister could dissent not only from cabinet but also from F.P.L.P. decisions if he considered that they were not covered by the Party's platform as approved by Federal *Conference,* the supreme ruling authority of the A.L.P. I said that a Minister who disagreed with a cabinet decision, and whose convictions were so strong that he could not support it, should resign from cabinet; he could always recontest the vacancy thus created. The Prime Minister said that generally Ministers should support cabinet decisions but this was not an inflexible rule; a technical right existed for a Minister to disagree with the ruling of cabinet and the action of Ministers was left to their own personal honour.

2.12   The principles of cabinet government discussed by conference
Conference report, 1919, pp. 40–2

CABINET GOVERNMENT
Mr McNamara (V.) moved—That in the event of a Labor majority being obtained, the system of Cabinet Government be modified so as to associate in the administration of each Department a committee of five members elected by the Caucus.

Mr McNamara stated that this proposal had been carried at the Victorian State Conference, and the idea was to alter the time-worn system of Cabinet Government in both the State and Federal spheres, but particularly in the Federal. He considered that the existing system of Cabinet, which had come down pretty well from the days of Cromwell, had outlived its usefulness, and although there had been some breakaways from it, the methods were still substantially the same. They wanted to get away from the present system so that the work of administration could be carried out by practically the whole party, and not merely by the eight or 10 men chosen for the positions, as obtained now. There were Cabinet Ministers today who did not administer their

departments at all in the proper sense of administration, and he would like to
see the work distributed so that proper attention would be given to the all-
important functions of administration. It should mean more effective administration than what the people got at the present time. Ministers drawing high
salaries had in a sense become a class apart, and they came to caucus in a solid
body—even when they had differences of opinion on subjects— and presented
their proposals in such a way that it did not always make for the best in
legislation, nor afterwards in administration. It would be better to divide up the
work amongst the members of the Party, so that the real aims and objects of the
Party could find effective expression in accordance with the platform upon
which the members of the Party as a whole had been returned.

Miss Daley (V.) formally seconded the resolution, which she considered
sought to give democratic expression to the principles upon which Labor men
were returned, but which did not always find performance in the ranks of the
Parliamentary party. Big salaries had helped to spoil some men, and in their
interests and the interests of the Labor Movement this reform should be
brought about.

Not practicable

Mr Tudor (Leader of the Federal Parliamentary Labor Party) did not consider
that the scheme as outlined was practicable, although he did think that there
could with advantage be an extension of the system of Assistant Ministers. That
he believed would make for better results in government, and would tighten up
the work of administration. It was a mistake, however, to suppose that
Ministers had not voiced objections to Bills, and there was one in particular
which took about a month to discuss in caucus before finality was reached.

Mr Lutey (WA) moved as an amendment that the words "of five members"
be deleted so as to read:— That in the event of a Labor majority being obtained
the system of Cabinet Government be modified so as to associate in the administration of each Department a committee elected by the Caucus.

Mr Lutey thought that an advisory committee elected by the caucus would be
better than delegating five members to Departments. The Committee would be
a connecting link between the Government, and keep its members always in
close touch with the aims of the Labor Movement and see that they were
expressed in legislation and administration.

Mr Willcocks (WA) seconded the amendment which he felt would safeguard
Ministers, and would lead to the proper fixing of responsibility. Something of
this kind would lead to the prevention of "mistaken judgments"—to put the
matter mildly—and go a long way towards purifying public life.

Dividing responsibility

Mr O'Loghlen (WA) opposed both the motion and the amendment. He did not
believe in dividing the responsibility of Ministers, nor did he believe, either, in
members of a party knowing always beforehand what was likely to happen in
certain matters. It would be idiotic, for instance, for a Minister of Customs to
tell what a Tariff was going to be, and there were other things which might
require just as close safeguarding. The best course, he thought, would be to have
advisory committees. When Labor had been in power there was little or no fault
to be found with the legislation, but there was a good bit that could be urged in
some directions against administration.

Mr Storey (NSW) predicted that if responsibility of a Ministerial character
was divided it could then not be fixed. How could responsibility be fixed on a

tariff if the whole of the party knew its contents—where, for instance, the additional impost of a penny might mean millions? They had had when the Labor Government was in power in New South Wales a "Bill" committee, the members of which used to go through the measures when they came from the hands of the Parliamentary draughtsman. The aim was to perfect the Bills as much as was possible. The proposal now made would not wipe out wrong-doing, and the remedy was, if there were Ministers who were not trusted that others should take their places. Ministers endeavouring to faithfully carry out the work of Departments had a good deal to do, and he considered that they might be relieved of a lot if there were Parliamentary secretaries appointed to assist.

Expert advice

The President, Mr Holloway (V.) (who left the chair for the time being) said that he was pledged to support this proposition. It had been found in Victoria that Ministers, when approached on subjects in the Departments which they were supposed to administer, that frequently there were matters they did not understand. Ministers of an all-round character were usually chosen in the Federal sphere with a view as nearly as possible to all of the States being repre-sented. If those Ministers had members of the party assisting them there would probably be the advantage of expert advice being forthcoming instead of a Minister trying to grapple with everything and not succeeding effectively in one thing. Where there were expert men in the Party their services should be availed of in the realms of administration.

MR. O'LOGHLEN (WA)—He would be a foolish Minister who would not consult such a man.

The President replied that there had been Ministers who would not consult members of the Party at all. The genesis of this whole idea was to make for expertness in administration.

"Destroying responsible government"

Mr Theodore (Q.), in opposing both motion and amendment, asserted that any such proposal would destroy responsible Government. Under the terms of the motion a Minister would be subordinate to a committee of five. He had to agree with them or get out, and, even if such a committee were merely consultative, where was the proposition going to land them? If a Minister accepted the view of the five members, Cabinet responsibility was destroyed, which meant removing the responsibility from a Cabinet of ten to a committee of five. Under the present system Cabinet had to account to the Party for any errors made. If a Minister committed an error of judgment then the Cabinet had to be taken to task. A team selected by members of the Party in caucus was supposed to be the ablest team, yet this proposal asked that a committee of five should be appointed to sit in judgment over men who had already received the endorse-ment of the party as the best men. No party or Ministry could make progress under such an unworkable proposition. In Queensland there were in the Party various committees which dealt with Education, Finance, Mining, Industrial, etc. for the purpose of watching the legislation proposed:—

SENATOR FERRICKS (Q)—All the Labor parties have that.

MR. THEODORE—Quite so; and the committees consulting with the Minister helped him as a rule. If one had to refer, say, industrial matters to a committee of five there would be delay, and it might happen that only about two decisions in a week would be given in matters requiring possibly quick handling. If a Minister led a Party into difficulties he should not remain a Minister, and Caucus had its remedy. The existing system which obtained in Queensland was adequate for all purposes and the proposals now made would hamstring the Party, a Ministry and all political progress.

The amendment was defeated on the voices, and the motion was defeated by 17 votes to 11 on the following division:—

For the motion: Messrs McNamara, Carey, Barnes, Sutherland, Lutey, Willcock, Jones, Graham, Stewart, and Holloway; Miss Daley.

Against the motion: Messrs Jelley, Gunn, Birrell, Grealy, Whitford, Makin, Ferricks, L. McDonald, Page, Theodore, Demaine, Storey, Gardiner, Farrell, Molesworth, O'Loghlen; and Mrs Storey.

2.13   Caucus rejects Chifley's budget
Caucus minutes, 29 October 1941

The P.M. then called on the Treasurer Mr Chifley to explain the Budget proposals to the Party. This was done at length & various Persons were thanked by the Treasurer for assistance given.

Mr Rosevear moved, Mr James seconded, That the Budget be withdrawn and it be an instruction to the Cabinet to reconstruct same in order to provide the payment of 25/- per week to Pensioners. (Carried.).

.   .   .

Moved by Mr Curtin, seconded by Mr Forde, that the motion of this afternoon dealing with Pensions be *committed*. (Carried).

It was decided to adopt the Treasurer's suggestion to bring down a fresh budget early in the new year granting £1.5.0 per week to Pensioners.

2.14   Whitlam rebuffed by caucus
Sydney Morning Herald, 20 September 1970

WHITLAM REBUFFED TWICE ON INCOMES
From Brian Johns, Political Correspondent

CANBERRA, WEDNESDAY—The Federal Parliamentary Labor Caucus rebuffed the Prime Minister, Mr Whitlam, twice today over proposals for a referendum to control incomes.

Caucus rejected a move, supported by Mr Whitlam, for a referendum to be held on the control of incomes as well as prices.

It also decided that if any of the Opposition parties brought forward a bill for a referendum on income control, it would meet again to consider the Government's stand.

This contradicts Mr Whitlam's firm declaration in the House of Representatives yesterday that the Government would not oppose an incomes bill supplementary to his prices referendum if the Opposition wanted to introduce it.

Answering a question in Parliament after the Caucus meeting this morning, Mr Whitlam said only that the Government was "willing to consider immediately any proposition that comes before the Parliament from any of our opponents" for an incomes referendum.

Caucus voted by 45 votes to 52 to reject a proposal put forward by Senator J. McClelland (NSW) that a separate referendum on wage control be held. Mr Whitlam and most of his ministers were on the losing side.

However, the Treasurer, Mr Crean, spoke and voted against the separate referendum.

The Government's bill for a prices referendum was introduced in the Senate—where its fate will be decided—last night and was debated late tonight.

It will be debated further tomorrow, but there is a feeling in senior Government quarters that no vote should be taken until next week, after the Parramatta by-election, to be held on Saturday.

The DLP introduced a bill in the Senate today for a referendum to enable the Government to control both prices and incomes. The issues would be put in a single question rather than separately as Mr Whitlam had wanted.

However, Caucus endorsed a recommendation today by Mr Whitlam that the Government should oppose the DLP's move.

Caucus did this by accepting a report from Mr Whitlam of his talks with DLP senators yesterday on the referendum.

Mr Whitlam repeated his publicly stated view that although he believed the Federal Parliament should have the power to control prices and incomes, he did not believe it was appropriate to have a referendum on the lines suggested by the DLP.

Apart from reporting on his talks with the DLP and giving his reasons for opposing its referendum proposal, Mr Whitlam did not speak during the two-hour Caucus debate this morning.

At an early stage the Minister for Works, Senator Cavanagh, moved that the Government should take an initiative in the Senate for a referendum on the control of incomes, but this resolution was over-shadowed by Senator McClelland's proposal.

Senator McClelland moved that the Government should immediately introduce a bill for a referendum on incomes control in the House of Representatives and rush it into the Senate.

He said the Government should not have its strategy determined by the DLP.

Senator McClelland's proposition opened a tense, closely argued debate in which usual Caucus groupings were shattered.

2.15   Caucus's performance reviewed
Courier-Mail, 15 September 1973

WHITLAM GOVERNMENT HAS ARRIVED AT CROSS-ROADS
This Week in Canberra—from Wallace Brown

CANBERRA—It simply had to come, this flexing of the muscles by the Labor Caucus, this revolt against the absolute authority Prime Minister Whitlam has been asserting since he took office nine months ago.

It was inevitable that the inexorable Labor Party system would eventually catch up with him, ever since the halcyon days between last December 2 and 19 when he formed his interim two-man Government with Mr Barnard and had to answer to nobody.

As a result, this week will go down as the most significant one since Labor came to power, because it has put the Whitlam Government at the cross-roads in its method of operation.

It means that either Mr Whitlam changes his system and lets the Caucus into the decision-making processes fully, or else the Caucus is likely again to over-rule Cabinet decisions it does not like, just as it did on Wednesday.

This sensitivity is not news to any political party, but particularly not to the

Labor Party. It is laid down in Labor's rules that the collective decision of the Caucus is binding on all members of the party.

Wartime Prime Minister, John Curtin found he had to conform to the wishes of the Caucus when limits were set in the areas to which conscripted servicemen could be sent.

Mr Chifley in the late 1940s found he had to follow a Caucus directive to lift wartime controls under which he was attempting to restrain inflation by pegging wages.

Caucus

Similarly, in Opposition, Mr Whitlam found that his 14-man Parliamentary Executive could only make recommendations to the full Caucus, which often rejected them or brought in something quite different.

Only last year for instance the Caucus, in joyous anticipation that it was about to divide up the spoils of office, directed that when Labor gained Government it would have at least 27 ministers—against the wishes of Mr Whitlam who wanted fewer than that.

And so into this week, a humiliating one for the giant of the Labor Party, for the man whose electoral charisma finally brought the party into office, for the Prime Minister who seeks to emulate the style of Sir Robert Menzies and sometimes succeeds.

A week marked by flat Caucus directives to compromise on interest rates; to back away from Galston as the site for Sydney's second airport; to draft legislation for a referendum on price controls.

Yet the internal Caucus turbulence, the feeling of discontent that it was not being consulted sufficiently, had been brewing for a long time.

It revealed itself when the rural rump of the party led by the Northern Development Minister (Dr Patterson) persuaded Caucus to direct that there be no further tariff changes without consultation.

Though the discontent has been general, it has been left to various individuals to ventilate it—such as Aboriginal Affairs Minister Gordon Bryant, Left-Wing Senator John Wheeldon of Western Australia, middle-roader Mr J. Berinson (W.A.) and Right-Winger Mr Paul Keating (N.S.W.)

And it was the veteran Labor man Mr Fred Birrell of South Australia who warned Mr Whitlam that he was in danger of losing control of caucus—which in turn spurred Mr Whitlam on his snap turnabout move for the prices referendum.

Yet the issue which upsets Labor men most—and remains unresolved until probably next week's Caucus—is Mr Whitlam's current procedure by which he announces Cabinet decisions to his Tuesday press conferences, fait accompli, before they have been endorsed by the Wednesday Caucus meetings.

His weekly press conferences follow a pre-election promise to the National Press Club that he would have such a conference every Tuesday he was in Canberra.

It is a promise he has honoured and to which the press corps is holding him.

For the media it is a welcome change from the system of previous regimes when Prime Ministers ran for cover.

But the Parliament in general, and the Labor Party in particular, does not see the situation in quite the same light.

3

The Leader of the Labor Party

The Leader of the party has always been elected by the federal caucus. In one case the conference invited a leading state politician to enter federal politics, but insisted that caucus alone could elect the leader (3.1). That right has remained unchallenged.

Leadership elections have been straightforward, as in Fisher's case (3.2), very close, as with Curtin (3.3), or easy, as when Chifley was elected (3.4). Naturally considerable significance is given to the leader because, although in theory he is only the first among equals, he has wide prestige, considerable influence inside the party and receives great publicity. Often the election of one man rather than another is seen as a significant victory for a particular section of the party. Whitlam's election was fairly simple in 1967 (3.5, 3.6).

One regular political dictum is 'Never resign, never explain'. Labor leaders have not always followed it. In 1905 Watson offered his resignation after two decisions of conference had, in his view, cast doubts on his ability (see later, 4.1). He was persuaded to withdraw the resignation. In 1943 Curtin, then prime minister, threatened to resign after he had been attacked in caucus; he withdrew the resignation after caucus had passed a vote of confidence in him (3.7, 3.8). In 1968 Whitlam resigned and sought re-election (3.9); he was opposed by Dr Jim Cairns (3.10) and the explanatory letters of the two men show the different ideas on leadership that each of them had.

While caucus elects ministers, the prime minister distributes the portfolios. But until recently it was assumed that prime ministers did not have the power to dismiss them without caucus's agreement. Curtin was given the power to dismiss ministers, but never used it, although he did suspend E. J. Ward (3.11). In July 1975 Whitlam sacked Cairns because, Whitlam claimed, he had misled parliament (3.12). Whitlam later received caucus support for his action.

Different leaders used a wide variety of tactics. Watson was prepared to commit his party in advance of consulting caucus because he believed, correctly, that they would support him (3.13). When Hughes was faced with a backbench revolt in the House, he first backed down, then referred the affair to a committee and finally persuaded caucus to accept an amendment to the committee's report (3.14). But such intrigues could only work occasionally. Chifley declared himself to be the servant of caucus (3.15), although he in fact manipulated it to ensure support. Whitlam believed in 'crashing through' obstacles and threatened to resign in some instances when faced with caucus opposition (3.16). Each leader has his own style to suit his personality.

3.1 The rights of caucus to select leaders debated
Conference report, 1919, pp. 103–4, 107–8

FEDERAL CAMPAIGN DIRECTOR
Mr. Watkins (T) then moved—
1. that, in view of the urgent importance of the forthcoming Federal elections

to the workers of Australia, it is desirable to set up a Campaign Directorate, and
2. That the Hon. T. J. Ryan (Premier of Queensland) be appointed Campaign Director, and that he be added as a member of the joint committee of the Inter-State Executive and the Federal Parliamentary Party Executive, to take part with them in the formulation of the policy statement of the Australian Labor Party at the forthcoming elections.

(At this stage Mr. Ryan left the Conference Room).

Mr. Watkins said this was a most urgent matter. The important problem was how to win the Federal elections.

Mr. Bramston (N.S.W.) seconded. If Mr. Ryan was placed in this position the people of Australia would have fresh hopes. They could win if Mr. Ryan was put in the position where he could throw his whole weight into the fight with voice and pen.

"A Unique Compliment"

Mr. Carey (V.) opposed the motion. It looked like surrendering the Labor movement to one man. Mr. Ryan was a good man who had done excellent work, but was that any reason why they should abdicate everything in favor of one man? Mr. Ryan himself did not want that. They had paid him a unique compliment—something that no other man had got. Let it rest at that. Of course, it all arose from good motives, but he was against this.

Mr. Morgan (W.A.) moved an amendment—That the words "and that he be appointed Campaign Director" be deleted. Mr. Corboy (W.A.) seconded.

Mr. Butterfield (S.A.) said the main reason for the motion was to have Mr. Ryan as the mouthpiece of the election. After the election his position would be determined by the Parliamentary Party. He opposed the amendment. They should place Mr. Ryan in a position where he would have to be accepted by their opponents in the fight.

Senator Barnes (V.) supported the amendment. By carrying the resolution they would be putting one man in the position where he could over-ride everybody else in Federal politics. They were making him a dictator in the Movement, and he for one would not be a party to that. There was no question about what he said being true. Where would the Federal Executive and the Federal Parliamentary Party stand if this motion was carried? The Federal Party had taken steps already, and would naturally get all the help they could, including that of Mr. Ryan. Why, then, pass this motion? It would be foolish to put Mr. Ryan in the position they were contemplating and he felt sure that Mr. Ryan did not want that himself. He would not place any man in the Labor Movement in the position of dictator.

.   .   .

"Wanted in Federal Politics"

Mr. Holloway (V.) said they all wanted Mr. Ryan in Federal politics. The only difference was as to the methods adopted. Mr. Tudor was the accredited leader, and would be so until the Federal Caucus displaced him. It was not for the Conference to say that Mr. Ryan should be leader. It was hard to see how anybody could oppose Mr. Ryan as leader, Attorney-General, and Prime Minister if Labor got into power at the next elections. But that was a matter for the Federal Party to determine. To do what had been decided on the previous day was, to his mind, in conflict with what had been done at the June Conference, when a committee had been appointed to superintend the Federal campaign. This Conference had no power delegated to it to upset what had been done then. What was done then would be largely nullified, and Mr. Ryan would be in the eyes of the party and the outside people the leader of the party. Mr. Ryan himself would see that, and had himself admitted that he would be no party to placing anybody in a false position. If he was elected Campaign Director he could only be looked on as the leader of the party, although Mr. Tudor was leader constitutionally. They all wanted to have Mr. Ryan in the lead, but he wanted to see it done in a constitutional way. He contended that the committee already appointed had the power to get the assistance of Mr. Ryan in the coming fight.

Regarding Authority

Mr. Ryan said they should not anticipate what the Federal Caucus might do. When a man went into Caucus he went there on an equal standing with his fellows. All he wanted to know was what Conference wanted him to do in the coming campaign. He did not want to make statements without the authority of the party, and he wanted to know if he had that authority or not.

DELEGATES: Yes, you have.

MR. RYAN: Well, that is all I want to know. Naturally, he wished to ascertain his standing in the matter, so that everything could be done in the smoothest possible way. He intended, at any rate, to make his position clear to the Federal Parliamentary Party. He would not "butt" in against the party on any account.

3.2   Andrew Fisher elected leader
Caucus minutes, 23, 30 October 1907

Spence moved, McGregor seconded, 'That the Party hears with very deep regret the decision of Mr. Watson to resign the Leadership owing to the severe strain upon his health, & that in deference to his expressed wish steps be taken to appoint his successor this day week.' Carried.

A discussion ensued on the question of providing a Secretary for the Leader, & it was decided That each member contribute 10/- per month (commencing next month) for providing assistance for the Leader of the Party.

Webster moved, Maloney seconded, That the motion carried last Wednesday relating to the filling of the Leadership be rescinded, & that nominations be received today & the election be held next Wednesday. Lost.

Watkins moved, Hall seconded, 'That the method of electing the Leader be by an absolute majority.' Cd.

It was decided that Senator De Largie & Frank G. Tudor take charge of the Ballot & that the Chairman be the returning officer.

A. Fisher	was nominated by	Dr Maloney,	secd.	O'Malley
W. M. Hughes	" " "	D. Hall,	"	T. Brown
E. L. Batchelor	" " "	G. McGregor,	"	W. Storey
W. G. Spence	" " "	P. Lynch,	"	D. Watkins

E. L. Batchelor withdrew, & after an exhaustive Ballot Hon. A. Fisher was elected.

W. M. Hughes then moved, Spence seconded, That A. Fisher be elected Chairman. Carried unanimously.

A. Fisher thanked the members for electing him.

3.3   John Curtin elected leader
Caucus minutes, 1 October 1935

Leader J. H. Scullin reported that he had received a cablegram from Messrs. Makin & Frost, in which Mr. Makin intimated his intention of nominating for the position of Leader.

G. Lawson stated he had also received a Telegram from M. Blackburn, asking him to forward a Ballot paper.

Mr. A. Drakford further reported he had received Correspondence from M. Blackburn appointing him as proxy and requesting him to record Mr. Blackburn's vote in accordance with his wishes as enclosed.

At this stage Mr. F. Brenan moved and J. Holloway seconded, that consideration of the appointment of a Leader of the Party be deferred until after the conclusion of Conferences designed to promote Unity, now about to be held, and until the return of Members of the Party now abroad.

Messrs. Martens, Curtin & Riordan opposed the motion. On being put to the meeting the motion was defeated.

The Ballot was then proceeded with, and Messrs. G. Martens and E. Green were duly elected scrutineers.

It was resolved on the motion of Dr. W. Maloney, seconded by C. Barnard, that Messrs. Makin, Frost and Blackburn be allowed a vote in accordance with their wishes. On the vote being taken the scrutineers announced the result as follows: Curtin 11 Votes, Forde 10 votes.

The Chairman J. H. Scullin declared J. Curtin duly elected Leader of the Party, and in doing so offered him his heartiest congratulations.

Mr. J. Curtin in taking the chair as Leader, thanked members for the honor they had confered upon him and stated he would at all times do his utmost to retain the confidence which members had placed in him, and would endeavour to the best of his ability to follow in the footsteps of the late Leader.

3.4   Ben Chifley elected leader
Caucus minutes, 5, 12 July 1945

A suggestion was made by Mr. Forde that the Party should meet on Wednesday next, 11th instant, at 11 a.m. After a brief discussion, Mr. Williams moved, and Mr. Conelan seconded 'That a meeting of the Party be held at 2.30 p.m. on that day.'

Senator O'Flaherty moved an amendment as follows: 'That the meeting take place at 11 a.m. on the 11th instant.' Seconded by Mr. Dedman. Lost.

Mr. Johnson moved a further amendment as follows: 'That a Party meeting take place on Thursday next, the 12th instant, at 2.30 p.m.' Carried. The amendment then became the motion and as such as confirmed.

Wires appointing Proxies were received from J. Langtry, T. Sheehy, D. Mountjoy, R. Pollard, Senator Nash and Senator Tangney.

Election of Leader

Mr. Williams moved 'That the election of Leader be postponed until the return of Dr. Evatt, Mr. Pollard and Senator Nash.' No seconder, the motion lapsed.

The question of validity of Proxies was raised. The Prime Minister ruled that these were in order.

Mr. James moved as follows: 'That owing to the absence of so many members of the Party from the meeting:

1. 'That the present Prime Minister, Mr. Forde, and the Cabinet carry on for a period of five weeks as from today.
2. At this meeting we then proceed only to elect a Leader and fill the vacant Cabinet position.
3. In the meantime, we request Cabinet to give consideration to recommending to Caucus the appointment of Assistants to those Ministers who are overworked, on similar lines to those adopted by the New Zealand Labor Government.
4. This question to be decided by Secret Ballot.'
   Seconded by Mr. Breen. Lost.
   Mr. Martens moved as an amendment, the following:
   1. 'That the eighteen members of the Cabinet be re-appointed.
   2. That we proceed to elect the Leader and then to elect a Minister to fill the Cabinet vacancy caused by the death of Mr. Curtin.
   3. That this matter be decided by Ballot.'
   Ruled out of order.

Election of Returning Officer

Mr. Rosevear was appointed Returning Officer.

Scrutineers: Messrs. Russell, Daly, Bryson and Senator Grant were appointed.

Election of Leader

Candidates: Messrs. Chifley, Forde, Evatt and Makin.

The Returning Officer reported that Mr. Chifley was elected with an absolute majority.

Mr. Chifley thanked members for the honor they had confirmed on him. He stated he would give of his best at all times and asked members for their co-operation in all matters, as success could only be assured if this were done.

Mr. Forde congratulated Mr. Chifley on his election and assured him and the Party that he would in future, as in the past, give him the fullest support, as he did in the case of Messrs. Scullin and Curtin as Deputy Leader.

3.5   Leadership prospects for Labor Party, 1967
Sydney Morning Herald, 7 February 1967

LABOR'S DAY OF DECISION
Canberra Commentary from Ian Fitchett

A last minute count of expected alignments in tomorrow's vital ballot for the leadership of the Federal Parliamentary Labor Party indicates that the present deputy leader, Mr. Whitlam, will come very close to obtaining an absolute majority over his other opponents.

But Mr. Whitlam's chances of gaining an absolute majority will be lessened if Mr. F. M. Daly (N.S.W.) decides to contest the leadership as part of an alleged pact with Mr. Whitlam's main challenger, Mr. F. Crean (Vic.), aimed at achieving the latter's victory with Mr. Daly as his deputy.

However, even if Mr. Daly runs it is expected that he will not be able to influence enough votes and preferences in favour of Mr. Crean to affect the final outcome; all that he would achieve would be to make Mr. Whitlam depend on preferences to become leader.

Any move by Mr. Daly against Mr. Whitlam by standing for the leadership in the present circumstances would almost certainly destroy his very good chances of becoming deputy leader.

The present state of Federal Caucus is such that it is now obvious that Tasmania and Queensland will dictate the final result, with Mr. Whitlam relying heavily on a bloc vote of seven of the eight Tasmanian votes.

The Labor Party has suffered such huge losses in Victoria since 1955 that this State, the second largest in Australia, can send only eight members and four senators, a total of 12, to a Caucus meeting at which it will put forward two candidates for the leadership, Mr. Crean and Dr. J. F. Cairns. There are 33 Victorian seats in the House of Representatives and 10 Senate places but Labor's numbers are so reduced there that Tasmania, the smallest State, will have only four votes less when polling begins tomorrow.

Although the party lost three seats in N.S.W. last November it still holds 17 seats there as well as five Senate places, compared with six seats and three Senate places in Queensland, three seats and six Senate places in South Australia, three seats and five Senate places in Western Australia and the A.C.T. seat. As a result there will be 69 votes at tomorrow's Caucus and Mr. Whitlam would have to secure 35 primaries to secure an absolute majority.

Mr. Whitlam's strength will lie to a large degree in the split in the Left-wing vote between Mr. Crean and Dr. Cairns.

The Victorian A.L.P. secretary, Mr. W. H. Hartley, is backing Dr. Cairns while the State president, Mr. W. Brown, has swung in behind Mr. Calwell's man, Mr. Crean, with the result that this hitherto ruthlessly dictatorial State executive no longer possesses the absolute authority to direct members and senators from that State how they should vote.

The upshot is a reported leakage of at least three if not four of the 12 Victorian votes to Mr. Whitlam, an action which will require some degree of courage on the part of those who intend defecting.

Votes

Mr. Whitlam should be assured of seven Tasmanian votes, seven of the nine Queensland votes and break even in both South Australia and Western Australia, thus gaining another eight or nine votes.

This leaves N.S.W., where Mr. Whitlam should secure a small majority of the 22 votes. He could also get three or four from Victoria and the lone vote of the member for the A.C.T., Mr. J. R. Fraser.

All in all Queensland and Tasmania should decide the issue and it appears likely that short of any last-minute disaster for Mr. Whitlam they should come in strongly behind him and give him the coveted leadership.

Obviously a false step for Mr. Whitlam would be to create any suspicion in the minds of the Tasmanian bloc that he had made any deals elsewhere for the deputy leadership as the Tasmanians are solidly behind one of their own members, Mr. L. H. Barnard, to fill that position.

As a result the deputy leadership fight could end up in a close contest between Mr. Daly and Mr. Barnard, although both Mr. Crean and Dr. Cairns will provide tough opposition in the likely event of their defeat in the main leadership ballot.

In Mr. Whitlam's favour tomorrow will be the desire of a big cross-section of Caucus to elect a leader who cannot be described as a "cliff-hanger", or one of whom two or three individual members might claim that their vote put him in office.

Responsible

These are the responsible Labor men who believe that the new leader should not have a questionable mandate. There can be no gainsaying the fact that Mr. Whitlam is the only candidate who could win outright in a very bitter struggle.

Every effort has been made by Mr. Calwell and his followers to exploit the undoubted element of anti-Whitlam feeling in the party but this attack has been blunted by the Left-wing split over the Crean—Cairns candidatures.

The N.S.W. Left-wing will support Dr. Cairns almost to a man, but their counterparts from Victoria will back Mr. Crean and this does not make for a united front against Mr. Whitlam.

Mr. Daly's position is still a mystery. If he runs for the leadership Mr. Whitlam's chances of an absolute majority must diminish, but enough of the preferences of those who might vote for him or for Mr. K. E. Beazley (W.A.) should flow back to Mr. Whitlam to return him the winner on preferences.

If Mr. Daly's candidature for the leadership should embarrass or handicap Mr. Whitlam in any way it would surely prove a false step. Mr. Daly is the one man who cannot afford to make last minute enemies if he is to defeat Mr. Barnard for the deputy leadership and his final decision will be made with this fact very much in mind.

3.6   Whitlam elected leader

Canberra Times, 9 February 1967

MR. WHITLAM LEADS A.L.P.

Labor's leadership ballots yesterday ended in an unexpected compromise. Mr. Gough Whitlam and his nominee, Mr. Lance Barnard, soundly defeated the left-wing candidates for Leader and Deputy Leader of the party.

Their victory was tempered by the success of the two left-wing supported candidates for the Senate positions. Senator Murphy, N.S.W. and Senator Cohen, Victoria, were elected Leader and Deputy Leader in the Senate.

Mr. Whitlam defeated Dr. Jim Cairns, of Victoria, for the leadership by 39 votes to 15 on second preferences.

There were five candidates for the leadership—Mr. Whitlam and Mr. Daly, N.S.W., Dr. Cairns and Mr. Crean, Victoria, and Mr. Beazley, W.A.

With one member of the Caucus absent because of the Hobart fires, Mr. Whitlam received 32 of the 68 first preference votes, against 15 for Dr. Cairns and 12 for the other left wing candidate, Mr. Crean.

On the first preference vote count Mr. Whitlam received one vote from Mr. Beazley's total of three, the other two going to Mr. Daly.

On the next count Mr. Daly was eliminated with six of his eight preferences going to Mr. Whitlam. Dr. Cairns had received no preferences at that final stage.

Three votes short

Last night Mr. Whitlam announced the results of the four leadership ballots but would answer only one or two questions. He will give a full-scale news conference this afternoon.

The Caucus began almost 1½ hours late. It had been scheduled for 2.30 p.m. but was adjourned to allow two delayed Tasmanian members, Mr. Duthie and Senator Poke, to attend. A third Tasmanian, Mr. Davies, returned to Tasmania from Melbourne when he heard that a relative's property had been destroyed in the fires.

The meeting took only about 15 minutes to elect Mr. Whitlam. On the first count he was only three votes short of an absolute majority and although the final result was decided by preferences it was never in doubt. Applause at 4.40 p.m. signalled his victory.

.   .   .

Details of counting

Leader Candidate	1st count	2nd	Final
Whitlam	32	33	39
Cairns	15	15	15
Crean	12	12	14 out
Daly	6	8 out	
Beazley	3 out		

3.7   Curtin offers his resignation
Caucus minutes, 24 March 1943

An argument developed on a Statement made by Mr. Calwell, as a result of which the P.M. retired from the meeting.

Mr. Forde took the Chair; He then read a letter from the P.M. as follows:

Prime Minister,
Canberra,
24th March, 1943.

Dear Mr. Forde,

In view of the accusation made against me by Mr. Calwell, i.e., 'that I will finish up on the other side (the anti-Labor side) leading a National Government', I invite the party either to dissociate itself from the accusation or appoint another leader. Obviously, if the charge has a semblance of justification, the party is in an invidious position in entrusting its leadership to a potential traitor.

Yours Faithfully,
John Curtin.

The Hon. F. M. Forde,
Canberra.

Mr. Calwell withdrew the statement he had made and expressed regret for what had occurred.

Senator Cunningham moved That this Party has complete confidence in our Leader Mr. Curtin. 2nd. Mr. Conellan; on being put to the meeting it was carried unanimously.

3.8   Curtin offers his resignation
Daily Telegraph, 25 March 1943

P.M. THREATENS TO RESIGN
CAUCUS CLASH WITH CALWELL

CANBERRA, WEDNESDAY—A threat by the Prime Minister (Mr. Curtin) to resign leadership of the party was saved by a vote of confidence at a meeting of Federal Labor Caucus today.

Mr. Curtin's threat followed allegations by Mr. Calwell (M.H.R. Vic.) that he had let down his party by compromising with the Opposition.

The clash between the Prime Minister and Mr. Calwell occurred over a Caucus Committee's report on the proposed extension of franchise to servicemen under the age of 21.

The chairman of the committee, Mr. Barnard (Tas.), said the committee had decided that franchise should be extended to all men in the fighting forces aged 18 or more, and all those of the same age liable to call-up.

Mr. Calwell, member of the Committee, challenged this statement, claiming the Committee had agreed the franchise should be extended to everyone aged 18 or more.

Mr. Calwell was supported by another Committee member, Mr. Rosevear (N.S.W.).

During Mr. Calwell's speech, Mr. Curtin interjected, accusing Mr. Calwell of being a Sham-fighter. Mr. Calwell than attacked Mr. Curtin for having comromised with Labor's opponents.

Vote of Confidence

"If you go on retreating like this, we will find you on the other side or leading a National Government," Mr. Calwell said.

In reply the Prime Minister said Mr. Calwell had been a member of the Labor Party for years, but had never figured in any fight for Labor principles.

"Since the age of 16 you have had a sheltered job," said Mr. Curtin.

"You have never fought for the Labor Party, and have never carried the Labor flag in any electorates except your own."

(Mr. Calwell is M.H.R. for Melbourne)

Mr. Curtin then contrasted his own service to Labor with Mr. Calwell's, and recalled the many fights he had been in for Labor causes.

When he ended his speech, Mr. Curtin left the room.

A demand by Senator Lamp (Tas.) that the Prime Minister be asked to withdraw his remarks, was not accepted by Caucus.

At the conclusion of the meeting the Minister for the Army (Mr. Forde), who had replaced Mr. Curtin as chairman, called members back to hear a letter he had first received from the Prime Minister.

The letter declared that Mr. Calwell had branded the Prime Minister as a potential political traitor, and that unless the rest of Caucus dissociated itself from the implication, it would have to find a new leader.

Mr. Calwell then expressed regret and withdrew his remarks, and the meeting carried a vote of confidence in Mr. Curtin.

3.9   Whitlam explains his intention to seek re-election
Advertiser, 25 April 1968

TEST OF LABOR LEADER'S LETTER TO CAUCUS

Following is the text of Mr. Whitlam's letter to all members of the Federal A.L.P. Caucus, setting out his reasons for throwing open the leadership of the party:—

As I undertook in my telegram of last Friday afternoon, I now set out the reasons which oblige me to take the unprecedented course of throwing open the leadership of our party, although my leadership has never been challenged inside Caucus.

The proceedings of Federal Executive on Wednesday morning, Thursday morning and afternoon and Friday morning had produced a thoroughly damaging situation for the party as a whole.

A direct and deliberate affront had been offered to the Tasmanian Conference, Tasmanian Executive and the sole remaining Labor Government.

Bitterness

The proceedings created a well and deservedly publicised impression of intransigence, factionalism and bitterness.

Federal Executive still has no rules for laying or hearing charges.

It can at any time invoke the emergency powers adopted 13 years ago.

The Parliamentary party bears the direct brunt of any loss of public confidence or esteem.

Its leader was in the minority at every stage and in all attempts to find a reasonable solution.

Nearly half the majority against me was provided on each occasion by four of our colleagues, including two of my fellow office bearers.

All these factors created a situation which I could not ignore if I am to retain any public credit or credibility as leader of our party.

Nor could the Caucus ignore them if it is to retain public credit or credibility as a future Government of this nation.

I do not contest the propriety of any member of the Caucus voting against me on the Federal Conference or Executive.

On the contrary, as you all know, I have resisted the whole concept of block voting at all levels of the party.

Responsibility

I do believe, however, that all members of Caucus have a special responsibility to promote the interests of the Caucus.

In particular they should promote our chief function, which is the formation of a Labor Government at the earliest possible moment.

Members of Caucus who are members of the Federal Executive and Conference solely by virtue of their positions in Caucus have a higher responsibility.

They are in effect the representatives of Caucus.

Where Caucus has declared a position on an issue, they are honor bound to express the wishes of Caucus.

Even where Caucus has not expressed a view or is not entitled under the rules of the party to express a view, they still have a very high responsibility to promote the interests of Caucus.

Certainly they have no right to promote the interests of a faction of a State executive at the cost of seats we hold or must win.

It was widely publicised and noted that I do not possess the confidence of the majority of members of Caucus who happened to be members of the Federal Executive.

This being so, I believe I am bound to refer to the Caucus to discover whether this majority reflects the majority opinion of Caucus.

Effective

Talk of personal dictatorship will not cut much ice in our Caucus and Caucus executive, which in the past 14 months have proved the most effective since the defeat of the Chifley Government.

During my leadership and with my support, the Caucus office-bearers and the six State leaders have come to be ex-officio delegates to our Federal Conference.

I have advocated a greater voice for electorates and affiliated bodies in the decision-making processes of our party.

My whole approach is based on the obvious premise that we cannot achieve significant economic, social and industrial reforms by political means unless we hold over half the seats in the House of Representatives and win over half the votes of the people of Australia.

3.10   Cairns seeks party leadership
Advertiser, 27 April 1968

DR. CAIRNS'S LETTER

MELBOURNE, APRIL 26—Following is the text of the letter by Dr. Cairns to all members of Federal Labor Caucus:

Mr. Whitlam has notified all members of the Parliamentary Labor Party that on Tuesday, April 30, he intends to resign the leadership and recontest it. I deeply regret that the leadership has been made an issue by his decision to resign.

A contest for leadership is not my choice. It is the result alone of Mr. Whitlam's decisions.

To permit Mr. Whitlam to contest the leadership unopposed would leave the incorrect impression that the Parliamentary party unanimously supports his stand.

Initiative

The initiative to pursue the course to resign remains alone with Mr. Whitlam.

If he proceeds with his resignation and recontests the leadership, I will also be a candidate in that contest.

His resignation and conduct have endangered our party because they brought completely into the public arena matters which should have been settled elsewhere within the party's constitutional procedures.

They have raised the question just how far can Mr. Whitlam go in defying majority decisions of the party authorities of which he is a member or with which he is associated. They raise the question: Whose party is this—ours or his?

Traditions

The historic traditions of the party are that its democratic processes should be preserved, widened and deepened, not placed more and more in the hands of one person.

In 1966, at a special conference of the party, Mr. Whitlam did two things. He apologised to the Federal executive for his public attack on it, and said, "I now undertake to work within the frame-work of the party and to accept the decisions of its properly constituted authorities."

Mr. Whitlam has failed to honor this undertaking by his present attack on party authorities, and by his resignation to seek authority to override them still further should the need arise.

I am opposed to any attempt by any man to centralise power or to dominate his party colleagues.

I cannot accede to the leader's demand that Parliamentarians must agree with him within the various party conferences and executives because, disguise it as he may, this is the demand he makes.

Parliament

These conferences and executives are the parliament of the Labor Party, that of the average man who wants to have a say in public affairs, for there is no better available for any one in Australia.

Tens of thousands of Australians have labored over many years to build up the consultative processes of the Australian Labor Party.

But there are those who believe they are being "modern" in seeking to replace this perhaps rough and ready, but basically sound, process, by one that places an elite—and even an individual—at the top on the assumption that it, or he, knows best.

Arrogance

This is intellectual arrogance and dangerous folly. Just this is what is involved in the present crisis.

It is vitally necessary that the Parliamentary party should work in harmony with the "constitutional" authorities of the party.

Mr. Whitlam has proved for three years, not only in the case of the Victorian executive but that of the Victorian conference and the Federal executive, that he cannot achieve this.

Unless harmony is established it must be obvious that the party will be in a continuing state of crisis, which will place in danger the seats of many of our present members, whose majorities will not stand this state of affairs.

This means that we will, without question, be pushed further into the political wilderness despite the incredible weakness of the Liberal-Country Party coalition.

3.11 Ward suspended by Curtin
Daily Telegraph, 25 June 1943

IMMEDIATE FEDERAL POLL: WARD RELIEVED OF OFFICE

CANBERRA, THURSDAY— A Federal Election will be held almost immediately, the Prime Minister (Mr. Curtin) announced in the House of Representatives tonight.

Mr. Curtin's announcement followed a decision by Full Cabinet to relieve the Minister for Labor (Mr. Ward) of his portfolio pending an investigation by a Royal Commission.

The Royal Commission will investigate Mr. Ward's allegation in Parliament on Tuesday that a War Cabinet defence document was missing.

Mr. Ward's suspension from office took place immediately.

In his announcement to the House of Representatives Mr. Curtin said that immediately Parliament had passed certain machinery measures, he intended asking the Governor General (Lord Gowrie) for a dissolution.

The Opposition Leader (Mr. Fadden) agreed that an election was desirable to solve the present unworkable state of Parliament.

Coles' stand

The decisions to release Mr. Ward of his duties and to appoint a Royal Commission were made at a hurried meeting of Full Cabinet tonight.

The Opposition had earlier demanded in the House of Representatives that a Royal Commission be appointed.

Before Cabinet met it was learned that Mr. Coles (Ind. Vic.) had told the Prime Minister he considered the whole missing document subject should be clarified before the House rose.

Mr. Coles added that until the matter was settled he considered Mr. Ward should either resign his office or be removed.

Mr. Coles' demand made it certain that unless the Government acted on his suggestion he would vote for the Opposition motion for a Royal Commission.

This would have resulted in the Government being defeated and being forced to resign.

It is believed that at the Cabinet Meeting Mr. Ward refused to resign his commission on the grounds that it might be regarded in some quarters as an admission he was at fault.

He told Cabinet, however, that he did not wish to embarrass the Government, and would be willing to be relieved of his duties.

Parliament met today in an atmosphere of tension, which increased as the afternoon wore on.

When the proceedings began, the Prime Minister announced he had instituted thorough inquiries, and had found no evidence to support Mr. Ward's charge that a defence document was missing.

Mr. Ward then announced that he accepted the Prime Minister's assurance that no document was missing.

The document he referred to, he said, must therefore be still in existence.

Opposition members expressed angry dissatisfaction with the two ministerial statements, and finally moved the adjournment of the House to discuss the whole matter.

After a bitter debate the Opposition adjournment move was defeated 29−28.

3.12   Cairns sacked over loans rumpus
Financial Review, 3 July 1975

Mr. Whitlam last night sacked Dr. Cairns as Deputy Prime Minister without in any way re-establishing the credibility of his Government in the whole loans affair.

Dr. Cairns at the same time revealed a very damaging point against Mr. Whitlam—that his department knew of the Harris loan letter, which has provided Mr. Whitlam's central justification for removing Dr. Cairns, a fortnight ago.

Mr. Whitlam knew of the letter then and immediately sought advice from the Attorney-General's Department.

Yet on Tuesday, Mr. Whitlam divulged the letter with the following deceptive preamble: "Yesterday I was shown a letter in the following terms . . ."

The whole affair plays even further into the hands of the Opposition, which is pushing for a full inquiry into Government loan operations—to cover not only those involving Dr. Cairns, but those of Mr. Connor as well.

Dr. Cairns divulged last night that whether intentionally or not, he will be an ally of the Opposition in that task.

Opposition leader, Mr. Fraser, hinted heavily on television last night that further information, implicating another Minister in the whole loans affair, was likely to emerge today.

His Deputy, Mr. Lynch, has already stated that there is further information to come out.

The Opposition is striving to have elucidation of the loan-raising activities of Mr. Connor and his permanent head Sir Lenox Hewitt, included in any inquiry.

Mr. Whitlam may have sacrificed Dr. Cairns, but the Opposition is gunning for Mr. Connor and, through him, Mr. Whitlam himself.

The tale as it is so far known, damaging as it is for the Government, is not in itself going to precipitate Opposition action to force a double dissolution.

Mr. Fraser is going to wait to see if he can implicate Mr. Connor and Mr. Whitlam.

The immediate point out of Dr. Cairns's letter of reply to Mr. Whitlam's "please explain" is that he could come up with no better explanation for the copy of a letter offering commission to Mr. Harris which Mr. Whitlam released on Tuesday than that he had no recollection of signing it.

Dr. Cairns told Mr. Whitlam: "The letter quoted in your press statement was presented to me for signature.

I rejected it because I found it unacceptable.

I replaced this letter with another one which I had dictated and later signed."

This second letter, which Dr. Cairns quoted in Parliament on June 5, read: "The Australian Government is willing to borrow funds from lenders on terms and conditions suitable to us."

It was on the basis of this reply to Mr. Whitlam that Dr. Cairns asserted his innocence of the charge implicitly laid by Mr. Whitlam on Tuesday that he had misled Parliament.

It was on the basis of it that Dr. Cairns refused to resign when asked to do so by Mr. Whitlam.

It was the same defence that Dr. Cairns relied on in a lengthy press statement issued last night.

That press statement contained a final epistolary word from Dr. Cairns to Mr. Whitlam after the Prime Minister had notified him that he was going to Government House to hand in his commission.

In it, Dr. Cairns said: "I reject your decision. It is arbitrary and unfair.

You have twice held me guilty of wrongful action without any inquiry, each of which has the most harmful consequences to me."

Dr. Cairns went on to say in his press statement that he had asked Mr. Whitlam to accord him the right of being judged by his peers—the Cabinet and the Parliamentary Party.

Whilst there is not much prospect of Dr. Cairns receiving an enthusiastic response from that quarter—there are, for one thing, still enough discrepancies in his story, and unanswered charges by Mr. Whitlam of conflicts of interest on the part of Mr. Philip Cairns, to leave doubts in the minds of most Labor parliamentarians—the statement, nevertheless, must delight the Opposition.

Mr. Fraser could not have put it more eloquently than Dr. Cairns did last night: "I believe there is extreme injustice in this case in which a Prime Minister has acted against his colleague closest in rank.

It is not the way to victory for a Labor Government. It is the way to defeat."

The fact is that the versions of Mr. Whitlam and Dr. Cairns about the Harris loan affair conflict in so many material regards that an inquiry is inevitable.

Either it is the quasi-judicial inquiry already promised by Mr. Whitlam if the versions of the affair do not coincide, or it will be a Senate inquiry initiated by the Opposition.

Mr. Whitlam has not solved the issue in any way by dismissing Dr. Cairns.

The deep pessimism of many Labor people about the future of the Labor Party in Government is confirmed.

3.13   Watson commits caucus to support Deakin
Watson to Deakin, 17 December 1906

As you know, our party is not anxious for office unless a programme worth having could be carried through, and I am not so sure that in the Parliament as at present constituted there is much chance of carrying much of the Labor party's programme. If not, we must be patient. At least you can rely that we shall do nothing against your Ministry while engaged in altering the tariff and in carrying other matters of a Democratic nature.

3.14   Hughes's intrigues to get his view accepted by caucus
Caucus minutes, 15, 17, 22 November 1910

Minutes of Meeting held Nov. 15th / 1910 at 7.15 p.m.

Mr. Hughes presided.

Mr. Hughes stated that he had called the meeting to consider the position created by an amendment which was carried in the Land Defence Bill.

After discussion Senator Pearce moved 'That the Acting Prime Minister proceed with the Naval Defence Bill and should a number of members require any Clause postponed for the consideration of the party it be postponed.' Carried.

The Meeting then closed.

Confirmed. W. M. Hughes, Chairman.

Minutes of Meeting held Nov. 17th 1910.

Mr. Hughes presided.

There were 48 members present.

Moved by Mr. Archibald and seconded by Mr. Ozanne That the party have the fullest confidence in the Ministry. Carried.

Mr. Hughes moved 'That when, during a discussion of any measure upon a matter not already decided by the party, strong objections are expressed in regard thereto and the Whip has ascertained that a majority of available members of the Chambers in which the matter is being discussed so desire, then the Minister in charge shall postpone the consideration of the Clause until a meeting of the party can be called to consider the case.' Carried.

Senator Pearce moved to amend the Land Defence Bill by inserting the following provision: 'provided further that persons who have served two years in the permanent forces may at any time before they reach the age of 23 years and after passing the prescribed examination covering the practice as well as the theory of Military service for entry, enter the military college for the purpose of becoming a graduate thereof.'

Mr. Hughes moved 'That the matter be referred to the defence committee along with himself for consideration and report to the party meeting to be held on Tuesday the 22nd instant.' Carried.

The Meeting then closed.

> Confirmed. W. M. Hughes. Chairman.

> Minutes of Meeting held Nov. 22nd / 10.

Mr. Hughes presided.

There were 51 members present.

The minutes of meeting held the 15th and 17th instant were read and confirmed.

Mr. Roberts presented a report of the defence committee which stated that the committee had recommended the following modification to the amendment made in clause 9 of the defence Bill: 'Provided further that persons who have served two years in the defence forces may after passing the prescribed examination for entry to the Military College and at any time before they attain the age of 25 years enter the college for the purpose of becoming a graduate thereof.'

Recommendation No. 2: That the modification be made in the Senate when the Bill is returned thereto.

Senator Givens moved 'That the report be adopted.'

Mr. Hughes moved as an amendment to recommendation Number one That the following words be substituted in lieu thereof: 'provided further that the regulations shall provide for admission to the Military College of any member of the forces over the age of nineteen years who shall pass the prescribed examination and be recommended by the Governor in Council'.

On being put to the vote the amendment was carried by 24 to 22.

The meeting then adjourned until 7.15 p.m.

> Confirmed. Andrew Fisher, Chairman. 30/8/11.

3.15   Chifley explains his public attitude to caucus
Commonwealth Parliamentary Debates, 6 June 1945, vol. 182, p. 2643

I am proud to be the mouthpiece of the Caucus of the Labor Government of this country. I have no objection to offer if my colleagues differ from me regarding some aspects of Government policy; we have a way of finally resolving our difficulties. The proposals I submit to the House have been submitted with complete sincerity and confidence in the united opinion of the Party.

3.16   Whitlam threatens to resign
Australian, 16 November 1973

LABOR RALLIES BEHIND P.M. ON COLOR T.V. ROW
Resignation Threat Pulls M.P.s in Line

Labor Ministers and M.P.s closed ranks behind the Prime Minister, Mr. Whitlam, last night to head off any crisis threatening to bring down the Government.

Amid theatrics and high drama, Mr. Whitlam yesterday confronted the Parliament and offered his party the ultimatum of either his resignation or its full support for Cabinet authority.

By 6 p.m. the crisis had lost its heat, at least in public. A key figure in the affair, Labor backbencher Mr. U. E. Innes, issued a public statement endorsing support for Mr. Whitlam's stand.

Twenty-four hours earlier Mr. Innes had precipitated the challenge by giving notice he was asking the Labor Caucus to restrict Cabinet's freedom of action in its decision on the color television controversy.

But last night his brief statement concluded: "For my part, there will be no conflict in Caucus over today's statement by the Prime Minister."

An hour later, the Minister for Secondary Industry, Mr. Enderby, went on TV to defend Mr. Whitlam's stand as "magnificent" and one which the party could not quibble with.

It is the second time this year that Mr. Whitlam has used the threat of resignation to force the Labor Party to accept his authority on a major policy issue.

Six months ago, in a private meeting at The Lodge, he told senior party officials that he would quit if moves to repudiate the Government's policy on U.S. bases was overruled.

This time Mr. Whitlam issued his challenge in public. Using the opportunity of a question in the House from a former Liberal Party minister, Mr. C. R. Kelly, the Prime Minister flatly asserted his support for the sole right of Cabinet to make major economic decisions.

Mr. Kelly referred Mr. Whitlam to press reports of Mr. Innes' move, and asked if it was a proper procedure for a government backbench committee to have prior knowledge of Tariff Board reports.

Low tariff

Mr. Whitlam replied in part: "It would not be a proper procedure, and it will· not be a procedure of any government of which I am leader . . .

If my party were to purport to rule that Tariff Board reports were to be seen before the Cabinet decision was made or announced, I would surrender the commission that I have to form a government."

Mr. Whitlam did not restrict the threat to his own position. He bluntly warned that he would dismiss any minister whom he learned showed any Tariff Board report to any other member of the Parliament.

4

The Federal Conference and the Federal Executive

The federal conference is the supreme policy-making body of the Labor party. It first met in 1902 and has since met every two or three years. In theory it could direct federal members to introduce particular proposals. In practice it had little power to force such action and had no real methods of punishing members who did not obey. Federal leaders also disagreed about its powers: Watson believed that it should leave the federal party with considerable freedom of action (4.1); Fisher did not object to being directed by conference (4.2), while Hughes argued that the day-to-day business of administration must be left to parliamentarians (4.3). The practical problems raised by these men have never been satisfactorily settled.

In 1915 the conference finally established a federal executive which had the responsibility for making binding decisions on matters of policy and organization between conferences. In 1912 a similar proposal had been rejected (4.4), but in 1915 its constitution and rules were accepted. For a long time its powers were challenged. The state branches often denied that the federal executive had the authority to intervene in their internal affairs. However in 1922, after a long and bitter debate over a split in the New South Wales state branch, the executive decided that it had the right to do anything which helped ensure the success of the Labor party (4.5).

The capacity of the federal conference and executive to direct caucus was often discussed. In the 1916 conference various proposals were put forward to control caucus (4.6) but nothing came of them. But if the federal bodies could not direct federal caucus effectively, they were determined that the state branches should not direct caucus at all. In 1922 the executive denied that the state branches had the right to force federal members to sign undated resignations; the state branch argued that, if the federal member's behaviour was unsatisfactory, it only had to date the letter and send it to the speaker of the House of Representatives. As a means of controlling members it may have had great effect, but the federal executive declared it invalid (4.7). In 1931 the prime minister quoted federal rules to illustrate that caucus must not bow to demands from the state branches (4.8) and in 1936, following a direction to Queensland members from the state executive to support referendum proposals of J.A. Lyons's government, the federal executive reaffirmed its stand (4.9). The important point was, as the debate in 1933 over the question of readmitting the New South Wales branch to the party (it had been expelled in 1931 for refusing to accept federal policy) showed, if a particular branch could direct its members, the federal caucus might be split six different ways, following instructions from the six state branches (4.10).

Ironically the federal conference is the one institution in the Labor party which does not follow the principle of 'one vote, one value'. Although the size of the state branches varied considerably, the six branches each had the same number of representatives to the federal conferences and the federal executive.

There was at first considerable debate about whether such a practice was democratic, but opposition from delegates from the small states ensured that the system was not changed (4.11).

4.1   J. C. Watson writes to members of caucus on powers of federal conference
Watson papers, 27 July 1905, National Library, Canberra

To the Members of the Federal Labor Party.

Gentlemen, Since the close of the Inter-State Conference I have given careful and anxious consideration to its decisions, and regret to say that I am compelled to regard one of its resolutions as a censure upon the Labor Party in the Federal Parliament and another as a censure upon myself.

I am aware that resolutions passed by the recent Conference have no force unless approved by the various State Labor political organisations, but one must recognise that the Conference was made up of delegates appointed by the State organisations, for the most part of long experience and including members of the Federal and State Parliamentary Labor Parties. It was therefore of a representative character, and its decisions will naturally carry weight amongst the supporters of the Party throughout Australia.

I may say primarily that the view I have held since the inception of Labor in politics is that the organisations should decide in conference what the policy of the movement should be, and lay down such conditions as may be necessary to ensure the solidarity of the Party. Once the Party enters Parliament it alone should, by its corporate voice, decide the course to be taken in any particular emergency. Having chosen its captains the party outside should be prepared to trust to their guidance while the battle continues. If they do wrong, that is a reason for selecting fresh men when an election comes round; but I contend that the men in Parliament are, or should be, the best equipped to deal with Parliamentary emergencies.

Coming to the first resolution to which I object, there is no need for me to detail the circumstances in which the alliance was entered upon between the Federal Labor Party and the Liberal Protectionists; suffice it to say that it was agreed to by an overwhelming majority of the Party as being the only wise course open to us at the time. An emergency had arisen, and without abandoning any part of our platform we secured the help of allies on a number of leading proposals. The resolution arrived at by Conference on this subject reads as follows: 'That the Federal Labor Party should not enter into any alliance that would extend beyond the then existing Parliament, nor grant nor promise immunity from opposition at election time.' This resolution, as I have indicated earlier, practically amounts to a censure upon the Party in Parliament, as we entered into an alliance for this Parliament and the next, and promised to do everything possible to secure immunity from Labor opposition for our allies at the ensuing election. If it is granted that alliances are sometimes justifiable, how ridiculous it would be, in a Parliament that stood for months on the brink of a dissolution, to propose an alliance for that Parliament only. Further, what other party would ally itself with us if, at the ensuing election, it had not only to fight the common enemy but also ran the risk of being shot from behind by one of our candidates. To ask any other party to enter upon that kind of alliance would be to insult its intelligence, and it is therefore farcical to talk of permitting alliances under the conditions named.

4.2   Fisher does not object to receiving instructions from conference
Conference report, 1912, p. 18

REFERENDUM PROPOSALS

Mr McDonald moved the following resolution from Toowong W.P.O., Q.:—
That the referendum proposals be again submitted to the electors at the next
Federal election.

Mr. Coyne seconded the motion.

Mr. Roberts moved as an amendment that the words "That it is a national
necessity" be prefixed to the motion. He said it was contrary to the general
trend of conferences to make anything mandatory, and he considered it prefer-
able to insert the words he had suggested.

Mr. Giblin seconded the amendment.

Senator Needham urged Conference to carry the motion, as it was highly
necessary that the referendum proposals should be submitted again at the next
Federal elections.

Mr. Fisher stated that he had no objection to the direct words of the
resolution as moved. The referendum proposals would be submitted all right if
they were alive.

Mr. Hannan thought it would strengthen the hands of Labor at the next
election if the resolution were carried.

The amendment was defeated by 19 votes to 7, and the motion was carried.

4.3   Hughes writes on powers of conference
Conference report, 1912, pp. 26−7

COMMONWEALTH POWERS

The following letter from Mr. W. M. Hughes, Federal Attorney-General was
read by the secretary:—

"With regard to the referendum, I do sincerely trust that the Conference will
not attempt to lay down any hard and fast rule, or define the questions which
will have to be submitted to the people, as it was prior to the last referendum.
Unless we get the full powers we ask for, an amendment will be useless and
worse than useless, because it will cover us with confusion and disgrace if we get
an amendment and legislate upon those lines, and are brought up with a round
turn by the High Court. What answer shall we give to the people who gave us
what we asked for? I should have liked to have been able to put my views before
the Conference, but, of course, that is impossible.

"My own idea is that if the Conference broadly approves of what we ask for
and broadly disapproves of the attitude of those State Labor parties that oppose our attitude, and declares that such alterations in the Constitution as are
necessary to give effect to the New Protection policy, that is to say, a fair and
reasonable price to the consumers, the regulation of trusts and combines,
together with, where necessary, their nationalisation, it will help us tremen-
dously, and will not hamper in the least.

"I would not have you believe that an expression of opinion by the Conference as to the lines the questions should take would be undesirable, but that
any formal resolution, and, above all, any attempt to precisely define those
questions, will hamper us, and will inevitably, in my opinion, bring about their
rejection. Of course, I do not for one moment say that we should put the
questions exactly as they were put before. I have my own idea what should be

done, but the moment such an idea is made public—at this stage, 18 months before the matter will be submitted to the people—it becomes at once a centre of criticism, and loses its virtue. We are asking for tremendous powers, and we are fighting tremendous vested interests. And we ought to try to go into the conflict with a united front.

"To that end I would strongly urge that the motion I moved at the New South Wales State Special Conference, which was rejected, should be affirmed by the Interstate Conference, viz: 'That the interpretation of all planks of the Federal platform should be the business of the Interstate Conference: that when the Interstate Conference has not so defined the meaning of any particular plank, the interpretation of that plank should, in the interval between the conferences, be the business solely of the Federal Labor Party, and that that interpretation should be loyally accepted by every member of the movement.

"Of course, the same principle applies in the interpretation of planks in the State platform. The interpretation of these should be the business of the various State conferences. Where there is ambiguity the particular State Labor Party concerned should interpret it, and all members, whether in the Federal movement or not, should loyally accept that interpretation, pending the alteration at the Conference, State or Federal, as the case may be, which must always have the last word, and be the final arbiter on all matters connected with their platform.''

4.4 Debate on proposal to establish a federal executive
Conference report, 1912, pp. 41−2

APPROVING OF AN EXECUTIVE

Mr. McDonald said that it was necessary that a Federal Executive should be established, so that the party should have such an authoritative body to interpret the planks of the platform in cases where there was a difference of opinion and to give decisions in disputes. For instance, they had found that the State Labor parties had differed recently in their opinions regarding such questions as the referendum and the Commonwealth Bank. From time to time between the sitting of the Conferences, difficulties arose regarding various matters, and it was necessary that some central body should deal with them. Mr. Ramsay MacDonald had recently suggested the formation of an international Labor secretariat, and the time had arrived when the Australian Labor Party should take its place on the council of the Labor movements of the world.

Mrs. K. Dwyer seconded the motion formally, holding that the principle was good. She believed that if the Labor Party had had such a body as this, many misunderstandings would not have arisen. For instance, the differences regarding the financial agreement and the referendum would have been avoided. Two representatives should be nominated by each State—one to represent the Federal Party and the other the State Party.

Mr. Hannan felt the proposed executive should consist of the secretaries of the governing political organization of each State. He moved that the executive be so composed.

Mr. Lamond suggested that they should first determine whether they would have an executive, and then discuss its composition afterwards.

Mr. Fisher moved—That a Federal Executive be established. He said that such an executive could arrange the agenda paper for Conference, and deal with other important matters. It was desirable to have an executive to whom the

State Labor parties could appeal when in difficulty. It would be the guiding body, and could settle differences of opinion without wrangling.

Mr. Carey seconded the motion.

Mr. Roberts thought the time had arrived when they should have a central body to deal with Australian matters. Apart from that, however, he did not think the time was ripe for an executive which should control.

Mr. Watson said that an executive body of this kind would have to be one that could be easily called together, and under present conditions the members of it would have to be convened from the various quarters of Australia. He did not favor the proposal put forward at the Brisbane Conference, as he thought the scheme as outlined there would be impracticable under present conditions. It would take too long to get a meeting of the executive in the case of an urgent matter arising.

Mr. Lamond said it would be unwise to create now an executive with anything like the powers set out in the Brisbane scheme. He agreed there should be an executive to consult in cases where differences of opinion arose. But he did not think it a good thing to vest the whole of the powers of the Australian Labor Party until such time as the question had been earnestly considered. The matter of expense would also have to be dealt with.

4.5   Federal executive determines it has right to intervene in affairs of any state branch
Conference report, 1924, p. 19

At the commencement of the proceedings a request was received from the Federal Parliamentary Labor Party, asking that a deputation, consisting of Messrs. Charlton and Fenton, should be given an opportunity to place a resolution before the Federal Executive which had been carried by the Federal Parliamentary Labor Party. It was moved that the delegation from the Federal Parliamentary Labor Party be admitted to deal with any questions they desire to place before the meeting.

During the discussion which followed it was claimed that if the deputation desired to deal in any way with the trouble existing in New South Wales Labor circles that the meeting should be so informed. After further discussion in which various delegates supported and opposed the motion the resolution was put and carried. Messrs. Charlton, Fenton, Blakeley, and Makin, M.sH.R., were then admitted.

Mr. Charlton, on behalf of the deputation, stated that he desired to place before the Federal Executive a motion which had been carried by the Federal Parliamentary Party. The Party desired to prevent any further brach in the Movement in New South Wales, knowing full well that such would extend beyond the limits of the State. It was apparent that quite a number of unions and leagues would not be given representation at the forthcoming New South Wales Labor Conference if the present attitude of the New South Wales State Executive was continued. The solidarity of the Movement was the only thing actuating the Federal Labor Party moving in the direction which it had done. He submitted the following resolution, which had been carried by the Party:—"That the Federal Executive of the Australian Labor Party should intervene to settle amicably the trouble which exists in New South Wales." He submitted the motion for the consideration of the Federal Executive.

The President stated that representation of the Federal Parliamentary Party would be given due consideration, and the deputation then withdrew.

Communications were received from a number of organisations affiliated with the Labor Movement in New South Wales, requesting the Federal Executive to intervene in the then existing dispute in New South Wales.

At the evening session the question of the power possessed by the Federal Executive was raised. It was claimed by the N.S.W. delegates that the Federal Executive did not have the power to intervene in a Labor dispute in connection with a State's operations.

After considerable discussion, the Chairman ruled that the Federal Executive could act in any dispute affecting the Australian Labor Party. He stated further that this would define the power of the Federal Executive, unless the ruling referred to was disagreed with. It was resolved. "That, in view of the correspondence received, asking that the Federal Executive should take action in an endeavor to bring about a settlement of a dispute in the New South Wales Labor Movement, and in pursuance of the power and authority vested in the Federal Executive under its rulings, we proceed to consider means by which a settlement of the differences in the New South Wales Labor Movement can be effected."

4.6 Proposals to ensure that caucus obeys conference decisions
Conference report, 1916, pp. 24–5

On the motion of Mr. Scullin, seconded by Mr. Dwyer-Gray, it was resolved to refer the following to the Australian Political Labor Executive:—

Special meetings of the party may be convened by requisition to the Secretary.
1. If Parliament is sitting, by 12 members.
2. If Parliament is not sitting, by one-third of the members.
3. In each case sufficient notice shall be given to provide for the meetings being convened.

Ministers and officers of the Federal Parliamentary Labor party shall be elected by exhaustive ballot, and portfolios allocated by the Caucus at a duly constituted meeting.

Every Labor Minister or officer, or member of any committee of the party, shall exercise his own judgement and vote in Caucus meetings, notwithstanding that a Cabinet or any committee shall have arrived at a majority decision. No action of any kind whatsoever will be taken to interfere with the freedom of a minority of a Cabinet or any committee in the Caucus meetings of the party.

All business arising at party Caucus meetings shall be decided by each member exercising his own unfettered judgement by speech and vote.

Provision shall be made for private members to inititate and complete public business, including legislation.

Simplification of Parliamentary procedure and Standing Orders to expedite public business.

Referred to executive
On the motion of Messrs. Dwyer-Gray and McCallum, it was agreed that the following solutions should be referred to the Australian Political Labor Executive:—

"That the Australian Political Labor Executive be empowered to appoint a representative who may attend all meetings of the Federal Labor Caucus, and supply confidential reports to the Central Executive of each State.

"That the Federal Parliamentary Labor party should furnish to the Australian Political Labor Executive a precis of general business done at each Caucus meeting."

4.7 Federal executive overrules New South Wales branch in its attempt to recall members
Conference report, 1924, pp. 25—6

An application was received from Mr. Charlton, leader of the Federal Parliamentary Labor Party, to appear before the Federal Executive in connection with the decision regarding the recall, which had been arrived at by the New South Wales Conference.

Subsequently Mr. Charlton, accompanied by Mr. A. Blakeley (secretary of the Federal Parliamentary Labor Party), attended, and dealt with the motion carried by New South Wales Conference, namely: "Candidates for endorsement by the General Executive shall sign and place in the hands of the General Executive an undated resignation. Any candidate or Parliamentary members who refused to execute the mandate of the party or its controlling body shall be immediately recalled, and his resignation as a member sent in."

A general discussion ensued. Ultimately Mr. Kenneally suggested that a conference between the officers of the State Executive and the Federal Executive be held, with a view of arriving at an amicable decision in connection therewith. This was adopted, and Messrs. Willis, Magrath, Tyrrell, and Carey (officers of the State Executive) attended.

The Federal president intimated to the officers of the State Executive that the decision arrived at by the New South Wales State Conference was in opposition to the laws governing the Labor Movement. At the same time it was not desirable that the Federal Executive should openly veto any such decision, provided it was possible for a mutual understanding to be arrived at by which it would not be put into operation.

After discussion, it was agreed that the Federal Executive should submit to the State Executive its idea regarding the application of the motion, and Mr. Willis stated that he did not anticipate any difficulty regarding the suitable settlement as he regarded the Federal Executive as the higher authority to deal with these matters.

The visitors then withdrew.

It was then resolved that it be a suggestion from the Federal Executive of the A.L.P. to the New South Wales State Executive that the resolution providing for placing in the hands of the State Executive by any candidate or Parliamentary member an undated resignation be suspended pending the next New South Wales State Conference, as it is inconsistent with the rules governing the Movement in other States of Australia. Further, in our opinion, it would be detrimental to the best interests of the Movement as a whole. Further, that the New South Wales State Executive be informed that the question of framing an adoption of a uniform pledge for the Commonwealth would be dealt with by the forthcoming Federal Conference.

4.8 The prime minister denies right of state branches to dictate to federal members

Caucus minutes, 18 February 1931

In connection with the position created in the East Sydney By-Election, & the domination of the N.S.W. State Executive, the Prime Minister indicated a ruling 'That the policy of the Federal Labor Party is that contained in the Federal Platform as interpreted by the Federal Executive.' He was not going to take dictation from any one section of the movement. He quoted the Federal Platform Rules to show the protection to Federal members.

4.9 Federal executive rules that state branches can not dictate to federal members

Conference report, 1939, p. 75

QUEENSLAND CENTRAL EXECUTIVE'S POWER TO DIRECT FEDERAL MEMBERS ON MATTERS OF FEDERAL PLATFORM AND POLICY QUESTIONED
Mr. Beasley asked for a ruling as to whether the action of the Queensland Central executive, in instructing the Queensland members of the Federal Parliament, was not a violation of the rules of the Party.

The Chairman said that he would not give a ruling because he was not in possession of all the facts. He was not aware that this matter would be raised at the Executive. Had he known it, he would have brought all the material evidence with him, and would have given a ruling.

Chair—Mr. Fallon vacated the chair at this stage in favor of the vice-chairman (Mr. Graves).

Mr. Beasley raised a point of order that, in the circumstances of the action of the Queensland Central Executive, the Queensland representatives were not entitled to be present at this meeting of the Federal Executive.

Vice-Chairman Graves ruled that Rule 15 of Standing Orders, as follows, applied: "All questions involving an interpretation of the Platform of the Party, or the direction of members in accordance with the principles of the Party shall be decided by a definite resolution which shall be voted upon as recorded, and not by a ruling of the president."

Resumption of Debate.—Mr. Graves moved the following resolution:—"That the Queensland Branch of the Australian Labor Party has placed itself automatically outside the A.L.P. because of its defiance of the Constitution of the Party by instructing, through the Queensland Central Executive, the Queensland Labor Representatives in the Commonwealth Parliament to support the marketing proposals of the Lyons Government for submission to a Referendum, irrespective of the determination of the Caucus of the Federal Parliamentary Labor Party on the matter.

Mr. Beasley seconded the resolution.

Motion defeated by 10 votes to 2.

FEDERAL AUTHORITY TO DIRECT ON QUESTIONS OF FEDERAL
PLATFORM AND POLICY
It was resolved:—"That the Executive declares that no State Executive may direct members of the Federal Parliamentary Labor Party in regard to matters affecting the Federal Platform and/or proposed legislation which the Federal Parliamentary Labor Party has to deal with in the Legislature."

4.10   Federal conference reasserts its supremacy in state branches
Conference report, 1933, pp. 30−1

STATEMENT BY INTERSTATE CONFERENCE OF THE AUSTRALIAN
LABOR PARTY IN RESPECT TO NEGOTIATIONS FOR GREATER UNITY IN
THE LABOR MOVEMENT
The Conference, therefore, has decided that it would apply itself to the task of
uniting Labor throughout the nation, so that at the earliest opportunity a
common and united front could be presented to the forces that frustrate welfare
for the workers and producers and recovery for the economic life of the
Commonwealth.

It has carried the following resolution:

"This Committee recommends that subject to the full and unreserved
acceptance of the platform rules and constitution of the Australian Labor
Party, the resolution carried in 1931 by the Interstate Conference for the
expulsion of the New South Wales Branch as then existing be rescinded, and the
members of the said branch be granted full continuity of membership."

"The Committee further recommends that, subject to the readiness of the
group concerned to act loyally to the obligations set out above that it be
empowered to negotiate provisions to ensure that the rights of the members of
the branch constituted by the conference in 1931 shall be preserved and maintained."

To the invitation thus extended, the State Labor Party of New South Wales
replied by an insistence upon its right to be the sole authority for the interpretation of the Federal Labor Party's Platform and Constitution in N.S.W.
This course would make the rank and file of the Labor Movement in every
other State subordinate to the State authority of New South Wales. The Conference defined its position in this respect in the following resolutions which
were conveyed to the State Labor Party:—

"That the State Labor Party be informed that the platform, rules and constitution of the Australian Labor Party provide for the self-governing rights of
the rank and file of the Labor Movement in each State, as assembled in its
General Conference, in respect to matters that are State in their nature and
character, and do not involve Federal action or the Federal Platform, which
subjects, by their nature and character, are reserved for the Federal Conference
as representative of the rank and file of the Labor Movement in the Commonwealth."

4.11   Representation of states at conference debated
Conference report, 1919, pp. 19−20

BASIS OF REPRESENTATION
The General Secretary then moved the first resolution from Victoria, as
follows:—

Federal Conference Rule 1 to be amended to read:—

"Each State shall be entitled to a delegate for every 200,000 or part thereof of
the population of such State."

If Rule 1, Federal Conference Rules, is amended as suggested, the respective
States will have representation on the following basis:—

New South Wales   10 delegates
Victoria   8 delegates

Queensland	4 delegates
South Australia	3 delegates
Tasmania	2 delegates
Western Australia	2 delegates

Mr. McNamara (V.) explained, in seconding the motion, that his reason for desiring a committee in the first place was to try and have, as a result of the committee work, a definite scheme upon which the basis of representation in its various aspects could be discussed. There was a feeling in Victoria that it might be a good thing to have representation at Conference on the strength of the Labor Movement in the different States as against the purely population basis.

MR. PAGE (Q.)   But this proposal is bushranging.

One vote, one value

Mr. McNamara said that he believed that representation on the membership in the movement would be a good basis upon which to adjust representation. The idea at the back of the proposal was democratic, and made for one-vote-one-value.

Mr. Clementson (W.A.) opposed the motion, which, he said, would, if given effect, have a bad effect on the Labor Movement in Western Australia. It was all very well to talk of the democratic principle of one-vote-one-value, but it was highly indiscreet to carry it to such an extent as to bring about centralisation. This proposal would, in its operations, penalise the less populous States, and in the big spaces thwart the progress of the outposts of the Labor Movement. Under the suggestion now made, New South Wales, with her 10 delegates, could always outvote three States, and very nearly four. That did not appear to be very democratic to him, and he would certainly be up against the motion in the terms in which it was now put.

Question of numbers

Senator Gardiner (N.S.W.) reminded Mr. Clementson, who had expressed fears of the dominating influence of New South Wales, that it was the vote of that State on the Conscription issue that had saved the Democracy of Australia. However, Mr. Clementson need not fear New South Wales, which would get only that to which it was entitled under this scheme. He still believed that representation on the basis of numbers was a good thing, and he did not think that mere arbitrary geographical boundaries should obtain in the Labor Movement. Once a Labor man came into the Senate he was recognised as a Labor man, whatever State he might be returned for.

Mr. Willcock (W.A.) moved as an amendment—

That Rule 1 be amended so that Federal Conference be composed of 30 delegates: each State to be allotted a quota of delegates in accordance with the affiliated Labor Movement in each State, such quota to be determined by the Federal Executive on the membership for year previous to Conference.

Senator Barnes (V.) seconded the amendment.

The General Secretary at this stage withdrew the original motion, and the amendment by Mr. Willcock now became the motion.

"Centralisation of power"

Mr. Makin (S.A.) was against any proposition of this kind, which would make for a centralisation of power, and was therefore undesirable. He did not wish to see any State with a representation that might mean a monopoly of seats at Conference, and as all Laborites shared the burden of the Labor Movement equally, there should be equality in representation. The views he had put forward might be called those of a "State Righter," but he urged that regard should be given to the rights of those who, although in less populous States were just as keenly interested and active in the Labor Movement as those in the big States. South Australians felt that the interests of the Labor Movement would be best safeguarded by continuing the existing system of equal representation, which had worked well in the past, and until faults could be shown in it, should be allowed to remain.

5

Women in the Federal Labor Party

PART II

The Federal Labor Party and Australian Politics

6

1901−1917

When the federal parliamentary Labor party first met in May 1901, its members came from individual state branches which had little common purpose or few common attitudes. In the first five years the members found where they agreed and in 1905 the party finally adopted a national objective towards which the parties should work (6.1).

But in the meantime the party had to decide what stand it would take on two major issues, the tariff and immigration. The non-Labor parties in the colonies had been divided primarily on the question of whether customs and excise duties should be raised to protect the goods made in Australia from outside competition or whether trade should be free, with customs duties being raised only to provide revenue. In federal politics the other two parties, the Freetraders and the Protectionists, were still divided primarily on this issue. But different Labor members supported both sides and, rather than risk dividing the party, caucus agreed to leave it an open question for all members to decide for themselves how they vote. The second major question was immigration of coloured people. The Labor Party favoured total exclusion of all coloured immigrants (6.2) and it justified its stand by a mixture of racial and industrial arguments (6.3).

During the period 1901−9, no one party could command a majority in the House of Representatives and therefore be sure of maintaining itself in power. Alliances with other parties, or at least promises of support, were essential. Just after the Labor party had formed its first minority government, in 1904, it offered an alliance to Alfred Deakin and his group of Liberal Protectionists. The offer was refused (6.4). In 1905 when Deakin regained power, he gave the Labor party a list of the proposals he hoped to introduce, in a bid to get their continued support. He was successful and the party promised 'general support'. But delegates to the federal conference were sceptical of the value of these alliances and believed that the ultimate aim of the Labor Party had to be a parliamentary majority. They believed that an alliance, particularly one which promised that the Labor Party would not oppose candidates who were prepared to support them in parliament, would stunt the party's growth (6.5). When the two non-Labor parties finally united in 1909, this problem was solved.

For the majority of the period 1910−16 the Labor party was in office, but there it found itself torn between two alternatives: careful administration or an active programme of social reform. This choice became even more difficult when the demands of war production slowed even more the rate of reform. Backbenchers in the party were often critical of the government (6.6) and tried to reassert the right of caucus to determine what action should be taken by the government, particularly when the party executive tried to censure in caucus some of its more outspoken critics (6.7). Delegates to conference were equally critical and accused the government of failing to introduce many planks of the party's platform, including the clause that promised preference in employment to registered unionists (6.8). Fisher and Hughes defended the government, the latter claiming that senior public servants were not sufficiently in sympathy with the Labor government's objectives (6.9). Fisher also expressed the common Labor view that the federal government needed greater power (6.10). His government twice held referenda seeking changes to the constitution which would have given new and wider responsibilities to the commonwealth, but the referenda were defeated both times.

The major battle was over conscription. As early as 1901, the opposition of the party to conscription for overseas service was expressed in caucus (6.11). In 1916 by a narrow margin the party agreed to hold a referendum asking the people whether they wanted conscription: but the party was bitterly divided (6.12). After the proposal was defeated, the party split, with Hughes walking out of caucus, followed by over twenty followers (6.13). There were several contradictory accounts of what happened in that meeting (6.14), but the comments of some of those members who walked out of the party, written just before or after the event (6.15), indicate how wide the gap was. A special federal conference was held in December 1916, at which all those who had supported conscription were expelled (6.16). The debate indicated clearly the views of some members of the party on the superiority of caucus (6.17) and on the idea that it was better for the Labor party to stay ideologically pure and out of office than to compromise its principles (6.18).

6.1 Party objective, 1905
Conference report, 1905, p. 10

LABOUR'S OBJECTIVE
It was unanimously decided that an objective should be adopted. The following objectives were proposed:
New South Wales and Tasmania
(a) The cultivation of an Australian sentiment based upon the maintenance of racial purity and the development in Australia of an enlightened and self-reliant community. (b) The securing of the full results of their industry to all producers by the collective ownership of monopolies and the extension of the industrial and economic functions of the State and Municipality.
Queensland
That the objective of the Federal Labour Party should be declared, and in these terms: The securing of the results of their industry to all producers by the collective ownership of the means of production, distribution and exchange, to be attained through the extension of the industrial and economic functions of the State and local governing bodies.
Victoria
The gradual nationalisation of the means of production, distribution and exchange.
Melbourne P.L.C.
Conference affirms that Capitalism is the enemy and destroyer of essential private property. Its development is through the legalised confiscation of all that the labour of the working class produces above its subsistence wage. The private ownership of the means of employment grounds society in economic slavery, which renders intellectual and political tyranny inevitable. Therefore,

Conference affirms that it is the object of the Australian Labour organisation to obtain control of all the means of production, distribution, and exchange, i.e., the means of employment-wealth production to be owned and controlled by the people in the interest of, and for the use of, the whole of the people, in contra-distinction to profit for a class.

Mr. J. C. Watson, M.H.R., moved, on behalf of the N.S.W. Executive, Political Labour League:

"That the objective read as follows: (a) The cultivation of an Australian sentiment based upon the maintenance of racial purity and the development in Australia of an enlightened and self-reliant community; (b) the securing of the full results of their industry to all producers by the collective ownership of monopolies and the extension of the industrial and economic functions of the State and muncipality.

Apart from loyalty to his own State, he preferred the objectives outlined by the New South Wales League, and carried by their Conference in January last. As to the wisdom of having an objective, he thought there was just as great a reason for the Federal Party—or rather the Labour party in the Federal sphere—to adopt an objective as there was for those bodies whose sole concern was State matters. It was a wise thing to direct the attention of the people to what they were really aiming at as a party. The great thing was to let the people know the good they were working for. The manner in which the Constitution circum-vented the Federal party in politics was an additional reason why they should have an objective on the programme. The matters coming into the arena of Federal politics must be fewer in number necessarily, and would not appeal in the same direct way as proposals in the various States. With regard to the first clause (a) in the motion, dealing with the cultivation of an Australian sentiment, etc., he thought such a proposal a very good one. In fostering an Australian sentiment, he did not mean that it should be one overbearing or arrogant, but that it should be cultivated in a true spirit of national pride. It was a good thing to inculcate a healthy sentiment of that kind in the people, for then anything that would be derogatory to them in the eyes of the other nations would not happen. Dealing with clause (b) he said such a proposal had the effect of impressing itself on the minds of the people. All could be done under this objective of the N.S.W. League that they could expect for some time to come. Whilst it might be a little ahead of what was possible today, it was not quite out of reach. It was sufficient that they were going for the collective ownership of monopolies, and understood their powers in that direction. Having done that he believed that they would have done all that was possible.

6.2 The Labor party and Immigration Restriction Bill
Caucus minutes, 31 July 1901

RESTRICTION OF IMMIGRANTS BILL
McDonald moved and Spence seconded 'That the Party work for the total exclusion of coloured people whether British subjects or not, and to prevent importation of labour under contract'.

Hughes moved and Brown seconded 'That the Party approves of the Educational test as to coloured British subjects, with such amendments as may seem necessary; but opposes absolutely the admission of all coloured aliens.'

6.3 J. C. Watson speaks on Immigration Restriction Bill
Commonwealth Parliamentary Debates, 6 September 1901, vol. 4, pp. 4633–4

As far as I am concerned, the objection I have to the mixing of these coloured people with the white people of Australia—although I admit it is to a large extent tinged with considerations of an industrial nature—lies in the main in the possibility and probability of racial contamination. I think we should gauge this matter, not alone by the abstract possibilities of the case, but by those considerations which appeal to our ordinary human weaknesses and prejudices. The question is whether we would desire that our sisters or brothers should be married into any of these races to which we object . . . If these people are not such as we can meet upon an equality, and not such as we can feel it is no disgrace to intermarry with, and not such as we can expect to give us an infusion of blood that will tend to the raising of our standard of life, and to the improvement of the race, we should be foolish in the extreme if we did not exhaust every means of preventing them from coming to this land which we have made our own. The racial aspect of the question, in my opinion, is the larger and more important one; but the industrial aspect also has to be considered.

We know that a few years ago businessmen, speaking by and large, looked upon the Chinese or other coloured undesirables as men who could be well tolerated, because they took the place of labourers, of men who might be unreliable, or not quite so cheap, but when it was found that these Orientals possessed all the cunning and acumen necessary to fit them for conducting business affairs, and that their cheapness of living was carried into business matters as well as into ordinary labouring work, a marked alteration of opinion took place among business men, so far as the competition of the 'heathen Chinese' were concerned.

In each and every avenue of life we find the competition of the coloured races insidiously creeping in, and if we are to maintain the standard of living we think necessary, in order that our people may be brought up with a degree of comfort, and with scholastic advantages which will conduce to the improvement and general advantage of the nation, some pause must be made in regard to the extension of the competition of the coloured aliens generally.

6.4 The Labor party offers alliance to Deakin Liberals, 1904
Caucus minutes, 1 June 1904

Mr Watson reported present position & read letter which he had forwarded to Mr. Deakin.

Tudor moved, Pearce seconded, That a copy of the letter sent to Mr. Deakin be entered on the minutes. Carried.

Correct copy of Watson's letter to Deakin. Argus. 2/6/04. F. G. T.

'26/5/04.'

Dear Mr, Deakin,

I have been empowered by the Labour Party, at a meeting held to-day, to enter into negotiations with you in reference to arranging an alliance by which the Liberal and Labour parties may be consolidated, sufficiently, at least, to ensure a programme of progressive legislation being put through Parliament in the immediate future.

Our party recognises the desirability of securing settled administration if it can be obtained without sacrifice of principle upon the part of those concerned.

Having this in view, I would suggest the following as a basis:

1. No definite arrangement to be arrived at until after the projected attack on the Government has been disposed of, preferably after a vote has been taken on the inclusion of public servants in the Arbitration Bill.

2. In the event of an alliance being arranged, representation in the Cabinet to be accorded your party on a numerical basis, the Labour party stipulating for a negative voice as to the individuals to be included.

3. Ministers and supporters to accept programme for this session announced by the Government.

    Note: The railway vote will have been decided.

4. Details of next session's programme to be submitted to joint party, with right of either section of joint party to withdraw from alliance if agreement impossible.

5. All questions relating to programme and conduct of affairs by Ministry to go before joint party.

6. Members of joint party to be supported at elections, after the manner usual in all parties, during the continuance of the alliance.

    Trusting you may be able to submit this suggestion to your party.

I remain, sincerely yours,

J. C. Watson

Copy of Reply Sent by Deakin

June 1st 1904.

At a meeting of the Liberal Party to-day it was resolved that present circumstances do not render advisable either of the proposed alliances or coalitions.

A. Deakin.

6.5   Conference delegates question value of alliances
Conference report, 1905, pp. 15−16

Mr P. Heagney moved the following addition to the Federal pledge:

After the words "caucus meeting" add the words "and not to form any alliance, coalition, or combination without such alliance, coalition, or combination having first obtained the sanction of the combined Labour organisations, to be determined by a special interstate conference".

He said that an alliance such as had taken place between the Labour party and Mr Isaacs was subversive of the best interests of the movement. They should come to some common course of action. Mr Watson had carried out his work with great skill under difficult circumstances, but the alliance was unwise when it attempted to obtain immunity from attack for those in the alliance who were not Labour members.

Mr Billson, M.L.A., seconded pro forma.

Mr Fowler, M.H.R., had from the first raised opposition to the alliance.

Mr Watson, M.H.R., said that the view he took was that the organisations outside laid down the policy upon which the Party was to work and decided what the platform should be. They arranged the pledge for each candidate to take before he submitted himself for election. But once the man was in Parliament they had to trust to his judgement to carry out their work. The alliance at any rate prevented a fusion of the two other parties, who could thus have presented a solid phalanx to Labour. The question of an alliance would only be determined by the immediate circumstances of the case. The alliance which they had made had more than justified itself.

Mr Fraser said that although they had come out of the initial alliance without disaster, still the proposition before them was in the right direction.

Mr Billson, M.L.A., said the great enemy to the cause was the man who was "as good as a Labour man", and in the alliance there had been individuals of that stamp. They might not always have a leader like Mr Watson, and it behoved them to be very careful regarding alliances.

Senator Turley said that alliances, so far as he knew them, had done no good for the Labour party. The men who came in with the Labour party generally did so to "get in out of the wet". He agreed that the alliance which Mr Watson had entered into had not affected the platform at all, although it affected outside organisations. If alliances were entered into he thought that they should not extend beyond the life of the Parliament in which they were formed.

6.6 Backbencher F. Anstey criticizes Labor ministry
Commonwealth Parliamentary Debates, 3 June 1915, vol. 77, p. 3667

I am here to uphold the principles of the Labour movement & not to support any particular government which does not uphold those principles. Honourable members talk about the referenda and of nationalizing monopolies, and yet they will not take a single step when they have unlimited power. Even with our present power in the matter of insurance and banking, no step has been taken; and the chances are that, when it is proposed to move, it will be found that there is no necessity, every state having taken action. A Government which is here to uphold the national existence can see men going to the war, and their wives and children practically starving owing to the enormously high prices of food, and all they can do is turn around and say they have no power to prevent it. That is absolute bosh, because they have the most extensive power possessed by a Government in any country. Under the Constitution the Government have domestic powers sufficient to enable them to protect the common people from the ravages of enemies without and within. The facts are plain and palpable to every man; and the Government and the Labour party could do what is necessary if they dared to take the chances.

6.7 Caucus reasserts its authority
Caucus minutes, 14 June 1915

REPORT OF THE EXECUTIVE
Mr. Charlton made a statement on behalf of the Executive on the attitude of certain members of the Party.

Mr Fisher and Senator Pearce having to leave temporarily, Mr. Hughes took the chair.

Mr. Hannan moved and Mr. Burns seconded 'That the debate be adjourned until Mr. Fisher and Senator Peace return.' The Motion was lost, and debate resumed.

Mr. Fisher again took the chair (3.35 p.m.)

Mr. P. J. Maloney moved as an amendment to the report of the Executive, and Dr. W. Maloney seconded,

1. 'That in future all Government measures be submitted for the consideration of Caucus before their presentation to Parliament, and that the nature of those measures when so presented to Parliament, shall be as a duly constituted caucus meeting by majority may decide.'
2. 'That in order to provide opportunity for giving effect to the foregoing resolution, arrangements be made for the holding of additional caucus meetings on alternate Tuesdays beginning at 2 o'clock.'

The amendment was Carried.

6.8   Conference delegates criticize government
Conference report, 1915, p. 30

ENGAGEMENT OF LABOR

Mr Cohen (V.) moved as an amendment the resolution from the P.L.C. Conference, Victoria—

That this Conference assembled protests against the unsatisfactory manner in which the policy of preference to unionists has been administered, and demand that the Government give immediate and full effect to the same. That in all future appointments of a permanent character applications shall only be received from financial members of affiliated trades unions, and all casual labor be engaged directly through the secretary of a recognised trade union.

He said that whilst Federal Ministers were sympathetic to preference to unionists, departmental heads were not. Since the present Government came into power he had been continually interviewing Ministers, asking that effect should be given to preference. In his opinion, only one department—that of Defence—was giving anything like satisfaction in this respect. When Messrs. Pearce and Jensen had been approached they had seen to it that difficulties had been properly adjusted. Of other departments the same could not be said. Week after week men came to the Trades Hall, Melbourne, who had never been in a Union, and asked to join because they had Federal employment to go to. This was a violation of preference to unionists, because it meant giving employment to those who were non-unionists, and yet there were capable bona-fide unionists out of work. He did not believe in that kind of compulsory unionism.

Dealing with Complaints

There were 130,000 unionists associated with the Trades Hall in Melbourne, and when application was made to place the position before the Federal Caucus they had been advised that the subject was one for the consideration of Victorian Senators and Representatives. In seeking to approach the Federal Labor Party, they were representing the unionists of Australia and not merely Victorian industrialists. There was never any difficulty in laying matters before the Victorian State Party. Personally, he would not cease to worry Ministers until full effect was given to preference. The regulation bearing on preference to unionists which had been issued by Mr Hughes did not properly meet the position. Departmental heads were endeavouring to rule in this matter of preference, but men were not going to be so ruled when they knew that the policy of preference should obtain in Federal work. Ministers surely should be more than rubber stamps, and assert themselves in administration. Mr Archibald, Minister for Home Affairs, did not extend even ordinary civility to deputations on preference to unionists. Although the Government policy was one of day labor, contractors had been running round the Home Affairs

Department endeavouring to obtain contract work, and pestering officials in order to do so. Departmental heads who disobeyed Ministerial instructions as to preference to unionists should be disrated. When Liberals took office they found the machinery well oiled because departmental heads were in line with their policy and method of doing things. Labor Ministers, however, should make the departmental officers do the work in accordance with the principles of the Government in power, and not allow the officials to do as they liked. Unionists were going to battle solidly for preference throughout Australia.

6.9 Fisher and Hughes defend government
Conference report, 1915, pp. 31, 34

GOVERNMENT POLICY—PREFERENCE

Mr Fisher (Q.) said he would be lacking in his duty if he did not defend Commonwealth Ministers. No Minister should be attacked individually but the Government as a whole, when fault was to be found. The policy of the Government was preference to unionists, and no departmental head had power to do things in contravention of Ministerial instructions. Mr Archibald had been attacked for the manner in which he had received deputations, but if that was to be urged against him it might also be said that Mr Cohen did not always comport himself in the best possible way. There should be established a Commonwealth bureau of employment, and unemployment, where every man could be registered according to occupation. There was no desire on the part of the Government to employ other than unionists when they could be obtained. No contract had been let which could be carried out by day labor. Individual instances might be different to this, but that did not disprove his statement of policy—it merely showed that the policy had not been perfected.

MR. COHEN: But the departmental heads are ruling.

MR FISHER: They do not rule, nor will they do so whilst the present Government is in power.

MR COHEN: But the departmental heads are laughing up their sleeves.

.   .   .

Mr Hughes said he was not at that particular moment defending administrative detail, and he hoped delegates would discriminate between the policy of the Government and any attempt by departmental heads to thwart it. No doubt there were flaws in administration. Labor Ministers could not immediately impress their opinions and authority on men who had for years been opposed to them. No doubt there were officials who were not in sympathy with the policy of preference to unionists. The Government had issued a regulation which widened the scope of preference to unionists making it apply to temporary as well as casual labor. The procedure was for the departments to notify the union secretaries of vacancies, and it was then necessary for the secretary to supply the labor. The business of the secretary would be to notify members to be at a certain place at a certain time. There should be a roster on the union books of unemployed members, in which every man took his turn. That surely was a fair thing. They were all agreed on the principle of preference—

MR COHEN: But how is it being carried out?

The Task of Administration

Mr Hughes said there were no doubt cases which required looking into. He admitted it was quite possible that there were high officials who looked upon the Labor Party with the hostile eye. No doubt this made the task difficult when sympathetic administration was so necessary.

A DELEGATE: Can't you deal with them?

Mr Hughes said if a man in his department deliberately failed to obey a Government order he would do his best to dismiss him.

MR McCUTCHEON: What does "do your best" mean?

Mr Hughes said that the Government could not dismiss an office boy, so one could see how securely entrenched leading officials would be.

MR GILL: Well, there should be an amendment of the Public Service Act making officers more amenable to instructions, or suffer the consequences.

6.10   Fisher explains why federal government should have greater power
Conference report, 1912, pp. 10−11

The States had complained of their functions having been usurped, and other complaints had been voiced. In his opinion the present Federal Constitution was not a workable one, not only from the Labor Party's point of view, but also from a national point of view. The present Constitution was altogether too restrictive in its nature, and prevented the representatives of the people elected on a broad franchise from giving effect to the people's will. While he did not proclaim himself in favor of this particular motion, he held that the time had arrived to give larger powers to the Commonwealth Parliament, so as to enable it to give effect to the will of the people. It would not be an outrageous proposition to lay before the people of Australia that a re-distribution of the powers of the Federation and the States would be a good thing and for their benefit. He did not think that the present division of Australia into six States would be of long continuance. He believed that, as far as his own State (Queensland) was concerned, more than one local body would be required for the proper government of that great territory. Some of the other states would find themselves in the same position. He invited the representatives of Labor to face this question boldly, and to recognise that all wisdom did not lie in the minds of the framers of the Federal Constitution. The cry of "Triumphant Democracy" raised in America had too much influence on the deliberations of the Federal Convention of 1890, and, in his opinion, the representatives who attended it took a step of too restrictive a character with regard to the relative powers of the national Parliament and the States. It was singular that they were the only British community which was so much hampered in regard to State and Federal activities. South Africa, after the experiences of the Australian Federation, unanimously decided to avoid the errors of a too restrictive Constitution.

A DELEGATE: Mr Watson made them do that.

Hampered at Every Turn

MR FISHER: That is all the more complimentary to one of our leaders. He asked delegates to remember that at present the Commonwealth and States were hampered at every turn in reference to questions relating to public health, shipping, railways, and other matters. The views on this subject that he was giving expression to were his own personal views, and he did not wish the Government to be committed to anything he said. Personally, he held that larger powers would have to be given by the people of the Commonwealth to the Australian Parliament, and the Labor Party would have to take its share in bringing these alterations about. All these required alterations, in his opinion, could be best carried out by amendments of the Constitution from time to time in a proper way. Unless this were done he predicted that in a number of years a party would arise which would appeal for a brand-new Constitution. He contended that it devolved on the Labor Party to take the lead in these matters.

6.11   Conscription and Defence Bill 1901
Caucus minutes, 25 July 1901

Clause 50: Batchelor moved and O'Malley seconded to alter the clause to read as follows: 'No members of the Forces shall be required unless he voluntarily agrees to do so, to serve beyond the limits of the Commonwealth except in the case of the Naval forces while on board ship.' Carried.

6.12   Caucus agrees to hold referendum on conscription
Caucus minutes, 25, 28 August 1916

On resumption Mr. Hughes made a complete statement on the position of Australia and the conduct of the War. Mr. Hughes also outlined a Policy for the Government in this connection. A number of questions were answered by Mr. Hughes.

Senator Lynch moved, Senator Needham seconded, 'That the proposal outlined by the Chairman be discussed and decided by this Caucus before they are further dealt with by the Cabinet.'

Discussion ensued.

Mr. Hughes replied to the various speakers and after further discussion made a proposition that the Government should not call up any men to the colors for training, until one month went by, but if the men responded by voluntary enlistment in sufficient numbers during this month and after, no men should be called up till after the referendum on conscription was taken. If on the other hand the number of enlistments was not sufficient, men should be called to the colors after the month had elapsed. The voting on Mr. Hughes proposal was Ayes 23, Noes 21.

6.13   Labor party splits
Caucus minutes, 14 November 1916

Minutes of Special Party Meeting held Nov. 14th 1916.

Mr Hughes presided.

There were present 64 members.

The Minutes of Meeting held on Sept. 27th 1916 were read and confirmed.

Mr. Hughes stated that the Meeting was called at the request of a number of Members by requisition and he would like to hear what they had to say.

Mr. Finlayson moved That Mr. W. M. Hughes no longer possesses the confidence of this party as Leader, and that the office of Chairman of this party be, and is hereby declared vacant.

Mr. Hannan seconded the motion.

Mr. Givens on a point of order submitted that the motion could not be moved until a previous decision had been rescinded on notice being given.

The Chairman upheld the point of order.

Mr. McDougall moved 'That the Chairman's Ruling be disagreed with.'

After discussion, Mr. Hughes stated that under the circumstances he would allow Mr. Finlayson to move his motion.

Mr. Turley moved and Mr. Russell seconded That each speaker's time be extended to ten minutes. Carried.

Mr. Charlton moved and Mr. J. Lynch seconded as an amendment 'That the respective state Executives of the P.L.L. be requested to appoint represent-atives to meet the Federal Labor Party to discuss the position as affecting the movement.'

Discussion ensued.

At one o'clock the meeting adjourned until two thirty p.m.

Meeting resumed at 2.30.

Debate resumed.

Mr. Hughes made a statement, after which he left the chair asking those who thought with him to follow him.

Mr. Finlayson moved and Mullan seconded 'That Mr. McDonald take the chair pro tem.' Carried.

Mr. Finlayson's motion respecting the position of Mr. Hughes as Leader was then put and carried unanimously.

Mr. Charlton's amendment altered as hereunder was then put to the meeting and carried: 'That the interstate conference be requested to meet with representatives of this party to consider matters affecting the future of the party.' Carried.

6.14   Three accounts of the caucus meeting of 14 November 1916

Argus, 15 November 1916

WITHIN THE CAUCUS
TENOR OF THE DISCUSSION
Mr. Hughes Remains Calm

There was not the reticence which usually characterises Caucus meetings, for although the strictest precautions were taken against anyone who was not a member of the party being near the room, members subsequently discussed pro-ceedings with a good deal of freedom, and a connected account of the sitting was not difficult to gather. No heat was displayed at any time during the dis-cussion. The quiet tone adopted by Mr Hughes at the outset was calculated to make the way embarrassing for those who were hostile to him. He made his appearance after most of the members had assembled, and when he walked to his seat at the head of the table he was greeted with hearty cheers by those who supported him. The majority of the members, however, made no demon-stration of any kind.

Mr. Hughes opened proceedings in a matter-of-fact tone by calling upon the secretary (Mr Watkins) to read the minutes of the last meeting. So much had occurred since the last meeting that members gave little attention to the minutes. For a few seconds after this formality there was a pause, in which tactical ground was being taken by the attacking and the defending forces. The Caucus waited for Mr Hughes, and the Prime Minister, after a short pause, called on the 'next business'.

As no one immediately rose, Mr Hughes said that the Caucus had been convened on a requisition by several members, and he invited some of them to open the proceedings. As a fact, the attacking party were ready. A section of them had met privately in a room in the city on the previous evening, and had not only drafted a motion of want of confidence, but had made preparations for meeting any other contingency which might have arisen. There is little doubt that it was a preconcerted plan that Mr Finlayson should launch the no-confidence motion. It was equally evident that it was in accordance with a pre-arrangement that the case against Mr Hughes was not to be sustained by argument. Mr Finlayson contented himself with indicating that the political line taken by Mr Hughes had disqualified him from the position of leader. There were some cries of 'no case' from Mr Hughes's supporters, when Mr Finlayson concluded a somewhat lame speech.

Mr Hannan, who seconded the motion, was more frank, inasmuch as he did not attempt to conceal the fact that the Caucus was bound to reflect the opinions of the organisations outside, and they had condemned Mr Hughes. This brought from Senator Givens the protest that they were a Federal Labour party, and that their solidarity would be ended if each State Executive were permitted to discipline members. Senator Givens also raised the point as to whether a motion of the kind could be moved without notice. Mr Charlton attempted to have the matter postponed until an interstate conference had considered the whole position.

A speech by Mr Carr is understood to have brought the debate back to the main subject. He said that there were evidently a number of members present opposed to the continuance of Mr Hughes as leader. There were also a number loyal to him, and he thought that it was due to Mr Hughes and to the party that nothing should intervene to prevent a decision on that vital subject. This view was generally accepted. It was apparent that those determined upon the condemnation of Mr Hughes had imposed silence upon themselves by general consent. These included nearly all the Victorians, although Mr Fenton, who has a strong admiration for the ability of Mr Hughes, is believed to have made an attempt to secure further consideration of the position.

The temper of the discussion was maintained, but as each speaker concluded there were loud cries of 'Vote', 'Vote', from the opponents of Mr Hughes. The Prime Minister, when he rose, remarked in a jaunty tone that he would like to say something on the motion himself. He made the point that on no occasion had he done anything without the consent of the majority of the Caucus. Whatever position he had taken was taken with the knowledge and approbation of many men who were now ready to denounce him. But the men who had demanded his disposition from the position of leader of the party were not there to hear anything which he might say in his defence, and those who were there were not free to weigh what he said or to adjudicate upon it. That being so, he would not remain.

Mr Hughes's dramatic retirement caused some surprise, and Mr McDonald was chosen merely to conclude the debate on the motion.

Argus, 15 November 1916

STATEMENT BY MR. HUGHES
Selecting the Ministry
EXTERNAL AFFAIRS PORTFOLIO DROPPED
The Political Situation

The Prime Minister (Mr Hughes) made the following official statement late last night regarding what had taken place during the day:

'The following motion was moved by Mr Finlayson (Q.) and seconded by Mr Hannan (V.).

"That the Prime Minister (Mr. Hughes) no longer possesses the confidence of the party as leader, and the office of chairman be and is hereby declared vacant."

Although the motion was out of order I permitted the discussion to proceed. I was asked to make a statement, but I said that I would prefer to hear the charge that was brought against me before I said anything. Mr Finlayson, in submitting the motion, stated that he did not propose to take up any time, as he said members had come there with their minds made up, and he would therefore content himself with moving the motion. A long discussion took place. An amendment was moved by Mr Charlton (N.S.W.) in favour of conciliation. Mr Charlton deprecated the action of the extremists, and urged that in the interests of solidarity the motion should be withdrawn. He moved as an amendment that representatives of various State Executives should be requested to meet the Federal Labour party to discuss the situation with a view to reconciliation.

Senator O'Keefe (Tas.) foreshadowed still a further amendment, which involved the maintenance of the status quo until an interstate conference could be called to deal with the situation. After some discussion, as the prospects of a modus vivendi seemed hopeless, I stated that, owing to the fact that members were acting under instructions from outside organisations, and were impervious to all argument, while expressing regret at severing a life-long connection with those members who were opposed to me, there was no course left open for me but to withdraw from the Chair, and request those who supported me to follow me from the room.'

Argus, 16 November 1916

REPLY TO MR. HUGHES
Labour Party's Official Statement

The following prepared by direction of the Federal Labour party by a representative committee, was handed to the press by the chairman, Mr Tudor, last night:

The statement issued by Mr Hughes concerning yesterday's proceedings at the party meeting so strains the facts as to amount to almost total misrepresentation.

The meeting was called by requisition, as many others have been called, in the following terms:

'We, the undersigned, are of opinion that a meeting of the party should be convened next week to consider the good and welfare of the party. We therefore request you to convene same, preferably for Wednesday next, November 8.'

The signatories comprising both conscriptionists and non-conscriptionists, explained that, in view of vacancies caused by resignation of Ministers and other political developments, they considered the meeting should have been called by the Chairman immediately after the referendum. Mr Hughes was invited to take the party into his confidence and to make a statement. This he refused to do. The following motion was then agreed to: 'That the Prime Minister (Mr Hughes) no longer possesses the confidence of the party as leader, and the office of chairman be and is hereby declared vacant.'

It is incorrect to say that the motion was not supported by speeches. Apart from the mover (Mr Finlayson), Messrs Hannan, Yates, O'Keefe, Hampson, Needham, Catts and Mathews set forth the grounds of no confidence, whilst Messrs Givens, Pearce, P. J. Lynch, Poynton, Carr, DeLargie, Senior, and Hughes replied. Messrs Charlton, J. Lynch, Fenton and O'Keefe spoke to an amendment favouring postponement of the debate until after the Interstate Conference met.

The main grounds of the no-confidence motion, as stated at the meeting, were:

1. The fact that Mr Hughes, as chairman, refused to accept any resolutions or amendments respecting a war policy, as against his dictation of a referendum for compulsory military service overseas, at the meeting of August 24 and succeeding days. After several days' sittings twenty-three members (a minority of the party) agreed at half-past 2 a.m. that the Prime Minister might pass the Referendum Bill, on the understanding that every member should have a free hand to either support or oppose before the public, and that the press censorship would not be exercised in a partisan manner. These conditions were not complied with. Ministers hostile to conscription were prevented from publicly opposing conscription unless they resigned from the Cabinet, and the censorship was administered in a ruthlessly partisan manner.

2. That Mr Hughes branded those advocating and supporting no conscription generally as traitors in the pay of Germany, as enemies of their country, and as being responsible for the policy of the I.W.W., and that a leader who would hurl such unfounded charges against a majority of his own party was unfit to be their leader.

3. That as Mr Hughes alleged that unless the Labour movement adopted his policy it was degenerate and unworthy, and that as the Labour movement did not endorse such policy, he should not continue to lead a movement he so maligned and misrepresented.

4. That the issue of regulations by Mr Hughes on the eve of the polling designed to intimidate voters from exercising the franchise, was a base betrayal of democracy, which showed him to be unfit to lead a great political party.

5. That Mr Hughes, by his assumption of the role of dictator, and his general conduct, was discredited throughout the country, and for the party to allow him to continue to lead it would mean ruin and disaster.

The only request made to depose Mr Hughes as leader was by the South Australian Political Labour Council. Six South Australian members refused to comply, whilst only one (Mr Yates) supported the 'no-confidence' motion. The allegation that his deposition from the leadership was sought by men not amenable to reason, but bound by instructions from outside bodies, is absolutely untrue. Two members of Mr Hughes's Cabinet, Messrs Mahon and O'Malley, were amongst those who were left perfectly free by their State Executives to deal with Mr Hughes as they thought fit, and both were prepared to vote for his removal from the leadership.

No question of expulsion from the party, or the platform, or framing the platform, was introduced, hence references made by Mr Hughes in this connection are merely designed to mislead the public.

Neither Mr Hughes nor any of his friends replied to the main charges made against him, and particularly failed to meet the accusation of tampering with the ballot. Mr Hughes pleaded his long association with the movement, threatened a dissolution, and then left the party room, calling upon his supporters to follow him.

6.15   Party members' attitude to the split
Fisher papers

Hughes to Fisher, 26 October 1916

To me it seems hopeless to mend the broken pot. It is now apparent that there are some elements in the Labor Party with which I have nothing in common, which is a fact I hate.

Pearce to Fisher, 21 November 1916

I could name you a dozen men who told me before the threats came (from the state executives) that they believed conscription to be the right thing who climbed down as soon as the gun was pointed at them.

Your old friend Higgs after endeavouring to run with the hare and hunt with the hounds chose the most inopportune (for us) moment that he could to resign.

However when we met we decided that we could not allow men like Anstey, Mathews and Catts etc., who had publicly declared that no matter what the Party did they would not support Hughes, to take part in the Party's deliberations and if it suited them accept its decisions and if it didn't turn them down. We therefore invited those members who were prepared to stand loyal to the Government to come with us and reconstitute the Government. 24 members have done so. We have reconstituted and I think we have a strong team. I believe it was inevitable and if it had not come at this question it would have come on some other later on.

T. Givens to Fisher, 22 November 1916

It is now evident that the description and crisis would have come apart altogether from the conscription issue. The individual leagues, unions, Political Labor Councils and Central Political Executives were dislaying such an amount of arrogance and domination on matters outside the platform and, in their desire to further their own power and authority, flouting the authority of the Interstate Conference and Executive—in fact showing such a spirit of disloyalty to the Australian Labor Constitution—that a crisis could not be avoided if a free parliament was to be preserved or any semblance of solidarity maintained in the Labor movement—and without that the party would be useless for any purpose.

6.16   Conference's motion to expel conscriptionists
Conference report, 1916, pp. 4—5

Mr Scullin moved: "That, as compulsory overseas military service is opposed to the principles embodied in the Australian Labor party's platform, all Federal members who have supported compulsory overseas military service, or who are members of any other political party, are hereby expelled from the Australian Labor movement."

Mr Scullin said that the pledge of the Australian Labor party asked that a man should conform to the principles of that party, and anyone who had not carried out the principles should no longer be allowed to be a member of that party. Whether the exact words were on the platform or not was merely a quibble, because there was no doubt as to the spirit of the Labor movement on this subject. It was only necessary to take the debates on the Defence Act, when the principle of overseas compulsion was sought to be introduced. There was not a man inside the party who would accept that proposition. Had Labor desired to accept overseas service, Labor members would have said so. The Citizens' Defence Force was quite another matter—laid down for the defence of Australia and not for overseas service at all. He was in Parliament when compulsory military training was brought in, but that was brought in for the defence of Australia. It was the corollary of home defence, and not overseas military service. It had been urged by some that there was nothing in the platform against overseas service, but the spirit of the Labor movement should be remembered always. To those who had urged this objection he would say that there was nothing on the platform against adult suffrage——

MR. RAE: Nor against chattel slavery, either.

MR. CORNELL: Or despotic rule.

MR. SCULLIN: No, nor such as they had had from Mr William Morris Hughes in the matter of despotic rule.

SENATOR LYNCH: What about the censorship in the Labor papers?

Dealing with the Issue

MR SCULLIN: The censorship which had been imposed upon Labor papers during the recent campaign would not have been tolerated in Russia. He had had experience in his own office of censorship conditions when word would come from headquarters that something or other was not to go in. Regarding the motion now before the chair he desired to say that no man could sneak away from the principles of the movement, merely because something was not written down in black and white. This Conference now assembled could deal with the issue. The whole history of the Labor movement had been against militarism, and militarism had been sought to be introduced by compulsory overseas service. Any man entering the Labor movement with the true principles of the movement at heart knew what compulsory overseas service meant——

MR. BURCHELL: Some have already been executed.

MR. SCULLIN: Any man violating the fundamental principles of the movement might expect to be executed. He saw around him men who had borne the heat and burden of the day——

SENATOR LYNCH: Hear, hear.

MR. SCULLIN: But that did not extend to them the license to break the principles of the movement.

6.17 Actions of caucus defended
Conference report, 1916, pp. 12—13

Senator Ready confessed that whilst opposed to the motion in its present form he found himself in strong sympathy with it. Matters of policy had to be considered. Conference should realise that a section of the Labor party had left and formed another party. That position should be faced at once; but this could hardly be done with the motion as now worded. Those members who had gone from the party had abrogated the first principle of the movement. They in the Labor movement had had to put up with a Dictatorship swollen by ambitions and personal ideas. Mr Hughes had declared that this was a non-party matter, but it was a vital question. Senator Lynch had spoken about some of them being brought down to the level of "poor dog Tray", but personally he would sooner sink with his party and principles rather than float with the tide with those principles suppressed. Why did Senator Lynch walk out of the Labor party room? Why? Because the party wanted a clear and definite understanding why Mr Hughes had treated them as serfs and placed the iron hand on Australia.

The Calling of Caucus

SENATOR LYNCH: What was caucus called for?

SENATOR READY: It was called to know whether Mr Hughes was going to run the party altogether or whether the party should not have some say in its affairs, and know why things had happened. Mr Hughes refused to recognise the supremacy of the party in caucus, the same caucus that had elected him as leader, and elected the Ministers. Who had elected Mr Hughes as leader, and who were his Ministers in the Government which had lately been formed? Did the members of the Hughes party have any say in it? Mr Hughes chose the whole bunch of Ministers and Senator Lynch had got his reward for his attitude of "poor dog Tray". Who, might he ask, were keeping these people in power at the present time? Were it not for Messrs Cook and Irvine Senator Lynch would not be a Minister of the Crown to-day.

6.18   Conference delegate defends purity of Labor party
Conference report, 1916, p. 5

Mr Blakely supported the motion. Conference, he said, should not take up any attitude of expediency or do anything that was palpably rotten. In New South Wales methods of expediency had been resorted to, with the ultimate result that they had had to expel a large number of Labor men in order to get a good party. If they did not have a proper party, of what good was it to the workers? To his mind it was far better to have half a dozen real Labor men in opposition than a whole Government in power if there was no attempt being made to put Labor principles into effect.

7

1917–1931

The electoral defeat of the Labor party in 1917 sent it into opposition for twelve years and temporarily estranged many members of the Labor movement from parliamentary solutions to the social and economic problems of the time. Many members began to espouse more extreme views or became more involved in the industrial unions. Further faction fighting became more bitter and for fifteen years splits in the New South Wales branch of the party were to hinder the federal party's chance of gaining power.

Typical of these more extreme views was the attack on the British Empire by the Irish-born Hugh Mahon, a former minister for external affairs. This speech was made just after Terence McSwiney, the mayor of Cork, had died after a prolonged hunger-strike, and it epitomized the anti-British views of the Irish section of the Labor party. For his speech Mahon was expelled from parliament, despite attempts by the Labor party to save him (7.1). He is the only member ever to be expelled from parliament.

The federal executive set a new precedent by calling a conference of trade unions in Australia, but the result was not strikingly successful (7.2). The most important debate occurred in 1921 when the conference adopted a new objective which demanded the socialization of industry, production, distribution and exchange. The discussion was lengthy (7.3). Not all groups accepted the objective and at one stage caucus wanted a special conference convened to reconsider it. By contrast the party rejected the idea of affiliation or any contact with the Communist party, which had grown rapidly in the early days after the Bolshevik victory in Russia (7.4).

When the party gained power in 1929, it faced widespread strikes, growing unemployment and an opposition majority in the Senate. Its period of office was one of trauma and disaster. Labour backbenchers became quickly dissatisfied with the government's lack of action. In 1930 the government tried to hold two referenda, one of which would have allowed parliament to change the constitution (7.5). The Senate rejected both proposals and later forced the government ignominiously to back down on a proposal to introduce preference to unionists, which was a fundamental plank of the party (7.6). Even a conference resolution that £20 million should be spent on public works to provide unemployment was shelved when it came to caucus (7.7).

The government's incapacity led to revolts and later splits in the party. Its decision to invite a Bank of England official, Sir Otto Niemeyer, to advise the government was condemned by caucus (7.8), while later in the year the acting prime minister and acting treasurer threatened to resign when caucus rejected their economic proposals (7.9). In January 1931 Theodore, who had been forced to resign from his post as treasurer six months earlier after his implication in a Queensland scandal, was reinstated, but only after a rowdy caucus meeting that led to five members leaving the party (7.10). In February the federal executive accepted Theodore's latest proposals and rejected those of J. T. Lang, the premier of New South Wales; but Lang refused to back down, a New South Wales splinter group separated from the party (7.11) and the branch itself was then expelled (7.12).

In June 1931 the government introduced a scheme called the Premiers' Plan, which was designed to reduce government spending. Since the plan included reduction of pensions it received an icy reception from sections of caucus and was only adopted by a narrow margin (7.13). The Scullin government was finally defeated in November 1931. It had never had the cohesion necessary to run a government in such difficult times (7.14).

7.1   Hugh Mahon expelled from parliament for attack on British Empire
Argus, 10 November 1920

Mr. Mahon, who presided at the demonstration, said in the course of his speech:

> They were told in the papers that Alderman McSwiney's poor widow sobbed over his coffin. If there were a just God in Heaven, that sob would reach around the world and one day would shake the foundations of this bloody and accursed Empire. There were no police in Ireland. There were spies, informers and bloody cutthroats. We read with delight that some of these murderous thugs had been sent to their account and he trusted that Ireland would not be profaned by their carcases.

Several resolutions were passed, one being that, 'in view of the policy of oppression and tyranny which had brought eternal disgrace upon the whole British Empire, of which Australia formed a part, the meeting pledged support to any movement for the establishment of an Australian republic'.

Caucus minutes, 10 November 1920

HUGH MAHON EXPULSION
Mr. Tudor raised the question of the threatened expulsion of Member for Kalgoorlie, Mr. Hugh Mahon. After discussion it was decided that in the event of Mr. Tudor not getting an adjournment until Mr. Mahon was present, the following was carried: Messrs. Blakeley & Considine: That as it has not been proved that the Hon. Member for Kalgoorlie, Mr. H. Mahon, used the words attributed to him in the Argus no further action be taken. Carried.

Caucus minutes, 11 November 1920

PROPOSED EXPULSION MOTION
The resolution carried at a special meeting held on 10th Nov. was recommitted. A letter was received from Mr. Mahon outlining his reasons for remaining away from the House and Party meeting.

Messrs. Catts & Considine: That all the words after 'that' be struck out with a view to inserting:

'this House whilst being opposed to all sedition and disloyalty and the subversion of constitutional means for the redress of grievances, is of the opinion that the allegations made against the Honorable member for Kalgoorlie, the Honorable Hugh Mahon, should not be dealt with by this House for the following reasons:

(a) The allegations made against the Honorable member do not concern his conduct in Parliament or the discipline of Parliament.

(b) That Parliament is not a proper tribunal to try a charge of sedition arising from the exercise of civilian rights of free speech at a public assembly of citizens.

(c) That the judicature is especially established and equipped and has ample power under the law to bring any person to public trial for the offence of sedition alleged against the Honorable member.

(d) That every citizen so charged is entitled to a public trial by a jury of his peers, where he would have the right to exclude by challenge biassed persons from the jury panel and that this fundamental principle of British justice should not be departed from in this case.

7.2   Federal executive convenes an all-Australian industrial conference
Conference report, 1921, p. 3

'Re All-Australian Industrial Conference—

'At this Executive meeting the members seriously took stock of the Movement and its relationship to the changed outlook of our members, and unanimously agreed that owing to this changing psychology of the great mass of the people in this country, and all other countries, the time had arrived when it was necessary to get a clearly-defined industrial policy which would be abreast of the times and be acceptable to the majority of our members in the industrial as well as the political wings of the Movement. With this object in view it was decided to convene through the various State branches an All-Australian Industrial Conference, and immediately after that an Interstate A.L.P. Conference to ratify or reject the decisions arrived at.

'This was done, as you are all aware, the result being that one of the most successful Conferences ever held took place in Melbourne on June 20th, 1921, when all schools of thought were present, all of whom agreed that unity was essential and could be brought about if an objective and policy suitable to the times could be arrived at. During the last days of this Conference the Executive met and decided that an Interstate Conference should be held in Brisbane on October 10th, 1921, this being the earliest date possible to fit in with the constitution of the Party, and that the Brisbane Conference should take the place of the ordinary triennial Conference of the A.L.P. Delegates no doubt have seen the report of the All-Australian Conference and the Executive have much pleasure now in submitting same to you with a recommendation that you make same the future objective and policy of our movement'.

7.3   Conference debates and adopts socialization objective
Conference report, 1921, pp. 6, 9, 25—6

Mr. Riordan (Q.) moved the first item, the objective: "That the socialisation of industry, production, distribution and exchange be the objective of the Australian Labor Party".

Mr. Murphy (S.A.) seconded the motion.

Mr. Theodore (Q.) said neither the mover nor seconder had stated what was desired to be accomplished by adopting the motion. Neither the report of, nor the resolutions of, the All-Australian Congress gave an indication of what was desired to be accomplished by altering the objective. He took it that the motion was to supplant the present objective of the Australian Labor Party. That would be a retrograde step. It was very essential, in the interests of the Movement, that they should have an objective that everyone knew the meaning of. One of the reasons for the objective was to proclaim to the world what they were striving for. He dared say no two delegates would agree as to what socialisation of industry meant. The originators of the phrase evidently took it to mean the control of industry by social organisation. They did not take socialisation to be interchangeable with nationalisation. Some would declare socialisation was what the Party were always striving for—collective ownership—and others would hold differently. The report of Congress seemed to imply delegates there meant something quite different from nationalisation and quite different from an industry managed and controlled by the State for the community. He did not think any logical argument could be brought to bear why the very important first clause in their present objective—the cultivation of an Australian sentiment: the maintenance of a White Australia and the development in Australia of an enlightened and self-reliant community—should be discarded at the present time. Clause 2 of their present objective embodies something which might be compared with the proposed new objective—the emancipation of human labour from all forms of exploitation, and the obtaining for all workers the full reward of their industry by the collective ownership and democratic control of the collectively used agencies of production, distribution and exchange. He admitted that the phraseology of the language of this clause, which was amended in June, 1919, was very vague, and that the meaning was somewhat obscure. It had only to be examined to show that they had not set out what they intended. It ought to be altered and simplified. He proposed as an amendment:—

"The emancipation of labour from all forms of capitalistic exploitation, and the obtaining for all workers and producers the full reward of their industry, by (a) the nationalisation of those agencies of production, distribution and exchange which are used under Capitalism to despoil the community; and (b) co-operative action in financing marketing, and distributing primary products".

Ultimate Socialism would be a similar phrase as long as they laid it down and understood what it meant. Socialisation as advocated by some in Australia was control by the workers through a supreme economic council. They must not regard themselves as being under some obligation to swallow the recommendations of the Melbourne Congress holus bolus. He was surprised to find in those resolutions such a lack of unanimity and harmony. Some were flatly contradictory in principle.

.		.		.

Mr. Riordan said that it was just as well to understand that the great trend of opinion at the All-Australian Congress was that a new order of society was necessary in order that the worker got a fair deal, and it was with that object in view the Congress re-drafted the objective. The opinion of that Congress was that socialisation could only be brought about by utilising the present system of Parliament to nationalise all industries. It was not intended, for example, that the State insurance should be socialised and handed over to the workers. It was intended that all industries should be first nationalised and then socialised. Under the new order there would be a central body. The coal miner would not hold up the new community. He may under the present system hold up the capitalistic system. There would be no danger of that under the new order, because the community would not tolerate him doing so, and if he did so would send someone to replace him and he would starve. Mr. Catts' argument was proof that some change should be made. Production for use and not for profit simply meant that the whole of the community's product would be used in the interests of the whole community, and that all the middlemen and exploiters who lived on the working class to-day would be cut out. The workers, under clause one, would see that the Labor Party had an objective. That was to release them from the bonds of wage slavery. For anyone to stand up and say they can do that under the present platform was ridiculous. Labor in power now only administered the farce of the capitalistic system. They had a clear demonstration in Queensland that as soon as they attempted to administer, the power of Capitalism had been effectively asserted. The first step under this scheme would be socialise credit and banking.

The amendment was defeated by 19 votes to 9.

7.4   Communist party members declared ineligible to belong to A.L.P.
Conference report, 1924, pp. 35−6

COMMUNISM

Item No. 43—South Australian Branch A.L.P.

'That Conference declares itself against the Communist Party as it exists in Australia to-day, with its idea of sudden revolution and foreign methods, that are not necessary in Australia: and that Conference declares itself in favour of practical Socialism through Federal and State Governments and Municipal and District Councils, and in favor of Pools and Co-operation to help the producers.'

Mr. Gabb (S.A.) in moving the adoption of Item 43, said he did so because he is of the opinion that we should be quite clear on this matter. It seems to me the Communist Party should be right outside our own: more or less it has threatened to become a separate party altogether from our party. Mr. Garden has made statements in New South Wales, and in my own electorate they tried to put it over me as if they came from this Conference. We should take a definite stand and if they the Communists form another party, well let it come. If there is to be another party, well the sooner the better: because we will then only have to put forward what the Labor Party stands for.

Mr. O'Halloran (S.A.) seconded the motion, and said that, although the wording was not quite as he had seconded, he would second same. He did not know whether the resolution would get very far. We as Labor men are pledged to the platforms of the Labor Movement. All we are doing is simply giving information to the public that we will not be responsible for anybody else's sins, unless they are prepared to stand by the platform of the Labor Party.

Mr. Painter (V.) moved an amendment. "That Conference declares itself against the affiliation of the Communist Party, as a party, with the Australian Labor Party".

Mr. Painter said: With the idea of the Communist Party in formulating their own ideas we can have no protest: but when they endeavor to use this party as their vehicle for their own propaganda, we must protest. Between this party—Australian Labor Party—and the Communist Party, as it is to-day, and as it is known, there is a wide diversity of opinion and objective. The Communist Party are Communist to-day, and in none of their economic theories have they the right to say they are the same as the Labor Party. It does not matter how much the Communists try to excuse themselves, they are damned by the results. They have every right to propagate their own principles, but their ways are not the ways of the Labor Party, and they must therefore stay out of the Labor Party. The endeavour to introduce the Soviet system into Australia—or any other country that has advanced along the lines of evolution as we have done—is like an endeavour to transplant a hothouse plant into the Antarctic. So with the Communists in Australia, the Australian Labor Party can have nothing in common because here there is a vastly different standard from that of Europe.

.   .   .

Mr. Theodore (Q.) said he was in agreement with Mr. Painter's amendment, but thought the amendment should go further, and therefore he would move a further amendment: "That no member of the Communist Party shall be eligible to become a member of the Australian Labor Party".

The Communists of this country are not bona-fide emancipators of the working class, but are in many cases the paid agents of the opponents of organised Labor in this country. But I believe that the vast majority are not actuated by being paid by disruptionists to see what disruption they can bring about in the Labor Party. Mr. Theodore quoted the rules of the Communist Party of Australia, whose headquarters are in Sydney and said he did not believe that any good can come from an attempt of this sort. Let them fight in the Communist Party, but do not let them come into the Labor Party for that purpose. Whiteanting is what it would be. It is not necessary to go into the history of what has been happening in the last two or three years to spread the Soviet propaganda throughout England and other countries. At this year's Conference in England the affiliation of the Communists was turned down by 98 per cent of the voting list—an overwhelming majority. You cannot mix oil and water. Has the time arrived when we are to hand over to people who have lately become members of the Labor Party, and who desire to use the Labor Party to get into Parliament or still to see the Labor Movement built up by the pioneers who have been pioneering for years. I say the time has come when the Labor Party must declare itself in favor or against the admission of the Communists to its ranks. The Labor Party is a democratic movement. There is no necessity for the workers to resort to violence. Where is the necessity in Australia? There may have been the necessity in Russia, where the workers had no hope of expressing their opinions. You might as well talk about unity in the Movement by bringing in the supporters of the Nationalist Party as bring in the Communist Party.

Mr. Blackburn (V.) in speaking against the motion and amendment, said: apparently what was wanted is an election placard against Communism, and I am not going to be a party to any declaration against Communism of that sort. If a man comes into your party as a Nationalist or Communist, I am going to watch the attitude of that person and judge him accordingly. The Labor Party stands for the freedom of speech and freedom of the press, and I appeal to Conference not to carry a motion simply as an election placard.

Mr. Riordan (V.) speaking in favour of the amendment, said: I have heard the different reasons given for refusing the admission of the Communists to the Labor Movement, and I do not believe or think that the majority of the reasons are because, as Mr. Blackburn says, "for an election placard". If you look up the report of a conference of the Communist Party held in December, 1923.

they declare they are not altogether opposed to the Labor Party, but do not believe the Objective can be achieved by Parliamentary action. Why should a body who contend that they are organised want to amalgamate with a party when they say they are not opposed altogether to that party, but say they do not believe that political action will do any good.

7.5   Referendum proposals put to caucus
Caucus minutes, 13 March, 2 April 1930

The Prime Minister reported that in connection with the proposed alteration of the Constitution That a Committee comprising Messrs. Brennan, McTiernan & Crouch (Legal Members of our Party) had sat, & made a recommendation to the Government, which was acceptable: That a new Section No. 129 be added 'That notwithstanding anything in the last preceding section, the Parliament shall have full power to alter the Constitution in the following manner: The proposed law for the alteration thereof shall, after the lapse of one month from its origination in a house of the Parliament, be passed by an absolute majority of each house of the Parliament, and be assented to by the Governor-General.'

It was put to the Meeting & Carried on the voices.

PROPOSAL ADD THIRD QUESTION. TRADE AND COMMERCE

The Prime Minister explained reason for calling Special Meeting of Party. A number of members of the Party had suggested that a third proposal 'Trade & Commerce' should be introduced as a Bill, & included in the Proposed Referendum. He reported that Cabinet had given consideration to the Question, and recommended that we bring down another Bill to provide for Trade & Commerce. He asked the Party to make a decision.

Moved Mr. Coleman, seconded Mr. McTiernan That the Third Proposal 'Trade & Commerce' be included in the Proposed Referendum & that the Government bring down a Bill.

A general discussion took place.

The Prime Minister said Bells were ringing calling the House together, and as there were members of the Party who were opposed to the idea, he would not take a snap vote; but adjourn the meeting until Thursday, 3rd April 1930, 11 a.m.

7.6   The government backs down over preference to unionists
Caucus minutes, 7 May 1930

The Prime Minister explained the reason he had called a Special Meeting. A political storm had arisen over the question of Preference to Unionists in Contract Labour, & the general questions of preference to Returned Soldiers.

The Prime Minister explained fully how the question had arisen, & how the matter had previously been referred to at Cabinet Meetings. He said the question was not big enough to fight the Senate, & go to the Country, & he now suggested that we make a graceful retreat, & endeavour to still affirm the principle of Preference to Unionists.

The Prime Minister then submitted to the Party a Statement re Preference to Returned Soldiers, which, if the Party agreed, he proposed to submit to Parliament.

.   .   .

Mr. Price moved, seconded Mr. Riley, Sr. 'That the Prime Minister's written statement on behalf of his Cabinet, & presented to Caucus, be endorsed.' Carried.

Mr. Crouch moved Amendment, seconded Senator Rae, in connection with Statement, 'That as between Returned Soldiers in the New Contract Condition, Preference be given to Returned Soldiers who are members of Unions.' Lost.

The Amendment was put & Lost. Motion Carried.

7.7 Caucus rejects proposal to implement conference decision
Caucus minutes, 14, 21 May 1930

Mr. Yates moved That the Government arrange to make £20 million available through the Commonwealth Bank for the purpose of supplying the wants of the States & Commonwealth for Public Works.

A General Discussion took place on Mr. Yates' motion 'That the Government arrange to make £20,000,000 available, through the Commonwealth Bank, for the purpose of supplying the wants of the States & Commonwealth for public works.' (Vote 14)

At 1.5 p.m. Mr. James secured the adjournment of the debate until 7.30 p.m. Meeting Resumed 7.30 p.m.

Senator O'Halloran moved an Amendment, seconded Mr. Crouch, 'That a Committee of seven including the Prime Minister, The Treasurer, & Mr. Anstey, together with four members of the Caucus, be appointed to consider the position, and report to the meeting of the Party on Thursday week.' (Vote 28).

The Amendment & Motion were put to the Meeting, & on the voices the admendment was carried. A show of hands was called for, which resulted, for the motion 14, Against 28.

7.8 Caucus deplores the advice of Sir Otto Niemeyer
Caucus minutes, 27 October 1930

Mr. J. A. Beasley moved, seconded Dr. Maloney, 'That this Caucus disagrees with the Tariff and Industrial Policy initiated by Sir Otto Niemeyer in his address published at the conclusion of the Premiers Conference in Melbourne, and affirms that the Tariff, and Industrial Policy of Australia are domestic matters to be determined by the people of Australia.' Carried.

7.9 Caucus rejects treasurer's advice
Argus, 12 November 1930

A serious crisis developed in the ranks of the Federal Parliamentary Labor Party at Canberra last Thursday night. As the result of certain financial resolutions carried by the Party, the Acting-Treasurer (Mr. Lyons) left hurriedly for Melbourne after intimating that he intended to consult with Prime Minister Scullin by wireless telephone on the question of resigning his portfolio. It is understood that Mr. Lyons informed members of the Party that he could not agree to carry through Parliament the financial plans endorsed by the Party.

The crisis arose as a result of a discussion regarding the meeting of loans maturing next month. These are a Commonwealth loan of £20,000,000 and State loans of approximately £9,000,000. As only £2,000,000 of this can be met from sinking funds, £27,000,000 has to be liquidated by other means. Mr. Lyons proposed to meet the indebtedness by raising a loan of £27,000,000 in about a month's time.

"Political Extinction"
Members of the Party supporting Messrs. Fenton and Lyons said they could not accept the resolution moved by Mr. Anstey. Mr. Lyons, in a lengthy speech, declared that a policy such as that proposed by Mr. Anstey and those supporting him would lead to financial disaster and political extinction. To this it was pointed out that the policy of the Labor government would be decided, not by the financiers, but by the Party itself, and that if it could not win on that issue then it was time it perished. It was also pointed out that if a new loan were raised, revenue derived from the recent additional taxation would have to be paid away in commission, brokerage and other charges. There would be a saving of at least £2,000,000 if the Commonwealth Bank were compelled to stand behind the loan.

How they voted
Mr. Anstey's motion was carried by 22 votes to 16.

Mr. Lyons left immediately the Party meeting ended, and caught the night train to Melbourne, with the intention of communicating with Mr. Scullin in London.

Statement by Mr. Lyons
Interviewed at Burnie, Tasmania, during the week-end Mr. Lyons said he had cabled a full account of the Caucus happenings to Prime Minister Scullin and had received a reply from Mr. Scullin. Asked what was in the message from the Prime Minister he said he could not communicate it direct, though it could be taken for granted that Mr. Scullin was right behind the policy that he himself and Mr. Fenton had sponsored. He added that the action he had taken was the only honest one. It was a question involving the honor of the Ministry, the honor of the country and his own personal honor.

Must keep faith
"A minority of the Cabinet is out for deferring the meeting of the loan which falls due next month: but the majority realise the folly of the scheme and its impossibility under existing conditions', said Mr Lyons. "The only way is the traditional way of keeping faith with the lenders, and giving them back their money when due, according to the letter of the bond.

7.10 Theodore reinstated as treasurer
Argus, 28 January 1931

Assertions that the Minister for Customs (Mr. Fenton) had resigned from the Cabinet as a result of Mr. Theodore's re-election to the Treasury were not borne out to-day. The Prime Minister (Mr. Scullin) said that Mr. Fenton had not tendered his resignation. Mr. Scullin refused to discuss the nature of a long conversation which he had with Mr. Fenton shortly after lunch to-day. In a subsequent interview Mr. Fenton intimated that nothing whatever would be done until next week.

Ministers have made many efforts to dissuade Mr. Fenton from the course of action which he appeared likely to take as a result of remarks passed in the heat of his resentment last night at Mr. Theodore's return to the Cabinet. It is hoped that Mr. Fenton will continue as a member of the Cabinet, although his resignation is quite possible.

The chief development to-day was the virtual resignation of Mr. Gabb (Angas, South Australia) from the Federal Labor party as a protest against Mr. Theodore's re-election. In a strongly worded letter to the Prime Minister, in the course of which he asserted that he believed a Minister of the Crown should be above suspicion, and that he had lost confidence in Mr. Scullin as a leader, Mr. Gabb intimated that he was not prepared to support the present Ministry any longer. Inevitably this means Mr. Gabb's departure from the party, for if he fails formally to resign the party will be forced to take steps against him.

Well-informed circles in Canberra are also expecting that the Postmaster-General (Mr. Lyons) will resign from the Ministry. Mr. Lyons has spent nearly all his time in Canberra since Mr. Theodore's re-election with Mr. Fenton, and he appears already to have dissociated himself from the majority of members of his party. To-day Mr. Lyons went into Queanbeyan, and in company with Mr. Guy (Bass, Tasmania) and Mr. Frost (Franklin, Tasmania) he spent the day driving and walking around the township. Clearly Mr. Lyons was desirous of having an opportunity of discussing and reviewing his position with Mr. Guy, his most intimate friend and devoted supporter.

Mr. Lyons left for Melbourne to-night after having refused to make any statement which would throw light on his plans, but his resignation from the Ministry will cause no surprise to those who have an intimate knowledge of the present situation.

Mr. Theodore's return

The Labor Party was given tacitly to understand that it had to choose either between Mr. Theodore or Mr. Lyons. The decision was unexpectedly forced upon the party, and it became a question of accepting either Mr. Theodore, who had professed views in accord with the desires of the 'Left Wing', or Mr. Lyons who, during his temporary occupancy of the Treasury, deeply offended the extremists of the party. It was made clear, firstly, that the Treasury had to be filled, for Mr. Scullin could not indefinitely carry both senior portfolios; and, secondly, that the only two men possessing the right to the Treasury were the two who had occupied it at successive stages in the last 12 months. On a vote which was distinctly of a 'snap' character, the Left Wing's blind antagonism to Mr. Lyons temporarily blinded it to the difficulties that lay in the path of Mr. Theodore's return, and in a division, which, in the circumstances was remarkably close, Mr. Theodore gained the day. Some members said that had anybody but Mr. Lyons been the alternative to Mr. Theodore, Mr. Theodore would certainly not have been elected. Members of the party keenly resent the manner in which such an important decision was sprung upon them. A proposal for a complete reshuffle of Cabinet positions came from Mr. Lyons. Again the Left Wing defeated Mr. Lyons. New South Wales members will not have Mr. Lyons on any terms.

7.11   Federal party splits
Caucus minutes, 19 February, 12 March 1931

Mr. Eldridge moved 'That N.S. Wales Members of the Federal Parliamentary Labor Party must comply with the directions issued by the N.S.W. Executive of the A.L.P. with regard to the East Sydney Federal By Election.'

The Chairman ruled the motion out of order.

The Prime Minister referred to the position of Mr. Ward, newly elected member for East Sydney and to the Federal Executive's Ruling. He ruled 'That any member elected on any other policy than [that of] the Federal A.L.P. cannot be a member of the Federal Parliamentary Labor Party. Further, that in view of the Federal Executive's Ruling and pending the holding of the Federal A.L.P. Conference, Mr. Ward cannot take part in the business of the Federal Parliamentary Labor Party.'

Mr. Beasley objected to the Prime Minister's ruling and refused to accept the ruling of the Federal Executive. He maintained that if Mr. Ward was to be excluded from Caucus meetings, other N.S.W. members who supported Mr. Ward's candidature must be similarly dealt with. Senator Rae moved dissent from the Prime Minister's ruling, Mr. Lazzarini seconded. Mr. Theodore occupied the Chair. A motion by Dr. Maloney 'That consideration of the motion dissenting from the Prime Minister's ruling regarding Mr. Ward's admission to Caucus be adjourned until the Federal Conference meets and decides the matter', was not accepted by the Chairman. A motion moved by Dr. Maloney, 'That the debate be adjourned', was lost.

The motion of dissent from the Prime Minister's ruling was put and his ruling sustained by 34 votes to 3.

In view of several statements being made during the course of debate that Mr. Ward was prepared to abide by majority decision of Caucus, the Prime Minister asked Mr Ward whether he was prepared to do so; but no reply was forthcoming from the Member for East Sydney.

7.12   New South Wales party to be expelled: president's address to conference
Conference report, 1931, p. 2

The New South Wales State Executive decided that the election should be fought on a policy foreign to that of the Australian Labor Party.

The Federal Executive and Parliamentary Labor Leaders, at the resumed conference in Sydney, at which Mr. Lang represented the New South Wales party, discussed the position, after which the Federal Executive met, and directed that the election be fought on the policy of the Australian Labor Party, as approved by the Federal Conference and interpreted by the Federal Executive; and, furthermore, pointed out that the Labor Party's policy did not countenance or support the policy approved of by the New South Wales Executive.

It further declared that, if the candidate in the then pending election supported the policy outlined by the New South Wales Executive, he would not be the representative of the Australian Labor Party.

The candidate, supported by the New South Wales Executive and some Federal members, supported the policy of the New South Wales Executive; and Federal members in New South Wales were circularised by the State Secretary, and informed that they were required to participate in the campaign, and furthermore, that they must support the policy enunciated by the State Executive, as against that of the Australian Labor Party.

The big majority of the New South Wales members refused to be false to their pledge, with the result that the New South Wales Executive is now endeavouring to penalise them for remaining loyal to the Australian Labor Party.

The issue to be determined is whether the Australian Labor Party shall continue on a Commonwealth basis, or become divided into different units, each limited in its operations by the various State boundaries.

If the right to determine Federal policy is ceded to any one State, Executive or individual, the same right would have to be similarly given in other States. Delegates can readily visualise what the result would be.

A Federal election fought on different policies promulgated by the various State Labor bodies would render uniform Federal Parliamentary action on behalf of the workers absolutely impossible. Hitherto, this has been obviated by the recognition of the Federal Conference as the body to determine the policy of the Australian Labor Party, and the recognition also of the Federal Executive as the authority to function on behalf of that body in the periods between the meetings of the Federal Conference.

At the previous meeting of the Federal Conference it was necessary to report that the New South Wales Branch had taken such action as indicated. It was not observing decisions arrived at by the previous Federal Conference.

Now we have before us the actions of the same branch in deliberately flouting decisions of the Federal Executive, and in a Federal by-election, propounding a policy entirely foreign to that approved by the representatives of the workers of Australia assembled in Labor's recognised Parliament.

I am convinced that this Conference will decide that the party shall continue on an Australian-wide basis; and this being so, it is essential that necessary action should be taken to provide the machinery and organisation by which those who desire to do so shall still be able to become and remain members of the Australian Labor Movement.

7.13   Caucus challenges Premiers' Plan
Caucus minutes, 4, 11 June, 23 September 1931

Mr. Makin raised the question of the Premiers' Conference reports wherein proposals for the reduction of pensions were alleged to be agreed to. The Attorney-General intimated that there was to be a meeting of Cabinet in Melbourne at the week-end when consultation with the Treasurer and Prime Minister would take place. Mr. Brennan stated further that it was the desire of the Prime Minister & the Treasurer to get the Premiers' Conference to agree to a concrete and comprehensive plan as quickly as possible. Mr. Yates moved that if any deviation is proposed either from the decision of the Federal Conference held in Sydney or the affirmations of this party in regard to wages and pensions, there be a call of the party members to a meeting to consider the proposals. Mr. Riordan seconded. Mr. Keane moved an amendment that the Acting Leader (Mr. Brennan) inform the Prime Minister that Caucus desires that no approval be given to any reduction plan without reference to Caucus. E. Riley seconded. The Attorney-General advised the party not to carry any resolution which could be misconstrued as one of suspicion or distrust of the P.M. & Treasurer who were taking part in the Conference discussions. Mr. Yates took a point of order on Mr. Keane's amendment which was upheld by the Chairman, Mr. Brennan, who ruled the amendment out of order. Dissent was moved by Mr. Lacey—the Chairman's ruling being sustained. The resolution moved by Mr. Yates was defeated. Mr. Keane moved his amendment as a motion which was carried by 14 votes to 9.

The Prime Minister reported the result of the Premiers' Conference and outlined the plan as agreed upon at the Conference. The Treasurer supplemented the remarks of the Prime Minister and explained the steps proposed to be taken to carry out the decisions of conference. Discussion of the Government's proposals was adjourned at 1 o'clock and resumed after the adjournment of the House at 4 p.m. Many questions were addressed to the Prime Minister and Treasurer, after which discussion ensued. The meeting adjourned at 10.25 p.m. until the following day at 10 a.m. The Prime Minister moved the adoption of the Plan as agreed upon at the Melbourne Conference. The Treasurer seconded. Mr. Lacey moved that we do not approve of any reduction of Old Age Pensions, Invalid or War Pensions; neither do we approve of any scheme which does not provide for adequate provision to employ the unemployed and make provision for necessitous farmers but suggest that other avenues be exploited with a view to savings being effected, especially in regard to the duplication of Parliaments, State & Federal Services, etc. The Prime Minister ruled that there could be no amendment to the motion, along the lines of Mr. Lacey's amendment. The Prime Minister declared that the Plan either stands or falls. Mr. Coleman moved an amendment, seconded by Mr. Makin, That an immediate dissolution of the House of Representatives and the Senate be sought and that the election be fought on the Fiduciary Bill and other proposals (Financial) of the Government. The amendment was lost by 25 votes to 14. The motion of the Prime Minister approving of the Premiers' conference plan was carried by 26 votes to 13.

Mr. Scullin gave an outline of the assistance rendered by the Banks, pointing out that the amount advanced for the last financial year & that promised for the year 1931—32 totals 50 million. In view of the changed position in Great Britain since the last meeting of the Party, the P. Minister said that it was becoming more difficult to come to a final decision and suggested that, in view of the new situation created by the overseas position, no decision or anything definite regarding the position of the Banks be decided upon for the time being.

Mr. Holloway moved, seconded by Mr. Makin, that this Federal Parliamentary Labor Party positive in its belief that the present National Crisis has been precipitated by the failure of those in control of the Monetary and Banking system of our country to meet the credit and currency requirements of the ever increasing Industrial Social and general economic activities of a growing population, the result being chaos and confusion with unprecedented want and suffering of our people. We therefore being convinced of the imperative necessity for the policy of Banking reform as indicated in Labor's Platform and supplemented by the decisions of Interstate Conferences of March and August of this year resolve that the Government

1. Reintroduce the Fiduciary Notes Issue Bill and, if rejected, an issue be made to the country at once upon Labor's complete policy of Banking Reform the first measure to cover—The complete recasting of the legislation known as the Commonwealth Bank Act to provide for inter alia—the complete control by the Nation of all issues of Bank credit and Currency.
2. The release of credits through the Australia Notes Act of amounts necessary to meet the requirements of Governments to finance present and new works and services. The marketing of primary products and to assist wheat farmers, Industry and Trade.

We therefore declaring that these reforms are essential to a restoration of public confidence, a revival of Industry and the re-employment of thousands of our workless, the restoring of the real wage standards, pension rate and social service advantages, call for the undivided support of the Australian public to give effect through the Commonwealth Government to this policy.

7.14   Warren Denning explains failure of Scullin government
Caucus Crisis, pp. 101-2

I believe that had not the downfall of the Scullin Ministry taken place when and how it did, it would have come soon after, and for some other flimsy reason, because in the Federal sphere Labor did not possess a fundamental unity of viewpoint and policy sufficient to enable it to continue efficiently in office. The dissolution of the party was inevitable once it came into direct contact with the exigencies of government.

While the period in Opposition lasted, it was easy enough to maintain an organisation which functioned as a Parliamentary Labor party with a reasonable measure of effectiveness, i.e., it opposed everything that reasonably could be opposed, occasionally embarrassed the government by well-timed sharp-shooting, and voiced a few generalisations of policy. Members then usually drifted off to bed about midnight, with the comfortable reflection that a day's work had been well done. But facing the pitfalls of office, a very different picture began to paint itself. Dormant ambitions, jealousies, and dislikes came to the surface. Political beliefs and points of view clashed, when the necessity arose of acting on the propositions that hitherto had required only brave talk. The comparative absence of responsibility while in Opposition made it possible for a red-hot Sydney Radical, inspired by extreme socialist or Communist organisation, to sit cheek by jowl with a conservatively minded Tasmanian, whose Labor philosophy was a dash of Karl Marx mixed with a splash of Fabianism, and a soupcon of Christian Socialism. But when those same individuals sat together around a Cabinet table, fully conscious that decisions were imperative and that those decisions would be carried into immediate effect by the administrative machinery of the country, and, what is more, accounted to the responsibility of the men making them, each looked at the position from his own point of view, often to make the startling discovery that there was a wolf in the fold. And therein lay the secret of the disruption which followed; the secret of the extraordinary indecision which caused this Ministry, on so many unhappy occasions, to be ridiculed throughout the country.

8

1932–1949

The Labor party was decisively defeated in the election of 1931. In the following decade it gradually improved its position. Much of its time was spent in considering foreign affairs. It spelt out its attitude to foreign wars when Italy invaded Abyssinia (8.1) and when World War II began in 1939 (8.2). But as party leader Curtin argued, however much the party members objected to the war policy of the government, they were obliged to obey the law (8.3).

After the war began, the prime minister, Menzies, tried to persuade the Labor party to enter a national all-party government. But Curtin opposed the proposal and at a special conference in 1940 persuaded delegates to accept a resolution that promised co-operation with the government but refused to agree to a national government (8.4). Following the direction of this resolution, caucus later adopted a similar stance (8.5).

In October 1941 the Menzies–Fadden government fell and Curtin became prime minister. Almost immediately caucus made its power felt by instructing the treasurer, Ben Chifley, to alter the pension proposals in his budget. The motion was withdrawn after Chifley agreed to introduce a larger pension as soon as possible (see 2.13).

Conscription proved to be one major problem, particularly when the Japanese forces reached Timor and New Guinea. At a special conference in 1942, Curtin sought party approval to introduce conscription for overseas service in the south-west Pacific region. This proposal was bitterly attacked by some members of the party and eventually referred to the state branches (8.6). Between conferences Curtin ruled that caucus had no right to discuss the question (8.7) although Calwell did attack the proposal in the House. (8.8). Eventually a majority of the branches supported Curtin's proposal (8.9).

Banking legislation proved to be another issue of major importance. One bill was introduced in 1945 and accepted by caucus after several attempts to amend it had failed. But the bill proved inadequate and in 1947 caucus readily accepted a proposal by Chifley to legislate for the nationalization of the banks (8.10). Chifley argued that the banks had seldom operated in the national interest (8.11).

One of the times when caucus made its influence felt most strongly was when the prime minister wanted Australia to sign the Bretton Woods agreement which had established the International Monetary Fund at the end of the war. At first caucus decided to refer it to a federal conference (8.12). Since the executive had agreed to the ratification of the treaty, a conference was the only body that could overrule its decision. But when a majority of branches were persuaded not to ask for the conference to be held, the question was returned to caucus which this time agreed to the prime minister's request (8.13). It provides an interesting study in the power of caucus.

The Communist party held considerable influence in the trade unions at this time and were often criticized by Labor leaders in caucus (8.14), and in conference (8.15). When the coal strike of 1949 threatened to bring industry to a halt, Chifley and the New South Wales premier, J. J. McGirr, strongly condemned the unionists and pledged themselves to support the arbitration system (8.16). Trade unions may be part of the Labor parties, but that does not prevent the interests of the two bodies often clashing.

Under Curtin and Chifley, the Labor cabinet was often a stormy arena in which strong personalities like Ward, Evatt and Calwell often fought with their leaders (8.17). Clashes of these types are perhaps inevitable where views are strongly held and personal ambitions important.

8.1   The party demands a policy of non-intervention in European conflicts
Caucus minutes, 23 September 1935

The following statement was then submitted by the Acting Leader F.M. Forde.

ABYSSINIAN DISPUTE

Australia has been looking to the Prime Minister to make a definite pronouncement as to his Government's attitude on the Abyssinian crisis. Weeks ago the other Dominions outlined their attitude. On the 8th September the Prime Minister of Canada was reported to have said: 'Canadians will not be embroiled in any foreign quarrel in which the rights of Canadians are not involved. We have bought and paid for security and peace, and we mean to have them.'

The Defence Minister of South Africa stated that no son of that Country would fire a shot without the people being consulted.

As uncontradicted statements appeared in the press that Australia had been committed right up to the hilt, there was a growing feeling that the Federal Government had blundered into a decision that might involve Australia in war.

While the Australian Labor Party's platform provides for adequate home defence against foreign aggression, it also contains a proviso against raising forces for service outside the Commonwealth, or participation or promise of participation, in any future overseas war, except by decision of the people. While I admire the efforts of countries that have been striving to settle the dispute in a peaceful manner, and particularly the way in which Great Britain has endeavoured to have Conciliation used in this dispute, I strongly hold the view that Australia should not allow the statesmen of any country to determine her course of action.

The Federal Government should instruct its delegate at Geneva that Australia will not be a party to war. Surely there is no more reason why Australia should become involved today than when four provinces were wrested from China by an original member of the League of Nations. If it were not for the oil fields of Abyssinia, and other rich natural resources desired by great vested interests, there would not be the mad manoeuverings for war. There would be the same apathy as was shown towards the invasion of Manchuria.

Only recently it was announced that Abyssinia had sold the rights to exploit the oil wealth of the country to American and English interests. The price to be paid was £ 0,000,000. Under pressure, however, the concessionaires withdrew. It is immaterial to the *masses of the* people of Australia how those oil fields are eventually distributed. Therefore we should keep out of this sordid quarrel over mineral and other wealth.

I sincerely hope that war will be averted. The control of Abyssinia by any country is not worth the loss of a single Australian life.

While the Australian Labor Party is opposed to Australia's participation in a foreign war over Abyssinia, it does not for one moment seek to justify Italy's attitude.

We should remember the price of the last war when 7,000,000 lives were lost and the financial cost was £40,000,000,000.

The price Great Britain had to pay for the holocaust was *a war debt of* £7,500,000,000. The cost to Australia according to the last Commonwealth year book, amounted to £812,000,000, including expenditure from war loans, and expenditure from consolidated revenue. The annual interest bill as a direct result is £8,000,000. There were also 60,000 of Australians killed, and 160,000 wounded. In addition to the tremendous burden of debt and interest, hundreds of thousands of our people were plunged into an abyss of grief and misery on account of the loss of their loved ones on the battle fields of Europe and Gallipoli.

Many of the economic problems weighing down the world today are the direct outcome of the last war which left a trail of misery unparalleled in history. Although we were told it was a war to end wars, the world today is on the edge of another grave cataclysm.

The attitude of the Australian Labor Party is clear and unequivocal. It wants no war on foreign fields for economic treasure. It wants Australia to be kept free of the entanglements leading to a repetition of the horrors of 1914−18. Therefore, the Australian Labor Party, for which I speak today, says '*non-participation*'.

After a lengthy discussion on the foregoing statement by Messrs. Dr. W. Maloney, F. Brennan, C. Barnard, F. M. Baker, J. Holloway, J. Curtin & D. Riordan, the Statement was submitted to the meeting and adopted unanimously.

Moved by A. Drakeford, seconded by G. Martens, that copies of the statement be supplied to the Press & all Labor Papers throughout Australia, on being put to the meeting the resolution was carried unanimously.

8.2 Labor party's attitude to outbreak of war
Caucus minutes, 5 September 1939

DECLARATION CONCERNING THE WAR

The draft of the recommendation with certain amendment as here follows was carried unanimously.

The Australian Labor Party affirms its traditional horror of war and of its belief that international disputes should be settled by arbitration.

It deplores the fact that force instead of negotiation and discussion has plunged the peoples into war. It believes that resistance to force and armed aggression is inevitable if attacks on free and independent peoples are to be averted. In this crisis, facing the reality of war, the Labor Party stands for its platform. That platform is clear. We stand for the maintenance of Australia as an integral part of the British Commonwealth of Nations. Therefore, the party will do all that is possible to safeguard Australia and, at the same time having regard to its platform, will do its utmost to maintain the integrity of the British Commonwealth.

As to the conduct of Australian affairs during this unhappy period, the Australian Labor Party will preserve its separate entity. It will give support to measures having for their object the welfare and safety of the Australian people and of the British Commonwealth of Nations.

We take the view that these measures should include the immediate control by the Commonwealth Government of all essential raw materials and the resumption by the Government of the factories associated with the production of munitions and war equipment.

There must be a rigid control of commodity prices and house rents so that war-profiteering will become impossible. Interest rates must be kept within bounds and the monetary system readjusted so that the National Debt be kept as low as possible.

The democratic rights of the people must be safeguarded to the maximum. The very minimum of interference with the civic liberties of the people should be the objective of the Government in carrying through its measures for national security. To ensure that this be done, it is essential that the Parliament of the Commonwealth should remain in session.

8.3   Curtin requires Labor party to obey law
Caucus minutes, 15 June 1939

The Leader (Mr. Curtin) reported that a meeting of the Labor Advisory Committee was held at Canberra last Friday, June 9th. The meeting had been called as a result of a letter having been received by the Secretary of the Party on June 8th from the Secretary of the Australasian Council of Trade Unions enclosing resolutions carried at a meeting of the full Executive of the A.C.T.U. held on May 21–23, 1939.

The letter from Mr. Crofts intimated that the decisions of the A.C.T.U. on the National Registration and Supply and Development Bills were forwarded to the Federal Parliamentary Labor Party with two requests:

(1) That all Federal Labor members should pledge themselves not to fill in the information as laid down in the National Registration Bill, and

(2) That the Party be requested to assist the Trade Union movement in its efforts to defeat the National Register Act.

Mr Curtin said that he had ruled that no member of the Federal Parliamentary Labor Party should give a pledge to any organisation of any sort or description, other than the pledge specified in the platform and constitution of the Party and which the member had signed as a candidate for selection by the A.L.P. There could be no other obligations entertained. He emphasised that the Party's constitution and platform prescribed that the Party was a constitutional Party and that changes in the laws were to be effected in accordance with procedure set out in the platform.

He had told the Advisory Committee that any request which he might receive as a member of the Party would be referred to the State Executive of Western Australia which was the only body to which he was competent to give a pledge, and he felt that as the matter was a Federal one that the Western Australian Executive in the nature of things would be obliged to refer the request to the Federal Executive.

'I told the Committee,' said Mr. Curtin, 'that it was treading dangerous soil to lay down a policy of revolt to a law. You ask us in effect to set ourselves up as a non-law observing party and thereby encourage the setting up of another "new guard". I would not allow the bankers or the Chamber of Manufactures to disobey the law were a Labor Government in power.'

After citing the motions which had been submitted by the A.C.T.U. Committee Mr. Curtin said that he had also directed attention to the resolution which provided that meetings should be called under the direction of the Trades Councils in the various States. He said that this course was not one that could be followed as the resolutions framed in such circumstances could be of a character which would not conform to the platform of the Party and that meetings held in this connection should be controlled by the State Executive of the States which was the organisation to which members of the Federal Parliamentary Labor Party had given their pledge and to whose authority they were subjected.

8.4 Conference accepts proposal that condemns National government
Conference report, 1940, pp. 20—2

Mr Curtin moved:—
"In order to effectively implement the policy agreed upon by conference and to achieve and maintain the maximum of national unity, and to ensure the preservation of the utmost degree of civil liberty consistent with the conduct of the war, this conference declares—
(a) That Parliament should be regularly consulted.
(b) That the Labor Party should maintain its integral identity in the people's interests.
(c) That a National War Council including representatives of Labor should be established to advise the Government in respect to the conduct of the war and in preparing for the post-war reconstruction.
Mr Curtin said that paragraphs (a) and (b) were in accord with the original declaration at the outset of the war. "The Opposition in the Federal Parliament can play a constructive and critical role, constructively and critically. Paragraph (c) rejects a National Government as a government. It is true that the Government could ignore such a National War Council, but a Government that was asking for a National Government could not ignore it." It could play a big part. It was a contribution Labor should make—a contribution he had in a humble way endeavoured to make since war broke out. He was impressed by Mr Richards' proposal, except for the rather large body Mr. Richards envisaged. The motion meant that Labor remained the watchdogs in the Federal Parliament for the time being, while making it clear that the utmost contribution that it could make would be made.
Mr. Makin seconded the motion.

8.5 Caucus promises co-operation in war effort but refuses to join national government
Caucus minutes, 15 October 1940

NATIONAL GOVERNMENT PROPOSAL. ADVISORY WAR COUNCIL
Mr. Curtin reported to the meeting concerning the consultation between himself and the Prime Minister in Melbourne and the inquiry of the Prime Minister as to whether the Labor Party would be prepared to consider the principle of a National Government. Mr. Curtin said he had not committed the Party in any way and that the caucus was quite free to make whatever decision it desired. He himself preferred the idea of a War Council or War Cabinet on the same lines as that instituted by the Labor Government in New Zealand. Mr.

Curtin further reported that he had received Messrs. Beasley, Rosevear and Mulcahy in Melbourne to permit conversations with this Group on the political situation. The discussion had revealed the impossibility of a Labor Government depending on this group for unconditional support. Their attitude seemed to suggest that the idea of a Labor Government dependent on their support was out of the question in his opinion.

Moved Dr. Evatt, seconded Mr. Morgan,

1. That the Federal Parliamentary Labor Party expresses its resolute determination to strengthen the war effort of the Australian nation and to ensure that Parliament as elected by the people shall be enabled to carry on effectively, particularly through the present grave and perilous situation; and, with that end in view, it hereby invites the co-operation of all other parties and all independent members of the Parliament.
2. That the Federal Parliamentary Labor Party is also of the opinion that, as an essential part of the war effort, steps should be taken to put into effect the substantial aims of Labor's electoral policy, as announced by its Leader (Mr. John Curtin); and to secure that end it also invites the co-operation of all other parties and all independent members.
3. That, with a view of securing the co-operation invited in resolutions 1 and 2, a committee of the Party be appointed to initiate discussions with the authorised representatives of all other parties and also with the independent members. That such committee shall report back to the Party.
4. That the committee shall consist of the Leader of the Party and other members.
5. That a copy of these resolutions shall be forwarded to the Secretary of each other Party and to each independent member; and shall also be handed to the Press.

The motion was carried.

8.6   Curtin proposes introduction of conscription to conference
Conference report, 1942, pp. 23, 32−5

By leave, Mr. Curtin made a statement regarding the use of Australian military forces. He referred to that part of the 1940 conference resolution which dealt with the disposition of Australian military forces. He said that the Government had recalled two A.I.F. divisions and were negotiating regarding the return of another division from overseas. The R.A.A.F. had been used in the Solomons operations. The R.A.N. went wherever it was required to serve. Mr. Curtin then dealt with the strength of Australian forces and the strategical position of the country in relation to Pacific operations. He said that only part of New Guinea could be defended by the A.M.F. The Government could not put the A.M.F. into Timor. To send troops outside Australia meant tearing battle-seasoned divisions into fragments and re-forming, thereby losing esprit de corps and team spirit. From the operational and organisational standpoints a homogeneous Australian army was, beyond dispute, necessary. The Repatriation Act created anomalies as between the A.I.F. and the A.M.F. Some A.M.F. had been in action, but would not receive the same benefits as A.I.F. who, although enlisted for overseas, had not seen service. There had been 83,000 volunteers from the A.M.F. to the A.I.F., but an extension of that number was not wanted because it was not desirable to break up A.M.F. divisions. There was no argument against one army. The minimum set for Australian operations was a further three divisions. Further, there had to be periodical relief of the force in New Guinea. The significance of Timor in respect of north-west Australia could not be denied. He asked conference for a definition of what were the territories of the Commonwealth for the purposes of defence and for political administration, and proposed that the following be added to the Defence Act:—"and such other territories in the South-west Pacific area as the Governor-General proclaims to be in the South-west Pacific area." The position had to be ended whereby a man could be sent to Darwin, where he could be bombed, but not to Timor to save Darwin from being bombed. An important consideration was that an homogeneous army would serve under the same conditions. He asked delegates to consider what he had said, and he would bring the matter forward next day.

Mr. Calwell raised a point of order. He said the matter was one not properly before conference. There was no resolution on it from any State branch, the Federal Parliamentary Labor Party or the Federal Executive. The danger was that, once power was given for conscription for the South-west Pacific area, further extensions would be sought. The matter should not be discussed by conference at all, but if anything were allowed to come before conference it should be then remitted to State branches before Federal conference committed the Labor Movement to what was conscription for overseas service.

The President said that the point of order would be dealt with when Mr. Curtin again raised the matter.

.   .   .

Amalgamation of A.M.F. and A.I.F. for use in South-West Pacific Area
Mr. Curtin said that voluntary enlistment and strategical requirements of Australia were the two main points of the party's policy, and he did not propose to alter that. What he did seek was an interpretation. The Government had brought two A.I.F. divisions back to Australia. It had to give regard to the islands surrounding Australia, not all of which were Australian territory. One of these was Timor.

Mr. Bryan raised a point of order as to whether leave should not first be granted.

The Chairman upheld the point of order, and Mr. Curtin then moved that he be given leave to move a motion dealing with a matter not included on the agenda paper, in the following terms:—

"That, having regard to the paramount necessity of Australia's defence, as set out in Section 5 of the special resolution adopted in June, 1940, by Federal Conference, the Government be authorised to add to the Defence Act, in the definition of the Commonwealth which at present defines the territories to which this Act extends, the following words:—'and such other territories in the South-west Pacific area as the Governor-General proclaims as being territories associated with the defence of Australia.' "

Senator Fraser seconded the motion that leave be granted to move the motion.

Mr. Curtin said he had little to add to what he had said at the previous day's sitting. The problem of Australian defence was a strategical one. If an area was vital to Australian strategy, then that area must be the one to which Australia must give full weight. The present difficulty could be circumvented by a proclamation annexing strategical islands, but that would be an abhorrent action. At the same time, were that done, it would be permissible to send the A.M.F. to those islands. U.S. and Australian forces which were in areas outside Australia should be released from doing work which A.M.F. pioneer battalions could do. He had opposed participation by Australia in oversea wars all his life, and he did not now ask for that, but that the definition of Australian territory be extended to cover areas vital to Australia. If the war went well, the U.S. forces would go north, and those forces must be replaced by Australian forces in areas not now Australian territory. The U.S. had saved Australia, and the Government had had a desperate fight to get aid for Australia. He did not want to live those months again. Now the position was that a barrage of criticism in Australia and the U.S. was directed at Australia that it would have Americans defend Darwin, but not Australians fight for the Philippines. He was asking conference to make certain that islands outside the political administration of Australia, but strategically vital to Australia, should be denied to the enemy by the strength Australia could put there. Because of the debt of gratitude owed to the U.S., Australia should be able to say that Australian resources would go on with them and maintain supplies and bases to them from islands close to Australia which, if not held, could be bases for the enemy to attack the U.S. forces.

Mr. Curtin gave an explanation of Japanese strategy in the Pacific and Indian oceans, and the constant threat to North-west Australia. Strategically, his motion was commonsense and had to be done. Further, the A.M.F. had seen action, but he defied anybody to amend the Repatriation Act to cover them. It was the first time Australia had had to fight for itself within the Australian area. Australia had an obligation to share in the defence of the Solomons.

Mr. Calwell asked, on a point of order: "Is it competent for any delegate to move a motion affecting the platform and rules of the party when no motion relating to the subject appears on the agenda paper."

The President ruled that it was competent for a delegate to move such a motion as Mr. Curtin had submitted, provided that the consent of two-thirds of the delegates was obtained.

Mr. Curtin raised a point that he was not seeking to alter policy, but seeking an interpretation of it.

.   .   .

Senator Cameron opposed leave on the the ground that the approach to the matter was wrong. Mr. Curtin's request should have come as the result of a Caucus decision or Cabinet consultation. There had been neither. The present procedure would result in a split in the movement.

Mr. Hanlon supported the motion. It was not a matter for Caucus to direct conference. Any delegate had the right to seek leave. A conference decision would avoid a split. Mr. Curtin had come to conference, which was unlike the position in the last war when the Prime Minister tried to bluff conference.

Mr. Calwell opposed leave. Mr Curtin had not consulted any section of the Labor Movement. Not one of the other 37 persons present at conference had been aware of it, and had had no opportunity to consult the State branches or the rank and file. The request was one for conscription for overseas service, and conference should not even entertain a debate on such a request, which, in any case, was not an urgent one. It was gross presumption if any delegate considered he could speak for the rank and file in favour of the proposal.

Mr. Walsh said the conference should discuss the matter on its merits, and at least enable it to go to the State branches. His view was that it was time the Labor Movement became realists on this matter, and, in any case, the Prime Minister had gone about his request quite properly.

Mr. d'Alton supported leave. He welcomed the opportunity to discuss the matter. Conference should have more talks with Labor's leaders on vital matters of policy.

Mr. Curtin (in reply) said that he thought the matter had been well debated. It should be considered by the Labor Movement. He had brought it to Federal Conference, and, if leave were now refused, conference denied the right to consider it to the very people it had been said should be consulted. It had been said that the matter had been "sprung," but there had been no time to have it placed on the agenda with the usual notice. The usual procedure could not be followed in war-time. He had been given no notice of the Japanese coming into the war, but, just the same, he had had to grapple with the new problem that involved. If the motion were introduced by leave, then conference could consider how best it should be dealt with.

The motion was put and carried by 28 votes to 8.

Mr. Curtin then moved the following motion:—

"That, having regard to the paramount necessity of Australia's defence, as set out in Section 5 of the special resolution adopted in June, 1940, by Federal Conference, the Government be authorised to add to the Defence Act, in the definition of the Commonwealth which at present defines the territories to which this Act extends, the following words:—'and such other territories in the South-west Pacific area as the Governor-General proclaims as being territories associated with the defence of Australia.' "

Mr. Curtin said the A.L.P. had properly always resisted conscription for overseas wars, but, with Japan coming into the war, the whole conception of the war had altered. He then gave a description of events, and also an appreciation of what the future trend of events might be. He said that conscription was the law in Australia for service in the defence of Australia. The interpretation he wanted was what was the "defence of Australia". He then gave his conception of what the defence of Australia involved. It had to be remembered that no preparations had been made in Australia for the defence of Australia before 1939. The Australian fighting force was now a great one, but the situation it faced was that in New Guinea the forces had to carry out a terrific amount of work—other than fighting. The U.S. fleet had stood between Australia and invasion, and Australia owed something to the U.S. for that. In the last two weeks the security of Australia had been completely established—but not permanently. The best the enemy could do now was to deny to the United Nations Australia as an offensive base. The enemy had consolidated in areas where rubber, petrol, oil and tin were located, and if these materials could not be recovered, then the war would not be won. An attempt had to be made to recover them. Further, if the Japanese were not driven out of island bases, it would be impossible to bomb Tokio. It was all right to say that the militia in Papua could ignore the A.L.P. platform as long as the policy did not have to be altered. Was Australia to say to the U.S. when it set out to recover its own land in the Phillippines: "Thank you, very much, but we will have to call for volunteers." He would not send suicide squads anywhere; he would send a real force.

He then gave figures of the requirements of Australian forces in the various islands, which could be met only with a homogeneous Australian army. He had never thought that he would have to ask the Australian worker to do the things he had asked him to do, but he had, and the task had come to him as Prime Minister, and what he had to do he had to do for the future. If there were any doubts as to his request, he had no objection to it going to the State branches, and Federal Conference remained adjourned in the meantime. He asked that the motion be not rejected during the present sittings.

Senator Fraser seconded the motion.

.   .   .

Messrs. Walsh and Taylor moved and seconded that the discussion be adjourned and the subject matter be referred to the respective State branches to give immediate consideration thereto, with a view to instructing their delegates on the issue, and that a special conference be held not later than the end of December to give further consideration to the matter. Motion for adjournment put and carried.

8.7   Calwell attacks conscription proposals
Caucus minutes, 9 December 1942

Minutes of Party meeting held 9/12/1942.

P.M. Mr. Curtin in the Chair.

The P.M. read a statement he intended to bring before the house tomorrow with the approval of the meeting; approval given unanimously.

Agreed after discussion that no amendment be accepted to the statement; if there is such, the Party to vote against same.

Mr. Calwell moved That this meeting of the Federal Parliamentary Labor Party is opposed to any proposals for the conscription of Australian Manhood for overseas service as being fundamentally the same in principle as those which the Labor movement rejected in 1916.

The P.M. ruled the motion out of order.

Mr. Calwell then moved that the ruling be disagreed with, Mr. Brennan seconded this. Mr. Forde took the Chair; after debate the motion of dissent was lost.

8.8   Calwell attacks in parliament proposals to introduce conscription
Commonwealth Parliamentary Debates, 10 December 1942, vol. 172, pp. 1713–14

As a youth I was an anti-conscriptionist in the 1916 and 1917 campaigns, and I am as much an anti-conscriptionist in 1942. I see no fundamental difference, and I moved a resolution at the meeting of the Victorian Central Executive of the Australian Labor Party expressing the view that there was no fundamental difference between the proposals enunciated by the Prime Minister (Mr. Curtin) in 1942 and those enunciated by the right honourable member for North Sydney (Mr. Hughes) in 1916. To me it does not matter where a man goes after he leaves Australian territory on compulsory service. To me geography does not matter. Whether the compulsion is for the South-west Pacific or for Europe, it is still military conscription for overseas service and, therefore, abhorrent to the traditional democratic principles of this country, and something that should be shunned and abhorred.

The Labor movement in this country is the expression in our time of the protest against the forces of reaction and privilege. The Labor movement in Australia has always obliged its parliamentary representatives to give an account of their actions to the movement which created them and made their political existence possible, and when it was displeased with their actions it told them that it no longer wanted their company. It did that to members of the party on the conscription issue in 1916, and the rank and file endorsed its action.

We on this side believe that the capitalist forces of society, who want to conscript the young manhood of this country to send them abroad, are concerned not with the defence of Australia, but with the interests of big business—those who provided the funds for the conscription fight in the last war—the land sharks and profiteers and all the other enemies of society. The people who support conscription to-day outside this Parliament are the enemies of Australia.

8.9   Views of state branches on conscription proposals
Conference report, 1943, pp. 39—41

LETTER FORWARDED TO STATE EXECUTIVES RE PROPOSED AMENDMENT TO DEFENCE ACT
Australian Labor Party—Federal Executive

23rd November, 1942.

To A.L.P. State Executives.
  (as addressed)
Dear Comrade,

Re Special Federal Conference

At the Special Federal Conference, held at Melbourne last week, the Rt. Hon. John Curtin, M.P., delegate from Western Australia, was granted leave to move the following resolution:—

"That, having regard to the paramount necessity of Australia's defence, as set out in Section 5 of the Special resolution, adopted in June, 1940, by Federal Conference, the Government be authorised to add to the Defence Act, in the definition of the Commonwealth which at present defines the territories to which this Act extends, the following words:—

'and such other territories in the South-west Pacific area as the Governor-General proclaims as being territories associated with the defence of Australia'."

After discussion, the following resolution was carried:—

"That the discussion be adjourned and the subject matter be referred to the respective State branches to give immediate consideration thereto, with a view to instructing their delegates on the issue, and that a Special Conference be held not later than the end of December to give further consideration to the matter."

I would be pleased if this resolution could receive the early attention of your State Executive in order that delegates to the Special Conference, which has been fixed by the Federal Executive to be held at the Trades Hall, Melbourne, on Monday, 4th January, 1943, may be instructed accordingly.

Yours fraternally,
D. L. McNamara,
Federal Secretary

REPLIES FROM THE RESPECTIVE STATE EXECUTIVES

New South Wales Executive

The policy of the Australian Labor Party has always been the adequate defence of our country.

The development of aerial warfare has made it essential that places adjacent to Australia should be defended in order to give effect to this policy.

We reaffirm our adherence to the principle of voluntary enlistment for service in areas beyond the requirements of the adequate defence of Australia.

Japan's threat to Australia makes it imperative that the Party's Defence Policy be implemented, and that those territories in the South-west Pacific adjacent to Australia necessary for our defence be brought within the provisions of the Defence Act.

In accordance with this policy the Executive resolves as follows:—
1. Therefore, we endorse the proposal of the Curtin Government to amend the Defence Act in order to provide security for the Australian people.
2. That youths under 21 years of age should not be posted on Active Service outside Australia.
3. The sacrifices involved in this total War must be spread over the whole community, and we request the Government to give effect to the Party's Policy of an excess War Profits Tax of 100%.
4. We further declare the necessity for the solidarity of the Labor Movement to defeat Fascist aggression and secure our policy of Post-war Reconstruction.

South Australian Executive

That this Special Convention of the S.A. Branch of the A.L.P. endorses the proposal of the Prime Minister to amend the Defence Act to permit the use of the A.M.F. in any area coming within the confines of what is officially termed the South-west Pacific Zone, and our delegates to the Federal Conference in January be instructed accordingly.

Victorian Executive

That this meeting of the Central Executive is opposed to any proposals for the Conscription of Australia's manhood for overseas service as being fundamentally the same in principle as those which the Labor Movement rejected in 1916. The Executive believes that the A.I.F. can be sufficiently expanded by voluntary enlistment to fill all its legitimate obligations, and therefore calls on all those who have subscribed over the years to Labor's traditional hostility to Conscription for service outside Australia and its territories to use their utmost endeavors to prevent conscription being imposed on the citizens of this country.

Tasmanian Executive

(a) The State Executive, Tasmanian Section, A.L.P., believing that the entire resources of Australia should be at the disposal of the Commonwealth Government for the urgent and adequate defence of Australia and the prosecution of the war, endorses the Prime Minister's proposal to widen the scope for service of the A.M.F. as necessary to the implementing of such defence, and as being in conformity with the defence policy of the Australian Labor Party as adopted at the Special Commonwealth Conference of the Party in June, 1940.

(b) That this Executive is of the opinion that any member of the A.M.F. who is desirous of transferring to the A.I.F. should be permitted and assisted to do so.

(c) That this Executive is of the opinion that every youth on attaining military

age should be permitted and encouraged to join the A.I.F. before being
compulsorily enlisted into the A.M.F.

(d) That this Executive is of the opinion that where the preponderance of
members (70%) of an A.M.F. unit desire to transfer as a unit to the A.I.F.,
facilities for the transfer on such a unit basis should be provided.

(e) That this Executive is of the opinion that provision should be made for the
utilisation, without interest, of the credit of the nation and the private wealth
which the defence of Australia seeks to protect.

West Australian Executive

That this special General Council of the West Australian Labor Party endorses
and pledges support of the Prime Minister's proposal that, having regard to the
paramount necessity of Australia's defence as set out in Section 5 of the special
resolution adopted in June, 1940, by Federal Conference, the Government be
authorised to add to the Defence Act in the definition of the Commonwealth
which at present defines the territories to which this Act extends, the following
words:—

"and such other territories in the South-west Pacific area as the Governor-
General proclaims as being territories associated with the defence of
Australia."

Messrs. Brooker and Cosgrove moved reception of report.

Mr. Bryan explained the position in regard to Queensland, stating that the
Queensland Executive decided to oppose the resolution submitted by Mr.
Curtin in respect to amending the Commonwealth Defence Act.

8.10   Caucus readily accepts 1947 banking bill
Caucus minutes, 16 September 1947

Mr. Chifley asked leave to introduce a Bill for the nationalisation of banking
(Banking Bill 1947). He stated that there was a recommendation from Cabinet
for the nationalisation of banking and he moved for its adoption. Seconded by
Senator McKenna. Carried unanimously.

8.11   Chifley introduces banking bill in parliament
Commonwealth Parliamentary Debates, 15 October 1947, vol. 193, pp.
798—9

The Labor party has maintained for many years that, since the influence of
money is so great, the entire monetary and banking system should be controlled
by public authorities responsible through the Government and the Parliament
to the nation. On this principle the Labor party has held further that since
private banks are conducted primarily for profit and therefore follow policies
which in important respects run counter to the public interest, their business
should be transferred to public ownership.

.   .   .

Time and again the policies of the private banks have run counter to national
needs for steady growth and high levels of employment. To go some years back
it is correct to say that the banks fed the boom and promoted unsound development in the twenties. When the depression came the banks as a whole restricted
new lending and called in advances . . . The effect of this was to accentuate the

protraction of business and the unemployment of those years. They helped but little in recovery during the thirties, waiting rather for improvement to come from other sources instead of taking the initiative and helping to promote recovery. They followed these courses because it seemed best and safest from the stand-point of their own interests.

Labor policy on banking has envisaged that, together with the elimination of private banking, the Commonwealth Bank would be strengthened to give it adequate control of monetary and credit conditions within Australia and its services would be extended to meet the needs of all sections of the people. The Labor party has in particular advocated the reduction of interest rates which, in the absence of control, were maintained at excessively high levels.

8.12   Caucus refers question of ratification of Bretton Woods agreement to conference
Caucus minutes, 27, 28 November, 4 December 1946

The Prime Minister moved 'That authority be given to the Government to introduce legislation to ratify the Bretton Woods Agreement.' Seconded by Mr. Dedman.

Amendment suggested by Mr. Falstein that the two propositions should be submitted separately. There being no seconder amendment lapsed.

Discussion of Motion proceeded until Meeting adjourned at 1 p.m. to 10.30 a.m. on Wednesday, the 28th instant.

Minutes of Adjourned Meeting of Federal Parliamentary Labor Party. Held 10.30 a.m. Wednesday, 28/11/46.

The Prime Minister, Mr. Chifley, in the Chair.

The Prime Minister declared the meeting opened.

Mr. Edmonds then asked the Prime Minister what was the position with regard to previous discussion on the Bretton Woods proposal in view of the resolution carried by the Federal Executive the previous day.

The Prime Minister stated he was not sure of the actual terms of the resolution but he would endeavour to obtain it as early as possible for the meeting, and he read the Federal Executive Rules—No.5 (Subsec. h)—which is as under:

'Rule 5 (Subsec. (h))—The Federal Executive shall have plenary powers to deal with and decide any matter which, in the opinion of at least seven members of the Executive, affects the general welfare of the Labor Movement, provided that no decision of the Federal Conference shall be abrogated under this rule. The Executive decision upon such matter shall be binding upon all members of the A.L.P., provided that any Branch or person affected shall have the right to appeal to next Federal Conference against such decision.'

During the discussion an amendment was moved by Dr. Gaha, seconded by Mr. Haylen, 'That the Bretton Woods Agreement be deferred until the terms of peace have been signed and made known to the world.'

Considerable discussion ensued and the meeting was adjourned at 1 p.m. to 10.30 a.m. on Wednesday, the 4th December, 1946.

Mr. Fraser received the call prior to the adjournment.

The Prime Minister read the actual terms of the resolution which was carried by the Federal Executive as forwarded to him by Mr. P. Kennelly: 'Having heard the Prime Minister on the matter and the reasons for and against the Bretton Woods Agreement this Executive believes that Australia should be a signatory to the Agreement.'

Minutes of Adjourned Meeting of Federal Parliamentary
Labor Party. Held 10.30 a.m. Wednesday, 4/12/1946.

The Prime Minister, Mr. Chifley, in the Chair.

Continuation of discussion of the motion of the Prime Minister that 'Authority be given to the Government to introduce legislation to ratify the Bretton Woods Agreement.'

During the discussion Senator Finlay foreshadowed further amendment 'That further consideration of the ratification of the Bretton Woods Agreement be deferred until the matter has been submitted to a Federal Conference of the Australian Labor Party.'

On the Motion of Mr. Edmonds it was agreed that the question be put at 1.5 p.m.

The Secretary, Mr. Sheehan, then outlined the motion by Mr. Chifley and the amendment by Dr. Gaha (seconded by Mr. Haylen).

On the amendment being put to the meeting it was defeated.

Senator Finlay then moved further amendment 'That further consideration of the ratification of the Bretton Woods Agreement be deferred until the matter has been submitted to a Federal Conference of the Australian Labor Party.' Seconded by Senator Amour.

Amendment was submitted to the meeting and declared Carried.

It was then submitted as a motion and declared Carried on the voices.

Meeting terminated at 1.15 p.m.

8.13   Caucus agrees to ratification of Bretton Woods agreement
Caucus minutes, 5, 6 March 1947

The Prime Minister then said that the Party was called together for the purpose of consideration of the Bretton Woods Agreement. The Federal Conference did not propose to deal with this matter and the Cabinet considered it of vital importance that the matter should be dealt with by the Party.

The Prime Minister then moved 'That authority be given to introduce legislation to ratify the Bretton Woods Agreement—entry being subject to Australia being allowed to join on conditions applied to original members.'

Seconded by Mr. Dedman.

Amendment moved by Dr. Gaha, seconded by Mr. Duthie, 'That the subject matter of Bretton Woods be taken into the House and that each member of the Labor Party be free to debate it and vote upon it as he thinks fit.'

Further amendment foreshadowed by Senator Nash, seconded by Senator Lamp, 'That the ratification of the Bretton Woods Agreement be deferred until a Federal Conference of the Australian Labor Party had decided policy in this matter.'

Discussion ensued until 12.50 p.m. when the meeting adjourned until 10.30 a.m. on Thursday.

Minutes of Adjourned Meeting of the Federal Parliamentary
Labor Party. Held 6/3/1947, 10.30 a.m.

The Prime Minister, Mr. Chifley, in the Chair.

Discussion ensued on the motion of Mr. Chifley, seconded by Mr. Dedman, 'That authority be given to introduce legislation to ratify Bretton Woods Agreement—entry being subject to Australia being allowed to join on conditions applied to original members.'

Amendment moved by Dr. Gaha, seconded by Mr. Duthie, 'That the subject matter of Bretton Woods be taken into the House and that each member of the Labor Party be free to debate it and vote upon it as he thinks fit.'

Amendment was submitted to the Party and Defeated.

Further amendment was submitted by Senator Nash, seconded by Senator Lamp, 'That the ratification of the Bretton Woods Agreement be deferred until a Federal Conference of the Australian Labor Party has decided policy in this matter.'

On being put to the meeting the amendment was Defeated.

Motion as submitted by Mr. Chifley was then put to the meeting and declared Carried.

8.14   Evatt attacks Communist party in caucus
Caucus minutes, 15 May 1947

Minutes of Meeting of Federal Parliamentary
Labor Party. Held Thursday 15/5/1947 at 10.30 a.m.

Senator Grant asked that Cabinet discuss the position of Russia in regard to the proposals to prevent work on the Rocket Bomb Range.

Dr. Evatt stated that the Communist Party had issued a pamphlet opposing the Range Bomb projects. In his opinion the Communist Party intended to torpedo the defence plan of Australia. There is no evidence that the Soviet Government has issued any instructions to the Communist Party but the Communist Party was acting in the interests of the Soviet in Canada, America and Australia. The Party is fostering animosity against the Australian Defence Plan and have a hymn of hate against Labor and against Australia. He did not consider that a Royal Commission would be of any value at the present time.

8.15   Communist party's tactics condemned by conference
Conference report, 1945, pp. 37-8

Mr. Ferguson moved:—

"This Conference declares that the struggles for improved standards, and in defence of principles, must be based on issues devoid of deception, and backed by the whole Labor Movement; and in the present dispute between the Federated Ironworkers' Association and the Broken Hill Pty. Co. Ltd. we note evidence of undeniable deception and contradictions that expose anti-Labor political attempts aimed at forcing a general strike, with the inevitable result of strengthening reaction.

"We consider that the unions involved in the dispute should accept the decisions of the N.S.W. Trades and Labor Council, directing reference to arbitration as the accepted means of settling disputes.

"We express the opinion that the proposed general stoppage in the coal industry would prove inimical to working-class interests, and we accordingly urge the Australian Coal and Shale Employees' Federation to refrain from forcing a general stoppage, which, if allowed to occur, can be defined only as a politically-inspired act against Labor Governments.

"We call on Australian unionists for support of our Labor Governments in this period of crisis as the surest means of preserving working-class interests."

Mr. McAlpine seconded the motion, which was carried unanimously.

Mr. Ferguson said he tabled the motion as a militant trade unionist, and one who was not a "Red-baiter". He detailed the history of the dispute. Commencing with the dismissal of a shop steward by the Australian Iron and Steel Co. Ltd., he said that the original dispute had been lost sight of while two great forces clashed. The activities of another political party in the matter placed a responsibility on the Labor Movement. The authority of the N.S.W. Labor Council had been defied; an unsuccessful attempt made to drag in the railwaymen; and a successful effort to bring in the miners. The whole position was a challenge to the Labor Movement, that had to be accepted. If the challenge was not accepted, it would mean a general strike, followed by a reaction which would be the same as had produced Fascism in Italy, Nazism in Germany, the sell-out by Britain at Munich, and the situation in Australia after the 1917 general strike.

Mr. McAlpine seconded the motion.

He warned delegates that the present situation was the outcome of a deliberate plan by Mr. E. Thornton of the Ironworkers' Association, to make a deal with the employers to replace arbitration with collective bargaining. Workers had had six years of continuous employment, and had made savings with which they could buy things to improve amenities. But the Communist Party did not want that, and were trying to engineer a general strike to wipe out workers' savings and make them desperate men, with misery and degradation.

The motion was carried unanimously.

8.16   Chifley and McGirr condemn coal strike
Daily Telegraph, 21 June 1949

Mr. Chifley and Mr. McGirr said in the statement 'The issues in this dispute are quite clear.The Australian Coal and Shale Employees' Federation filed with the Coal Industry Tribunal (Mr. Gallagher) a log of three claims.
(1) 'Long Service Leave: The Tribunal which has concluded its hearing of this claim, said on June 9 that it would announce a draft award in relation to this matter on Tuesday June 14.

Between those two dates the mining unions decided to hold aggregate meetings on June 16 and those meetings decided on a general strike on June 27 unless all claims were met in full.

The Tribunal withheld the draft award because of the stop work threat.
(2) Thirty-five hours week: The hearing of this claim was in progress and nearing completion. It was adjourned at the request of the Federation.
(3) Thirty shillings a week wages increase: This claim was withdrawn by the Federation itself almost immediately after it was lodged.

In these circumstances the decision to stage a general strike on June 27 is a wholly unreasonable and unjustified repudiation of conciliation and arbitration at a time when those processes are in actual course of effective functioning.

The decision, if adhered to, will lead to mass unemployment for workers in many industries not immediately connected with the coalmining industry.

The miners themselves will be heavily involved in loss and inconvenience.

Let this be thoroughly understood: This dispute must finally be settled by the proper arbitral tribunal and not otherwise.

No threats or strike, however prolonged, will influence the Government's policy in this matter.'

8.17   Clash between Curtin and Ward over leaks to press
Caucus minutes, 11 March 1941

Mr. Curtin emphasised the seriousness of the leakage of information from the Party room and stated that at the luncheon adjournment he had refused to see the press. At the dinner adjournment the press had, as usual, waited upon him, and although he had been given to understand that the press knew the text of the resolutions proposed at an earlier sitting, he did not make any comment thereupon, but only indicated the actual resolution that had been passed. His position made it essential for him to grant an interview to the press (it had always been the practice that had been followed) but he had only communicated actual decisions made by the Party without any comment.

Mr. Ward stated that he had an equal concern regarding the leakage of information. He pointed out that no information could have been given by either Mr. Morgan or himself because during the whole period of the debate they had not left the room.

.   .   .

At this stage Mr. Ward indicated to the meeting that the reports in the morning Press were unsatisfactory to him and that they sufficiently misrepresented his attitude that he felt he would be justified in making a statement. He did not regard the practice of the Leader giving statements about the business of the Caucus as desirable. Expression of opinions inevitably associated themselves with the giving of decisions to the Press. Mr. Curtin warmly denied that he had by inference or otherwise conveyed any expressions of opinion to the Press. He had done as he always had done when interviewed by the Press after Party meetings, conveyed to them actual decisions when such decisions were ready for release. Because of the criticisms he had safeguarded himself by having another member of the Executive present when giving these interviews. Mr. Curtin further stated that the previous evening he had actually seen another member of the Party in consultation with a Pressman and perusing the report of that pressman before sending same on to his paper.

Mr. Ward stated that although he had been seen in the presence of a Pressman and perusing his report he did not convey any information from the Party room. Whatever he had done was openly done for anyone to see and he had no reason to apologise for anything he had done.

9

1949 – 1974

The election defeat of 1949 unleashed internal forces that were to disrupt the Labor party. In the late 1940s communist influence in trade unions had increased and during the 1949 election campaign the Liberal and Country parties had emphasized the communist menace that they believed threatened the country. In 1951 the Liberal government introduced a bill to outlaw the Communist party. The Labor party was divided on the issue; some argued that, although the party opposed communism, it should concentrate on more positive reforms (9.1), while the federal executive, more conservative than caucus, instructed it to pass the bill in an amended form (9.2). When the act was declared invalid by the High Court, the Menzies government held a referendum to change the constitution to enable the government to ban the Communist party. Sections of the Labor party, led by Evatt, campaigned vigorously against the proposal, arguing that it was an infringement of civil liberties (9.3). Their passionate rhetoric was successful and the proposal was defeated.

The party finally split in 1955, after the right wing gained control of the party in Victoria. In a famous statement Evatt accused the Industrial Groups, organized by B. A. Santamaria to combat communist influence in the unions, of trying to infiltrate the Labor party. He claimed their ambitions were responsible for the party's defeat in 1954 (9.4). The federal executive investigated the charges and supported Evatt (9.5). Soon afterwards the party split in Victoria and Queensland. That split, and the eventual formation of the Democratic Labor party from the people expelled from the Labor party, was to help keep the Labor party out of office for a further seventeen years, even though it came within one seat of victory in 1961.

In the 1960s two issues dominated debate within the party, foreign affairs and state aid to non-government schools. A special conference held in Canberra condemned the continuation of nuclear tests and the establishment of bases in Australia that were controlled by United States personnel (9.6). But that conference also did great harm to the reputation of the Labor party because its parliamentary leaders, Calwell and Whitlam, were photographed outside the conference room, waiting for the decisions on party policy and unable to influence it (9.7). The conference was immediately labelled a meeting of 'thirty-six faceless men'. In 1966 the conscription of national servicemen for service in the undeclared war in Vietnam became a major election issue and Calwell, a veteran of the conscription battles of 1916 and 1942, led the Labor party's condemnation of the scheme during the 1966 election campaign (9.8). Vietnam remained a major issue for the next six years.

State aid to non-government schools also caused divisions within the party. After the federal executive interpreted a conference decision on state aid in a way that some members, and particularly Whitlam, considered to be a reversal of the policy adopted by conference, Whitlam attacked the decisions, and narrowly escaped expulsion. He defended his actions (9.9), but in an interview called the executive 'twelve witless men' and showed the impatience and the tendency to crash through obstacles with supreme self-confidence which have marked his career since.

In 1968 a further crisis erupted when a Tasmanian delegate to the federal executive, Brian Harradine, accused some of his fellow delegates of being 'friends of the communists' (9.10). In retaliation the executive refused to accept his credentials as a Tasmanian delegate (9.11). In the ensuing crisis Whitlam resigned his leadership of the parliamentary party and narrowly defeated Cairns in the ballot that followed (see documents 3.9 and 3.10).

In 1970 the Victorian branch, dominated by left-wing unions, tried to expel one of its leading parliamentarians when he supported the official federal policy on state aid. Using this opportunity, the federal executive devised a series of reasons to intervene in the Victorian branch and reconstruct it (9.12). From then on, the Labor party's fortunes improved.

In 1972 Whitlam launched the Labor party's electoral campaign with a speech that rang with promises and hope and raised the expectations of the Australian people (9.13). But the party's period of office was seldom calm. Ministers made public statements outside subjects covered by their portfolio; policies were introduced at a hectic pace, often without sufficient planning; and several bad mistakes were made, with Murphy's botched raid on the Australian Security Intelligence Organisation headquarters being the most obvious of them. Inflation soared. At the same time the Liberal—Country Party—D.L.P. majority in the Senate rejected some important bills. Then, in an attempt to gain a majority in the Senate, Whitlam appointed the leader of the D.L.P., Senator Vincent Gair, ambassador to Ireland (9.14). The opposition reacted by breaking a long-standing convention and using their numbers in the Senate to block supply. Whitlam immediately called a double dissolution and, listing his triumphs, appealed to the electorate for a continued mandate (9.15). His government was returned, but without a majority in the Senate. After that it was frequently threatened by the Senate's numbers. An early scandal was caused by the appointment of Junie Morosi as Cairns's secretary.

9.1   Federal president opposes moves to ban Communist party
Conference report, 1951, pp. 4—5

PRESIDENTIAL ADDRESS
Hon. J. Ferguson, General President, delivered his Presidential address.

The close of 50 years of Federation calls to mind those men and women whose courage, vision and belief made solid the foundations upon which our progressive and democratic organisation now stands.

I salute the memory of our pioneers who, down the years, helped to build a great Movement and a better Australia.

Labor has a record which we regard with pardonable pride, and recognises that its successes are as much a reflection of the work and sacrifices of the builders of the Movement, and it is a monument to the ability of men and women and past Conferences in helping to weld together a great united Movement. We must face up to current problems and gear for the future as our compliment to the past.

Labor achievements have given us a better Australia and, with it, a greater degree of responsibility, which we must accept and exercise if we are to retain all which we have gained over the years. To do this meant that Labor must forever remain Labor. There is, unfortunately, evidence of weakening belief, revealed in the actions of a few who would repudiate vital Labor fundamentals, lowering the Movement to the level of a Party without an effective policy, and at a time when we should be explaining and defending Socialist principles as the real means of solving current economic and world problems. Even now we find the Menzies—Fadden Government compelled to acknowledge the need for controls in the planned economy akin to what they described as socialist and used against Labor.

It seems that too many of our people are encouraged to believe that hatred of Communism is the only condition to good membership in the Labor Party. Opposition to Communism is an important political incidental to membership, but not the only condition of good membership—the test of which is true belief in Labor principles as a whole, and this in turn is the surest bulwark against totalitarian tyranny. Although committed to the struggle against Communism and other forms of totalitarianism, Labor must, at all times, guard against any tendency to join forces with those possessing nothing more in common with us than opposition to Communism. It would be fatal for Labor to fight Communism by associating itself with reaction. We should remember that every self-confessed opponent of Communism is not necessarily a friend of democracy.

Labor must continue its fight against Communism with even greater intensity. To ban their party and drive them underground is not the answer.

Exposure, not repression, must be our aim, and this calls for more active work in the Trade Unions. Communists cannot obtain power in the Trade Union if unionists are alert, informed and are offered correct leadership built around a progressive realistic program of action. The apathy and indifference of the average trade unionist explains Communist successes in the Trade Union Movement, and this apathy will be intensified once the trade unionist is encouraged to believe that the Communists can be legislated out of action.

Hitler and Mussolini provide the historic example of the failure of the repressive measures to destroy ideas. I repeat, that effective opposition to Communism is an informed, alert Trade Union Movement, subject to the political guidance of the Australian Labor Party. It requires more than conference resolutions, Parliamentarian speeches and Legislative Acts to stop Communism. Labor must accept its historic responsibility right now and commence a determined crusade among trade unionists, explaining policy, Labor achievements and exposing Communist duplicity. We must strengthen relations between the industrial and political sections of the Movement. Labor must get back to first principles and fortify its intentions by constructing a positive program of economic and social action to eliminate causes accounting for Communism. We must popularise and defend all that is decent in our way of life, and campaign in every workshop, factory, mine and work depot throughout Australia. Labor must stimulate its functions as the people's movement and as a medium for strengthening moral fibre and national integrity.

9.2   Federal executive gives instructions to caucus on Communist Party Dissolution Bill
Conference report, 1951, pp. 6-7

CLAUSE 2—COMMUNIST PARTY DISSOLUTION BILL
The most important question dealt with by your Executive was Labor's attitude towards the Communist Party Dissolution Bill.

At the meeting on May 9, 1950, your Executive carried the following resolution:—

"That the Australian Labor Party expresses its adherence to the Australian democratic way of life. We therefore declare that any proposal for the banning of a political party because of hostility and objection, no matter how repugnant such may be, is a negation of democratic principles. Nevertheless, consistent with our belief in democracy, and together with our knowledge that the policy and actions of the Communist Party demonstrates that its method and object aim at the destruction of the Australian way of life, justifies approval of the action of the Federal Parliamentary Labor Party favoring amendments to the Communist Party Dissolution Bill."

This resolution was followed by one advising the Leader of the Federal Parliamentary Labor Party that in the opinion of this Executive the amendments foreshadowed by the Parliamentary Party should be persisted in.

.   .   .

It has regard to the fact that in June last the Labor majority in the Senate passed the Bill in a form which enabled the Menzies Government—if it so wished—to do all the following things:—

(a) To ban the Australian Communist Party and appropriate its assets.

(b) To ban organisations which supported or were agents of the Australian Communist Party, and to appropriate their assets.

(c) To render liable to imprisonment for five years any person doing any act in support of the banned organisations or their objects.

(d) To remove Communists from the Commonwealth Public Service and from office in Trade Unions.

The Federal Executive has also regard to:—

(a) The refusal of the Menzies Government to accept Labor's amendments designed to ensure the application of the fundamental principles of both British and natural justice in respect of declared organisations and declared individuals;

(b) The entirely untruthful statements of the Prime Minister and members of his Government alleging that Labor supported Communism and sought protection for Communists; and

(c) The Bill contains drastic provisions which were not disclosed to the people during the election campaign.

The Federal Executive asserts that the Menzies Government wishes to avoid responsibility for giving effect to the main purposes of the Bill; to avoid its election pledges in relation to Communism and to conceal its abject failure to take effective steps to prevent the great ills that flow from the spiralling cost of living.

The Federal Executive has decided that, to contest the sincerity of the Menzies Government before the people, and to give the lie to its false and slanderous allegations against the Labor Party, that the Bill should be passed in the form in which it is now before the Senate.

The Federal Executive affirm that the Federal Parliamentary Labor Party is fully justified in its criticism of those controversial clauses of the Bill, and the amendments proposed thereto.

However, in the light of consideration already set forth, it directs the Federal Parliamentary Labor Party to withdraw its opposition to the Bill in the form in which it is now before the Senate, while leaving all members of the Federal Parliamentary Labor Party free to criticise the controversial clauses.

9.3   Labor party's pamphlet advocating 'No' vote in referendum to change constitution to allow government to ban Communist party

THE CASE FOR NO
ARGUMENT AGAINST THE PROPOSED LAW
The Australian Labor Party asks you to read this case and to vote no.

Labor is utterly opposed to communism. Labor has taken the only effective action to combat communism in Australia.

But the question is not whether you are against communism but whether you approve of the Menzies government's referendum proposals which are unnecessary, unjust and totalitarian and could threaten all minority groups.

Repeating President Truman's pledge, the Australian Labor Party refuses to "turn Australia into a Right Wing Totalitarian country in order to deal with a Left Wing Totalitarian Threat. In short, we are NOT going to end democracy."

Mr. Chifley's Warning
In his very last speech, Mr. Chifley warned Australia against this Menzies referendum. You should heed the warning of this great statesman who gave his life to the service of Australia.

Mr. Chifley was strongly opposed to Communism but he was convinced that the powers asked for would injure groups and persons who had no connection whatever with Communism.

Distinguished Church leaders have shown their grave concern on these questions. Thus Bishop Moyes said:

"For the Australian Commonwealth to develop an order that has even a faint resemblance to the police state of totalitarian countries, with its hunting for victims, is to give Communism its first victory. For we shall be adopting its methods and using Satan to cast out Satan."

So too, King's Counsel Eric Miller, of Sydney, says:

"In the view of Church and State, Communism is evil. The way to fight this evil is by the criminal statutes—amended wherever necessary—and not by throwing overboard the rule of law or the principles of British justice."

Three Proposals—Only One Vote
In this referendum there are three distinct proposals—but only one vote.

FIRST PROPOSAL
The first proposal would give Parliament power to re-enact the Menzies Act of 1950 without any alteration. But that Act was declared illegal and unconstitutional by six High Court Judges largely because the Parliament and the Government were trying to usurp the judicial functions of the High Court.

The Act of 1950 was a lengthy document. You haven't been given an opportunity of reading it, yet you are asked to vote for it; totalitarianism again!

The High Court's decision was that the Government already possesses full power to deal with and punish all persons and organisations concerned in subversive activity. See particularly the judgments of Sir Edward McTiernan, Mr. Justice Williams, and Sir William Webb.

It follows that the first proposal is quite unnecessary as well as dangerous to democracy.

SECOND PROPOSAL

This would give power to make a law in terms of the Communist Act of 1950 with such alterations and amendments as relate to "a matter dealt with by that Act".

This carries the first proposal to fantastic extremes.

Anti-Communists Threatened: The definition of "communist" could be extended to include anti-Communists who favour any form of social organisation. For instance, supporters of the Australian Labor Party and members of trades unions, and supporters of many other political and religious groups might be "declared" and deprived of employment or office.

Raids on Homes: Searches: A second illustration is the power of Commonwealth officers to search persons and homes. The original provision of the Menzies Government for search aroused wide protests and it was modified. But under this new proposal the Government could go back to the original provision conferring an unlimited right to search homes and persons within it. What an opportunity for a totalitarian Gestapo!

THE THIRD PROPOSAL

This would give Parliament power to make such laws "with respect to communists or communism" as Parliament may consider necessary or expedient for the defence or security, etc., of Australia. This proposal is even more outrageous than the other two.

Mr. Menzies attacks High Court's Judgment

Here for the first time we have a Government asking the people to deprive the High Court of its fifty-year-old jurisdiction to determine whether a particular measure relates to defence.

So the Menzies Government wants to strip the High Court of its constitutional functions and make a legislature's decision on "defence" unchallengeable.

Confiscation of Property

The result of a YES vote would be that any person or group who could be brought within the wide description of "communist" could be deprived by any Government of their property without compensation. The High Court could do nothing about it.

New power may be used to help Communism!

But the present proposal goes further still. It will come as a shock to you, but it is undoubtedly true that under this third proposal, legislation could be framed NOT to discourage or suppress, but actually to encourage or promote communism. For the proposed power is to make laws "with respect to communism" and a law encouraging Communism would be "with respect to" Communism just as much as a law discouraging it. Remember, that this is not a temporary alteration of the Constitution, but a permanent one.

Our Advice—Take No Risk

You should vote NO. The ballot paper should be marked 1 and 2 according to your choice. We advise you to vote NO by placing the figure 1 opposite NO and the figure 2 opposite YES in the ballot paper thus:

DO YOU APPROVE of the proposed law for the alteration of the Constitution entitled "CONSTITUTION ALTERATION (Powers to deal with Communists and Communism) 1951'"?

2   YES
1   NO

The three proposals are all dangerous. They are definite blows at Australia's
system of justice. And non-Communists are threatened with unjust treatment.

Existing Powers Adequate

The present Constitution and the existing laws give a Government prepared to
deal with Communists all the powers it needs.

Mr. Menzies has not acted. He has talked.

The Commonwealth Crimes Act contains provisions for the Courts to
declare any subversive body an illegal organisation and dissolve it.

Communism Is a Menzies Smoke Screen

Mr. Menzies knows all this.

Mr. Menzies keeps talking about Communism. It is a smoke screen to
conceal his failure to halt inflation and reduce the cost of living.

The Menzies Government is drunk with power and thirsts for still more
power.

In time of peace Mr. Menzies has actually instituted government by regulation enabling Ministers to control any industry, any business, any trade, or any
service in Australia. He has grabbed this power under the Defence Preparations Act.

Stop Menzies' "Grab for Power"

Now is the time for you to stop Mr. Menzies getting any more power.

An emphatic "NO" majority will stop him before it is too late.

Consciously or unconsciously, the Menzies Government is heading fast
towards totalitarianism in Australia.

Under the extreme powers of the Defence Preparations Act, Mr. Menzies has
power in time of peace to close down any trade or business at his pleasure.
Totalitarianism again!

British Legal Traditions Smashed

The Referendum proposals are calculated to smash all British legal traditions.
As recently as August 6th last, Lord Chancellor Viscount Jowitt, the head of
the British judiciary, said in Australia: "We don't believe in taking steps to ban
Communism because that is against British traditions."

9.4   Evatt's statement condemning activities of 'groupers' within Labor party
Press statement, 5 October 1954

The strong and determined desire of the overwhelming majority of trade union
officials and membership for solidarity within the movement has been given
eloquent expression at the Labor Day celebrations in New South Wales.

But the matter is of such Australia-wide importance to the Labor Movement
that I have come to the conclusion that I must say more about the present position, especially so far as the Commonwealth Parliament is concerned.

At the recent Federal elections on May 29 we put forward a policy of development and we polled a majority of the people in Australia. We made gains in every State except Victoria.

All this was achieved by the self-sacrifice of tens of thousands of voluntary workers for Labor.

It was achieved, too, despite the thinly-veiled use against Labor of the opening speech before the Petrov Commission—the statement of which seemed to be distant many poles apart from the truth of the matter so far as it has been more recently revealed by the sworn evidence of many witnesses.

But in the election, one factor told heavily against us—the attitude of a small minority group of members, located particularly in the State of Victoria, which has, since 1949, become increasingly disloyal to the Labor Movement and the Labor leadership.

Adopting methods which strikingly resemble both Communist and Fascist infiltration of larger groups, some of these groups have created an almost intolerable situation—calculated to deflect the Labor Movement from the pursuit of established Labor objectives and ideals.

Whenever it suits their real aims, one or more of them never hesitate to attack or subvert Labor policy or Labor leadership.

A striking example of this at the elections was the attack upon Labor's proposal to abolish the means test. That proposal had been approved, not only by myself but by the authorized representatives of the Federal Executive, the ACTU, the AWU and the leaders of the Parliamentary Labor Party in both Houses.

In spite of that, there were further attacks on the agreed policy. These attacks were eagerly seized on by anti-Labor parties, as though by a preconceived plan, and advertised from one end of the country to the other.

Since the elections, nothing has been done officially to deal with those responsible for the disloyal and subversive actions to which I refer.

In addition, it is my clear belief that in crucial constituencies members of the same small group, whether members of the Federal Parliamentary Labor Party, or not, deliberately attempted to undermine a number of Labor's selected and endorsed candidates, with the inevitable and intended result of assisting the Menzies Government.

Similar attempts at subversion have recently been taking place in the Federal Parliamentary Labor Party. In that Party the group concerned is small, almost minute, in numbers. But repeated attempts have been made to make use of minor and unimportant incidents in the Caucus.

For instance, it was falsely reported to the Press that three members, having nothing to do with the group, were resorting to fisticuffs.

Incidents were deliberately created and then followed by an almost instantaneous relay of distorted and sometimes invented accounts to a naturally receptive anti-Labor Press.

It seems certain that the activities of this small group are largely directed from outside the Labor Movement. The Melbourne News Weekly appears to act as their organ. A serious position exists.

Since the referendum of 1951 Labor leadership has become very patient with some of these outbursts, solely in the interests of solidarity. But our patience is abused and our tolerance is interpreted as a sign of weakness.

The Labor Party cannot yield to the dictates of any minority which functions in a way contrary to the overwhelming majority of the rank and file of the Labor Movement.

The procedures adopted cannot be accidental. They are deliberately planned. They are causing a rising tide of disgust and anger throughout Labor's supporters.

I cannot overlook the fact that in somewhat analagous circumstances Mr. Chifley was subject to sniping and snide attacks which helped to undermine his health and strength.

The feeling of the rank and file of Labor throughout Australia is strong and determined. Thousands of messages have come to me from Labor leagues and trade unions.

They are almost all to the effect that this planned and somewhat desperate attempt to disrupt and injure Labor leadership is really intended to assist the Menzies Government, especially in its attempt to initiate in Australia some of the un-British and un-Australian methods of the totalitarian police state.

Having in view the absolute necessity for real, and not sham, solidarity and unity within the movement, I am bringing this matter before the next meeting of the Federal Executive, with a view to appropriate action being taken by the Federal Labor Conference in January.

Ninety-five per cent of the rank and file of the Parliamentary Labor Party are absolutely loyal to the movement. There is not the slightest reason why their efforts should be undermined by a tiny minority.

9.5 Federal executive examines charges and counter-charges made by Evatt and 'groupers'
Conference report, 1955, pp. 7—10

Report, findings and decisions of the Federal Executive, Australian Labor Party, in respect to submissions, allegations and charges made by a number of persons affecting the general welfare of the Labor Party.

At 3 p.m. on the 27th October, 1954, the Federal Executive met at the Kingston Hotel, Canberra, to commence a Special Meeting as a consequence of a number of press statements by members of the Party, including the Federal Parliamentary Leader, the Rt. Hon. Dr. H. V. Evatt, M.H.R., which, in the opinion of the Executive, affected the general welfare of the Labor Movement as referred to in Rule 9 (a) of the Federal Executive Rules.

The Executive met subsequently in Melbourne on the 10th November, 1954, and again on the 29th November, 1954.

The submissions made to the Executive by a number of persons, all members of the Party, not only involved individuals, but contained charges against the Central Executive of the Victorian Branch of the Party.

.   .   .

The Executive investigation may be placed under four main headings:—
1 Disunity and lack of discipline in the Federal Parliamentary Labor Party.
2 Charges and counter charges involving individual members of the Party.
3 That, in effect, the Central Executive of the Party in Victoria is dominated and/or influenced by an outside body referred to as the "Movement" to the detriment of the Labor Party's basic principles.
4 That industrial group organisation has developed away from its original

purpose, and is being used as a vehicle to further the political aims of an outside body referred to as the "Movement".

It is proposed to deal with them in that order.

1   There can be no doubt as to the alarming disunity and lack of discipline in the ranks of the Federal Parliamentary Labor Party, and many factors have played a part in creating this condition.

It is not intended to critically examine all those factors. Sufficient for the purpose of the Executive is to say that it is accepted as a fact.

Having regard for the fact that the Federal Executive is the administrative authority to carry out decisions of the Federal Conference and to interpret the Constitution and Federal Platform vide rule 9(a) of the Executive Rules, it has become imperative for the Executive to exercise that authority for the purpose of issuing a directive to the Federal Parliamentary Labor Party to ensure that members will conduct themselves in accordance with the basic requirements of membership of this Party.

This directive is issued in the following terms—

(a) That the Executive of the Federal Parliamentary Labor Party shall accept the responsibility of reporting to the appropriate State Executive the behaviour of any member of the Federal Parliamentary Labor Party which, in the opinion of the Executive, warrants disciplinary action.

(b) The Executive of the Federal Parliamentary Labor Party shall at the same time notify the President of the Federal Executive of its action under (a).

The matter shall be placed before the Federal Executive, who shall, if it be deemed necessary, call for a report from the State Executive concerned.

(c) In the event of a majority of the Federal Executive deciding that the State Executive concerned has not taken disciplinary action in keeping with the offence alleged by the Executive of the Federal Parliamentary Labor Party, the Federal Executive shall take whatever action it deems fit under the provisions of rule 9(h) of the Federal Executive Rules.

(d) Providing that this directive is not to be construed as in any way amending or disturbing any existing rules of State Branches.

2   In regard to the matters falling under this heading which involve Dr. Evatt, Messrs. Keon, Mullens and Bourke, the Executive, after a full examination, have reached the following conclusions:—

(a) That the charges preferred against Dr. Evatt are not sustained.

(b) In the case of the allegations affecting Messrs. Keon, Mullens and Bourke, it must be noted that no specific charges were made against them by Dr. Evatt before the Executive.

It should be further noted that the handling of the controversy by the daily press was largely responsible for the widely held belief that charges against them would be laid before the Executive by Dr. Evatt. As a consequence of these circumstances, we are now compelled to find that whilst the conduct of the three members named have on occasion been in conflict with the welfare of the Labor Movement, the fact that the responsible bodies concerned, including the Federal Executive, failed to take action against them at the time, does to a material extent condone such conduct, and as a consequence it is not intended to press these matters further other than to direct their attention to the Executive directive under (1) of this Report.

3   The Executive's examination of this—the most vital question before it—involved voluminous submissions from a number of persons in varying forms of allegations, some of them being extraneous to the question.

In addition, the Executive sought the assistance of a number of people in its deliberations, notably the Premier of Victoria, Mr. Cain, his Deputy, Mr. Galvin, and the Secretary of the A.C.T.U., Mr. Broadby. We feel that the information and balanced objective views presented by these gentlemen materially assisted in the formulation of our conclusions.

They are set out hereunder—

(a) That a Special Conference of the Victorian Branch of the A.L.P. is directed to be held on a date to be named, and on the following conditions laid down by the Federal Executive.

(b) That with the exception of the Secretary and Assistant Secretary and Woman Organiser, all officers and members of the Central Executive, as referred to in Rule 5 of the Central Executive Rules, shall be declared vacant as from 9 a.m. on the date fixed for the Special Conference referred to under (a) hereof.

.   .   .

4   (a) That the Constitution covering A.L.P. Industrial Groups as referred to on pages 101 and 102 of the current Constitution and Rules of the Victorian Branch, shall be deemed to be non-existent after 31st December, 1954.

(b) That it be agreed that this Executive shall submit a recommendation to the next Federal Conference in respect to the overall question of Industrial Groups organisation in Australia, having particular regard for its original purpose of combating Communism in the Unions, and that pending a determination by Conference there shall be no recognition of this type of organisation by the Victorian Branch after 31st December, 1954.

9.6   Labor conference opposes nuclear testing and establishment of U.S. bases in Australia
Conference report, 1963, pp. 15—16

NUCLEAR DISARMAMENT AND NUCLEAR-FREE ZONE:

C. T. Oliver moved:

"The Australian Labor Party declares that the hope of mankind lies in agreement through the United Nations for total world disarmament. It supports the view of the Commonwealth Prime Ministers in March, 1961, that every effort should be made to secure rapid agreement to the permanent banning of nuclear weapons tests by all nations and to arrangements for verifying the observance of the agreement.

"It deplores the breach of the three years moratorium on nuclear tests and the resumption of tests without any end in sight.

"It declares its opposition to nuclear tests at any time by any nation and believes that the Australian Government should take all necessary steps to initiate a conference of the Antarctic Treaty Powers, China, Japan, India, Pakistan, Ceylon, Burma, Malaya, Thailand, Laos, Cambodia, Vietnam, the Philippines, Indonesia and all countries in Africa and South America directed towards making the Southern Hemisphere a nuclear-free zone.

"The Government should assure the United Nations that Australia in its submissions to the conference to make the Southern Hemisphere a nuclear-free zone would declare that it would agree not to manufacture, acquire or receive nuclear weapons.

"Australia now has its own bases capable of being used by itself and its allies in war.

"A defence radio communications centre capable of communicating with submarines operated by an ally in Australia would not be inconsistent with Labor policy if:

(i) Australian sovereignty were maintained;

(ii) Australian citizens engaged at the station were subject to Australian law;

(iii) the radio communications centre is under the joint control and operation of the Australian and U.S.A. governments and the facilities are available to Australian forces;

(iv) Australia's involvement in war is a question for Australia alone to decide at all times and under no circumstances and under no agreement should Australia become automatically involved in war;

(v) In the event of the U.S.A. being at war or threatened with war by another power, Australian territory and Australian facilities must not be used in any way that would involve Australia without the prior knowledge and consent of the Australian government;

(vi) The radio communications centre did not become a base for the stockpiling of nuclear arms in times of peace.

"Labor is opposed to foreign owned and operated bases for the supply or holding of defence equipment in Australia in peace time and declares it will not be the first nation in the Pacific to stockpile nuclear arms in its territories in peace time.

"The Labor Party shares the fears expressed by President Kennedy concerning the possible spread of nuclear arms to those nations not now possessing them. President Kennedy said on 17 May, 1962: 'We do not believe in a series of national deterrents. We believe that a NATO deterrent, to which the United States has committed itself heavily, can provide adequate protection. An increasingly dangerous situation will result if nation after nation feels that its expression of independence requires it to build up its own nuclear deterrent'."

Mr. Oliver was granted an extension of time and subsequently a further extension.

D. A. Dunstan seconded the motion.

Secretarys Amendment

The Secretary moved an amendment: "That all words after the fourth paragraph up to 'in its territories in peace time' be deleted and the following inserted: 'And that the A.L.P. is opposed to any bases being built in Australia that could be used for the manufacture, firing or control of any nuclear missile or vehicle capable of carrying nuclear missiles'."

The Secretary was granted an extension of time, and subsequently a further extension.

F. C. Grenfell seconded the amendment and was granted an extension of time.

C. Jones' Amendment

C. Jones moved a further amendment: "That the nuclear-free zone statement be endorsed, subject to the following:

"(a)   Recognition of the fact that it cannot be achieved unless approved by the nuclear powers, the U.S.A. and Russia;

"(b)   That on becoming the government, Labor will immediately take steps to initiate a conference of the Southern Hemisphere powers with the aims of establishing a nuclear-free zone in the Southern Hemisphere and determining Australia's attitude to the future of any established base in relation to the nuclear deterrent policy of the nuclear powers, U.S.A. and Russia, as it applies to this area.

"It is clear that the Menzies Government, without any regard for the consequences, has committed Australia to the establishment of a base in Western Australia and the responsibility therefore rests squarely upon the Menzies Government.

"Furthermore it is clear that the Menzies Government has committed any future government to the base. However, while recognising this fact, Labor in government will require that:

"(1)   Australian sovereignty shall be maintained at all times;

"(2)   Australian citizens engaged at the station shall be subject to Australian law;

"(3)   the radio communications centre shall be under the joint control and operation of the Australian and U.S.A. governments, and the facilities are available to Australian forces;

"(4)   Australia's involvement in war shall be a question for Australia alone to decide at all times, and under no circumstances, and under no agreement, shall Australia become automatically involved in war;

"(5)   in the event of the U.S.A. being at war, or threatened with war by another power, Australian territory and Australian facilities must not be used in any way that would involve Australia without the prior knowledge and consent of the Australian government;

"(6)   the radio communications centre does not become a base for the stockpiling of nuclear arms in time of peace;

"(7)   it shall be clearly understood that Labor is opposed to foreign owned and operated bases for the supply or holding of defensive equipment in Australia in peace time, and declares it will not be the first nation in the Pacific to stockpile nuclear arms in its territories in peace time."

9.7   Calwell and Whitlam wait for decision of 'thirty-six faceless men'
Daily Telegraph, 21, 22 March 1963

Conference rose at 2 a.m. today after being in continuous session since 10.30 a.m. yesterday.

Mr. Calwell and his deputy, Mr. Whitlam, had sweated out the result for hours.

Up to midnight they waited in their offices at Parliament House.

Then they went to the Hotel Kingston where the conference was meeting and waited outside under a street light.

Thus they shared in the weird conference which marks the all-time nadir of Labor parliamentary leadership.

Periodically delegates emerged from the A.L.P. Federal Conference to speak to Mr. Calwell and Mr. Whitlam.

Shortly before 1 a.m. Mr. Calwell and Mr. Whitlam retired to a parked car to await the decision.

At 1.15 a.m. Mr. Calwell and Mr. Whitlam went into the Hotel Kingston.

They sat with reporters in a lounge near the conference room waiting for delegates to make a decision.

By 1.45 a.m. when conference had still not reached a decision they left the hotel and went home.

At one stage Mr. Calwell had tried through an emissary to get through the conference a motion "the question be put" so that he would be put out of his anguish.

But the motion was overwhelmingly and contemptuously defeated.

·   ·   ·

The pictorial record opposite—Mr. Arthur Calwell's night watch—is a sad commentary on the decline in status of Labor's parliamentary leadership.

It shows Mr. Calwell and his deputy Mr. Whitlam, waiting in the midnight darkness outside Canberra's Kingston Hotel yesterday.

Inside the hotel, 36 virtually unknown men—delegates to the A.L.P. Federal Conference—were deciding a question of international importance.

9.8   Calwell condemns conscription for service in Vietnam
Age, 11 November 1966

The Opposition Leader (Mr. Calwell), opening the Labor party's election campaign last night, said the most important issue was conscription and the threatened extension of conscription.

Speaking at St. Kilda town hall Mr. Calwell said:

"The most important issue in this campaign is conscription, the conscription of a section of our 20-year-old youths, against their wishes and their wills, to kill or be killed in the undeclared civil war in Vietnam and the threatened extension of conscription to all 20-year-olds and other age groups to increase our unwarranted and unnecessary commitments.

"We can prevent all this happening by defeating the menace on next Saturday fortnight.

"The Menzies Government made the first blunder over Vietnam nearly two years ago. It blundered equally badly over Suez in 1958. The Holt Government is determined to increase the extent of the Vietnam blunder.

"So unimpressed are our men of military age, about the need to fight in the war in Vietnam, that none of them will volunteer. No one can deny this fact; not even our own bellicose Prime Minister.

"The Government having failed to attract volunteers, has resorted to conscription to maintain our army. It asks for your endorsement. I hope you will refuse it most emphatically.

"Conscription is immoral, it is unjust and it is a violation of human rights. It must and will be defeated.

"There are 600,000 Australian mothers with sons between 15 and 20 years of age, and many of these boys could be sent away to die or be wounded in the long, cruel, dirty war that is raging in Vietnam.

"I call on those 600,000 mothers and their husbands and their other sons and daughters to tell Mr. Holt that the lives of their eligible sons are too precious to be squandered by the man who has pledged this country to go all the way with L.B.J.

"I doubt if any one of the Government's senators and representatives who voted for conscription, and that includes the splinter group duo, has a son fighting in Vietnam.

"It is so easy, therefore, for all these anti-Labor members of Parliament to regard the lives of other people's children as expendable and to dispose of them in any way they think fit and without remorse or regret.

"There is no difficulty in separating conscripts from members of the regular army and so we will act in consultation with the American authorities, immediately we become the Government, to withdraw all conscripts in Vietnam. Our first act as a Government will be to abolish conscription and give orders that all conscripts in camp in Australia shall be discharged forthwith.

"The remainder of our troops will be brought home at the earliest practicable moment after consultation with our allies and so as not to endanger the lives of any Australian or allied troops. While our troops are in Vietnam, we undertake to give them any support they might need. We will never let them down.

"As it is immoral to conscript our youths to die in Vietnam, so it will be immoral not to withdraw them when we become the Government. This we will do.

"The Labor views on Vietnam are supported by opinions expressed by the late President J. F. Kennedy, and by other distinguished Americans like his two famous brothers, Senators Robert and Edward Kennedy, and by Senators Fulbright and Mike Mansfield, and 24 other outstanding senators."

Speaking of defence generally, Mr. Calwell said Australia must possess its own independent foreign policy and defence policy to enable it to honor United Nations and Commonwealth obligations and to carry out treaty obligations with other countries.

"Australia's dependence, for its defence, on other nations is due to the failure of the Menzies and Holt Governments to develop Australia's defence capacity to the full," he said.

"We are spending too much money on expensive sophisticated defence equipment, purchased overseas, the financial cost of which appears to rise beyond reason and beyond the control of the Government and with its value suspect.

Labor policy provided for a voluntary defence force properly equipped, and possessing modern weapons of war; being capable of great mobility within Australia and its own environs; having sufficient range and strike power to deter aggressors; being capable of use as part of United Nations forces for the maintenance of peace.

"We will raise Citizen Military Forces which can be rapidly mobilised in time of war."

9.9 Whitlam attacks decision of federal executive
Conference report, March 1966, pp. 56—7

REPLY OF MR. E. G. WHITLAM TO THE FEDERAL EXECUTIVE 3 MARCH, 1966

This is the fourth successive Executive meeting at which I have been under attack. In the current dispute let me say at the outset that I regret the impression which certain personal references may have given. I apologise unreservedly for these references. The Australian Labor Party, however, is greater than the personal hurts and grievances of any one of us.

It is my firm belief that the last Executive purported to make new policy. The last Conference said that "No (educational) benefit which is currently established shall be disturbed". An examination of the constitutionality of all State aid is a preparation to disturb established benefits. To oppose future extensions of Science Laboratories grants is to disturb benefits established more than a year before Conference. My own State Executive said that the Executive decision "contravened decisions of Federal Conference . . . (and was) wrong in principle". Has the Deputy Leader no right to support Conference policy?

The decisions of the Executive placed the Parliamentary Party in an impossible position. We were directed to oppose matters in Parliament which we had earlier supported and Conference had already endorsed. One anti-American proposition was referred for an inquiry by Caucus and another for a statement by the Leader. I am pleased that the N.S.W. Executive has asserted that "the elected representatives of the people should be free to declare in Caucus assembled their attitudes on Parliamentary action and to decide by majority vote without fear of coercion from outside bodies how the aims and objectives of the A.L.P. should be implemented".

Nothing could have humiliated the Parliamentary Party more than the selections for Executive Committees. Is the Parliamentary Party to have no status, no voice? I felt obliged as the Deputy Leader to speak up for it.

It is alleged that I made attacks on individual members of the Party. At the last Executive you had before you an item in which a public attack was made upon me by a prominent member of the Party. The Executive took no action. Unbridled and repeated attacks had been made on me in a journal conducted by men whose conduct was to be examined by you at my instigation. Again, the Executive took no action. Surely it cannot be that attacks only become important when made by me.

I do not believe that my stand in recent weeks has damaged the "general welfare" of the Party. I believe its welfare is at stake. I sought to promote its welfare. The disruption is not caused by drawing attention to breaches of policy. It is caused by making breaches of policy. The gravity of any situation determines the response. I have been as conscious of the party's welfare in the current situation as I have been on unity tickets, which have gravely affected the "general welfare" of the party for many years.

I have constantly striven for the party's welfare. I will go anywhere in Australia, if I am invited, to support the Labor cause. Two State Executives, however, have banned me from party gatherings for the last year. I have worked hard to assist State branches, as the present and former State secretaries among you well know. I have assiduously attended almost all Executive committees. I have sought to establish a basis of co-operation with the Executive.

I affirm my loyalty to the Australian Labor Party, its principles and objectives. I repudiate any allegations to the contrary. I am determined to help build the A.L.P. into a broadly-based socialist party with a radical and modern programme which can win power in this country. Labor members and supporters demand this. I have attended Executive meetings for the last two years. I believe that throughout that time my propositions to you have been in accordance with Conference decisions and Caucus wishes. Conference decisions will never be fully implemented until there is a Labor government. The public will never elect a Labor government until the party shows greater confidence in its parliamentarians.

9.10   Harradine attacks 'friends of the communists' in Labor party
Australian, 19 April 1968

ACCUSERS TRYING TO SILENCE ME, SAYS HARRADINE

The anonymous document which sparked the Harradine incident was circulated among senior members of the Labor Party in all States during the first week of April.

Apart from its attack on Mr. Harradine's past, the document also severely criticised the Tasmanian Labor Premier, Mr. Reece, and the deputy Federal Opposition Leader, Mr. Barnard.

On April 7, Mr. Harradine circulated to members of the Tasmanian State executive of the A.L.P. a lengthy denial of the charges against him.

In this document, he claimed the authors of the anonymous letter were "communists and friends of communists".

He added: "They published their anonymous attack because they know that on the Federal executive I will support Gough Whitlam if he seeks an inquiry into the conduct of the Victorian A.L.P. executive."

But the paragraph that stung the left wing majority on the Federal executive to move against Mr. Harradine was one in which he said:

"When I go to the meeting of the Federal executive on April 17, the friends of the communists intend to try to silence me.

"I have been informed that they will try to exclude me from the Federal executive meeting so that there will be one vote less in support of Gough Whitlam."

In a three-page covering letter attached to the denial, Mr. Harradine rejected the charges of his past associations with the Democratic Labor Party as a red herring.

He named the Victorian A.L.P. State secretary, Mr. W. Hartley—a member of the Federal executive—and Senator J. M. Wheeldon, of Western Australia, as having been former members of the Liberal Party.

He named a Victorian trade union leader who had allegedly once been a member of the Communist Party.

He also said an official of the Victorian A.L.P. executive had been a member of the Eureka Youth League, a communist front organisation.

"There are a number of even more interesting and startling examples of previous political associations of other prominent party members, which I do not intend to raise unless they provide the opportunity," Mr Harradine's letter added.

But it was the attached denial that provided the Federal executive with its ammunition against Mr. Harradine, and which it now insists he must withdraw and for which he must "unreservedly apologise".

The text of the denial is:

"Why should the anonymous scribblers of the document seek to discredit officials of the Tasmanian A.L.P. and trade union movement?

"There is a very clear and definite reason.

"The authors of the document are communists and friends of communists. We are opposed to communism and to communism's exploitation of Australian trade unionists. That is what they cannot forgive.

"The document is not published to help the Labor movement. It is not published in a vacuum. It is published because Gough Whitlam has decided to cleanse the Labor Party of communist influence.

'Split Unity'

"The communists are trying to save themselves—as always—by raising the sectarian issue to divide Australian workers, to divert the attack from themselves and to maintain their influence in the A.L.P.

"They publish their anonymous attack because they know that on the Federal executive I will support Gough Whitlam if he seeks an inquiry into the conduct of the Victorian A.L.P. executive, which last year he called 'destructive, disloyal and disruptive'.

"How can Federal Labor ever hope to gain office while the situation in Victoria remains?

9.11   Federal executive refuses to accept Harradine as Tasmanian delegate
Sydney Morning Herald, 18 April 1968

A.L.P. EXECUTIVE SPLITS OVER SEAT FOR DELEGATE

In an extraordinary scene yesterday, the A.L.P. Federal executive refused to allow one of its 17 members to take his seat while inquiries were made to see if he was a "fit and proper person" to serve on the executive.

It took this action against the delegate, Mr. R. W. B. Harradine, of Tasmania, because of his past D.L.P. membership and because he had said that when he went to the executive "the friends of the Communists intend to silence me."

Late yesterday, when the Federal executive's challenge to Mr. Harradine was referred to it, the Tasmanian A.L.P. executive stood firmly behind him and refused to replace him.

The two bodies are now on a collision course.

If the Federal executive refuses to accept Mr. Harradine's credentials this morning, the Tasmanian branch may ask for a special A.L.P. Federal conference to deal with the dispute.

The executive's action was a major blow to the Leader of the Federal Opposition, Mr. E. G. Whitlam, who fought hard yesterday to have Mr. Harradine accepted at once as a delegate.

Anger

Many of the Labor Leader's supporters had forebodings last night that the situation could approach the party debacle in February, 1966.

Then rows over State aid and other vital issues at a meeting of the Federal executive in Canberra nearly led to Mr. Whitlam's expulsion.

Yesterday's heated quarrel split the Federal executive 10−6 at its first meeting since it was broadened from 12 to 17 members last August.

The quarrel arose as soon as the meeting began when the president of the Party's South Australian branch, Mr. M. H. Nicholls, M.P. demanded the right to question Mr. Harradine on his former D.L.P. membership.

As the argument developed, delegates were angered when Mr. Harradine produced a document which stated "When I go to the meeting of the Federal Executive of the A.L.P. . . . on April 17, the friends of the Communists intend to silence me.

"I have been informed that they will try to exclude me from the Federal Executive meeting so that there will be one vote less in support of Gough Whitlam."

Mr. Harradine told the executive that this document was attached to a letter he sent to the Tasmanian executive after an anonymous circular attacked him and other Tasmanian members of the party.

10−6 Vote

In effect, the circular had charged him with being a secret agent of the National Civic Council, associated with the D.L.P.

It had also charged the Deputy Leader of the Opposition, Mr. L. H. Barnard, the other Tasmanian delegate to the Federal Executive, with being "a Right-wing reactionary on foreign affairs."

Mr. Harradine strongly repudiated the charge and said his only association with the D.L.P. had been for about 18 months in the years 1956 to 1959.

More than an hour was spent in an argument about this which was reported to have favoured Mr. Harradine.

His critics on the executive then switched to the document and there were angry statements about Mr. Harradine's reference to "friends of the Communists".

Several delegates were reported to have asked heatedly if he was inferring that they were friends of the Communist Party or came under its domination in any way.

Finally, Mr. F. E. Chamberlain (W.A.) and Mr. Nicholls moved: "That all delegates credentials be accepted other than Mr. Harradine's.

"That Mr. Harradine's credential be deferred to enable a full examination of Mr. Harradine's credential to see if he is a fit and proper person to serve on the executive and that the examination be undertaken by the full Federal executive."

The voting on the motion was 10−6. Mr. Whitlam, Mr. Barnard, the two N.S.W. delegates, Messrs C. T. Oliver and W. R. Colbourne, Mr. C. H. Webb, M.P. (W.A.) and Mr. D. Lowe (Tas.) opposed it.

The 10 voting for the motion included the Leader of the Opposition, in the Senate, Senator L. K. Murphy, and his deputy, Senator S. H. Cohen.

9.12   The federal executive intervenes in the Victorian branch
Age, 15 September 1970

HOW VICTORIAN BRANCH WAS KNOCKED OUT

The Federal executive of the A.L.P. yesterday decided to dissolve its Victorian branch and set up a caretaker administration.

The resolution for dissolution was moved by Mr. C. R. Cameron (MHR, South Australia) and seconded by Senator K. Wriedt, of Tasmania, it was carried by 10 votes to seven.

The resolution said:

1. The Federal executive, having decided "that the Federal executive finds that the Victorian 'phasing out' policy on State aid was contrary to the Federal constitution, platform and policy of the party and finds that the State branch and State executive have acted in a manner which the Federal executive deems to be contrary to the Federal constitution, platform and policy as interpreted by the Federal executive," the Federal executive, pursuant to its powers under Federal Conference rule 7(c)(viii), hereby

   (a) Declares that the Victorian branch of the A.L.P. no longer exists;

   (b) Shall set up in place of the Victorian branch as an organisation competent to carry out the Federal constitution platform and policy of the A.L.P.;

2. Further and independent of the proceeding resolution (a) to (m) the Federal executive having resolved as follows—

"The Federal executive finds that the TUDC has been permitted to dominate the Victorian branch and the Victorian executive but finds no evidence that any person who has taken part in the compilation of the TUDC ticket at A.L.P. Victorian conferences was not a member of the A.L.P. The Federal executive recognises that sectional groupings are common to all political parties in Australia but that with a proper basis of representation and system of voting at conferences no such group can ever unduly influence or monopolise a party. The fact that the TUDC has unduly influenced and has dominated the A.L.P. Victorian branch and Victorian executive is a condemnation of the rules and structure of the Victorian branch. For these reasons the Federal executive finds that the rules and structure of the Victorian branch adversely affect the general welfare of the Labor movement."

9.13   Whitlam opens Labor campaign in 1972
Blacktown, 13 November 1972

Men and Women of Australia!

The decision we will make for our country on 2 December is a choice between the past and the future, between the habits and fears of the past, and the demands and opportunities of the future. There are moments in history when the whole fate and future of nations can be decided by a single decision. For Australia, this is such a time. It's time for a new team, a new program, a new drive for equality of opportunities. It's time to create new opportunities for Australians, a time for a new vision of what we can achieve in this generation for our nation and the region in which we live. It's time for a new government—a Labor Government.

My fellow citizens—

I put these questions to you: Do you believe that Australia can afford another three years like the last twenty months? Are you prepared to maintain at the head of your affairs a coalition which had lurched into crisis after crisis, embarrassment piled on embarrassment week after week? Will you accept another three years of waiting for next week's crisis, next week's blunder? Will you again entrust the nation's economy to the men who deliberately, but needlessly, created Australia's worst unemployment for ten years? Or to the same men who have presided over the worst inflation for twenty years? Can you trust the last minute promises of men who stood against these very same proposals for twenty three years? Would you trust your international affairs again to the men who gave you Vietnam? Will you trust your defences to the men who haven't even yet given you the F-111?

We have a new chance for our nation. We can recreate this nation. We have a new chance for our region. We can help recreate this region.

The war of intervention in Vietnam is ending. The great powers are rethinking and remoulding their relationships and their obligations. Australia cannot stand still at such a time. We cannot afford to limp along with men whose attitudes are rooted in the slogans of the 1950s—the slogans of fear and hate. If we made such a mistake, we would make Australia a backwater in our region and a back number in history. The Australian Labor Party—vindicated as we have been on all the great issues of the past—stands ready to take Australia forward to her rightful, proud, secure and independent place in the future of our region.

And we are determined that the Australian people shall be restored to their rightful place in their own country—as participants and partners in government, as the owners and keepers of the national estate and the nation's resources, as fair and equal sharers in the wealth and opportunities that this nation should offer in abundance to all its people. We will put Australians back into the business of running Australia and owning Australia. We will revive in this nation the spirit of national co-operation and national self-respect, mutual respect between government and people.

In 24 hours Mr. McMahon will present to you a series of proposals purporting to be the Liberal Party program. But it is not what he will say in 24 hours that counts; it is what could have been done in the past 23 years, what has happened in the last 20 months on which the Liberals must be judged. It is the Liberal Party which asks you to take a leap in the dark—the Liberal Party which dispossessed the elected Prime Minister in mid-term, the Liberal Party which has produced half-baked, uncosted proposals in its death bed repentance, it is the Liberal Party whose election proposals are those which it has denounced and derided for 23 years.

By contrast, the Australian Labor Party offers the Australian people the most carefully developed and consistent program ever placed before them. I am proud of our program. I am proud of our team. I am proud to be the leader of this team.

Our program has three great aims. They are:

—to promote equality

—to involve the people of Australia in the decision making processes of our land and to liberate the talents and uplift the horizons of the Australian people.

We want to give a new life and a new meaning in this new nation to the touchstone of modern democracy—to liberty, equality, fraternity.

9.14 Whitlam appoints Gair ambassador to Ireland
Sun, 3 April 1974

SNAP POLL THREAT TO WHITLAM OVER GAIR JOB OFFER
From Laurie Oakes

CANBERRA—The Federal Opposition may try to force a general election as a result of the appointment of the former D.L.P. leader Senator Gair to [a] diplomatic post.

The Country Party leader, Mr. Anthony, said last night the appointment strengthened his view that the Whitlam Government should be forced to the polls.

He received strong support from angry Liberal and D.L.P. Senators, who argued that the Opposition should reject crucial money Bills while it still had control of the Senate.

Debate

The announcement yesterday that Senator Gair had been appointed Australian Ambassador to Ireland shocked the Opposition and led to angry recriminations.

The Prime Minister, Mr. Whitlam, confirmed the appointment in the House of Representatives, touching off more than an hour of bitter debate.

The Federal Opposition Leader, Mr. Snedden, said last night Mr. Whitlam had acted "shamefully and with no political morality" in an attempt to gain control of the Senate.

Mr. Anthony described the appointment as "an act of cynicism unrivalled in the political life of this nation".

The D.L.P. Leader, Senator McManus, said that "in gangster language, Mr. Whitlam has adopted the attitude of Mr. Big.

"He has let out a contract on the D.L.P."

Last night, the Liberal Party's parliamentary executive held an urgent meeting to discuss ways to retaliate against the Government.

Liberals conceded privately that the appointment of Senator Gair was a political master-stroke which could lead to Labor winning 30 seats in the May 18 poll.

This is because Senator Gair's resignation from the Senate today will mean that six Senate vacancies instead of five will have to be filled in Queensland.

With five vacancies, the Government could have won only two Senate seats in Queensland, but now it is almost certain to win three.

If it also manages to win three Senate places in N.S.W., Tasmania, and South Australia, and two each in Western Australia and Victoria, it will leave 30 senators—enough to give it a measure of control.

A strong section of Liberal, Country Party and D.L.P. politicians believe the Opposition has nothing to lose by taking a gamble and forcing the Government to the polls.

The Opposition could use its Senate majority to reject two Appropriation Bills introduced in the House of Representatives last night by the Treasurer, Mr. Crean.

The Bills are to provide more than $170 million for the Government administrative expenses and capital works and services between now and the Federal Budget on August 20.

9.15   Whitlam's appeal to the people in 1974

Men and women of Australia,

Just 17 months ago, I stood here, and from this place and from this city I asked you to choose for Australia a new team, a new program, a new drive for equality of opportunities. You gave us a clear mandate to go ahead with our program for the next three years. For 17 months we have driven ourselves to carry out your mandate, to carry out the program I placed before you. Now the government you elected for three years has been interrupted in mid-career. Our program has been brought to a halt in mid-stream.

Everything we promised, everything we have achieved, everything you expected of us—your expressed hopes for yourselves, your families, your nation—all this is suddenly threatened. It is threatened by the actions of the men you rejected a mere 17 months ago. It is threatened by the actions of men elected to the Senate not in 1972, but in 1967 and 1970. It is threatened by men who refused to stand by the umpire's verdict—your verdict—to give us a chance, to give you a chance, to give Australia a new chance.

These men who have falsified democracy now ask you to turn back. Turn back to what? Think again how it was when you elected us in 1972. Unemployment was at its worst for ten years. Our rate of growth was one of the world's worst—a paltry 2%. The Australian dollar was grossly undervalued.

Foreign money was flooding in to buy up Australian resources and Australian industries on the cheap. Accelerating numbers of migrants were leaving in disillusion. Australia was still deeply involved in the war in Vietnam. Our whole foreign policy was based on hostility to China. We were running an army on the cheap by conscripting young men. There were young men in prison for their conscience. Australia was a deeply divided nation. Our young people were becoming alienated from the mainstream of Australian society. The disrespect in which our national leadership—the Liberals—were held at home had spread to disrespect for Australia abroad.

Think again, indeed!

Mark today's contrast. The Australian economy is one of the most buoyant and vigorous in the world.

Full employment has been restored, business activity is at its highest for a decade, company profits are at record levels and business expectations are at an all time high. Through our economic policies and our social security program, Australia's prosperity is becoming more fairly shared than ever before.

Abroad, Australia has never stood so tall. We have buried old animosities. We are held in new respect by old friends and allies. Never in her history has Australia been more secure.

We have ended national divisions, national disunity by ending our involvement in Vietnam, and ending conscription.

We have opened up new and expanding markets for our farm products.

By placing family reunion for migrants above mere recruiting, we have stopped the migrant drift.

For the first time Australia has a government determined to promote Australian ownership and control of Australian industries and resources.

For the first time for a generation Australia has a government dedicated to equal opportunity for all its citizens. We have more than doubled spending on schools. We have abolished fees at universities, colleges of advanced education and—going one better than our pledge—at technical schools.

For the first time Australia has a government determined to make the conditions of life more equal for all Australians, wherever they live in Australia.

For the first time Australia has a government seriously concerned to give equality of opportunity to women.

For the first time Australia has a national government involving itself directly in the affairs of our cities.

For the first time Australia has a government ready to give local government direct access to the national finances.

For the first time Australia has a national government prepared to co-operate in renewing our decaying urban transport system.

For the first time Australia has a national government determined to fulfil its constitutional obligation towards the aboriginals.

For the first time Australia has a government determined to preserve, protect and enhance Australia's national estate—our natural and historical inheritance, what we keep from our past, what we transmit to the future.

For the first time Australia has a national government which recognises the significance of the arts and artists in our society. Our support for the arts has released an unparalleled burst of creativity in this nation.

These achievements are just some of the fruits of programs based on expert advice. We sought and obtained the co-operation of the most highly qualified

Australian men and women to enquire into and to report upon basic requirements in Australia's social and economic structures. These reports are public.
The work of these enquiries and commissions is the basis of a continuing,
coherent, comprehensive program. The new initiatives I announce tonight are
the new dimensions and expanded fruits of this work.

9.16   Cairns appoints Morosi — then re-appoints her
Age, 6, 30 December 1974

SECRETARY 'PERSON OF HIGH ABILITY'
The Deputy Prime Minister, Dr Cairns, told Parliament yesterday that Miss
Juni Morosi had been appointed his private secretary at a normal salary and
that she was a person of considerable character and integrity.

He said he would not be influenced by campaigns which had an element of
the scurrilous and that if he had chosen a man, or a woman who was not good
looking, perhaps nothing would have happened.

.   .   .

The Prime Minister, Mr Whitlam, also spoke. He said, "It is a particularly
miserable and cowardly practice to cast aspersions on ministers in general and
ministerial staff in general.

If people are making allegations about ministers or minister's staffs they
should have the decency and courage to be specific."

Mr Whitlam said that over the many years that he had known and worked
with Dr Cairns, he had never had the least doubt, or reason to doubt, of the
integrity, honesty, and propriety of his deputy.

The appointment of Miss Morosi, an application on her behalf for a
government flat, and the linking of her name with two companies in the tourist
industry in NSW were also raised in the senate.

In the Senate the Attorney-General, Senator Murphy, confirmed that Miss
Morosi's husband, Mr David Ditchburn, had been appointed to the Film Board
of Review.

.   .   .

BACK AGAIN
Cyclone Juni strikes again. It has to be said that the Treasurer (Dr Cairns)
shows an impeccable sense of timing. After acting properly and promptly in the
early stages of the Darwin relief operation, he has once more turned attention to
the disaster area that is the Labor Government's public standing. Yesterday Dr
Cairns announced the reappointment of Miss Juni Morosi to his staff as
private secretary, calling at the same time for an end to the "campaign of
innuendo and pressure".

There has been much innuendo surrounding the Morosi affair, and that must
be regretted. But this is not at the centre of concern about Miss Morosi's
appointment to a key post on the staff of a key Minister. Consider instead the
questions of Miss Morosi's accommodation, her business activities and her
husband's Government appointment.

10

Epilogue: The Fall of the Whitlam Government

In 1975 inflation and unemployment continued to rise. Several Labor appointees were heavily criticized. The appointment of Juni Morosi to the treasurer's office by Dr Cairns became the centre of a political storm. Further, the appointment of three of Whitlam's former private secretaries to the status of permanent head was seen as a challenge to the neutrality of the public service. The slide of the Labor party towards electoral annihilation can be dated most obviously to the overseas loans affair which blew up in mid-1975. The initial result of this was the dismissal of Cairns from the ministry (3.15). Then the former deputy leader of the party, Lance Barnard, resigned from parliament and his seat of Bass was lost at the by-election with a massive swing away from the Labor party.

In March 1975 Malcolm Fraser had been elected leader of the Liberal party. He had then stated that a government should be allowed to serve out its full three-year term of office as long as it maintained its majority in the lower house, unless extraordinary and reprehensible circumstances occurred.

After the loans affair, against a backdrop of spiralling inflation and high unemployment, the polls began to show a decline in support for the Labor party. Encouraged by the results of the Bass by-election, Fraser began looking for some circumstances which he could call 'extraordinary and reprehensible'.

In October, as the budget was being put before the Senate, Fraser was under pressure from some elements within the Liberal party to block the budget. He explained the difficulties he faced in deciding whether or not to force an election (10.1).

The 'extraordinary and reprehensible circumstances' for which he was looking were provided for him by a resurgence of the loans affair. New evidence indicated that Connor had lied to parliament over his continued attempts to obtain overseas loans and he was forced by the prime minister to resign (10.2).

Fraser decided to block the budget bills in the Senate until an election was called. Whitlam refused to be 'blackmailed' into calling an early election. He stated that 'the basic rule of our parliamentary system [is that] Governments are made and unmade in the House of Representatives' (10.3).

This stalemate continued for a month. There was widespread speculation over how long the government would be able to meet its financial commitments and over whether all Liberal senators would continue to support the blocking of the budget bills. Finally the prime minister decided to call a half-Senate election but instead of responding to the prime minister's advice the governor-general sacked him (10.4) and explained the reasons for this sudden and unexpected action in a public statement (10.5).

This unprecedented action led to scenes of outraged anger on the steps of Parliament House where angry demonstrators massed and were addressed by Labor leaders (10.6).

During the election campaign Labor concentrated on the constitutional issue despite the fact that the polls showed this to be declining as an issue compared with inflation and unemployment. The Labor party was annihilated at the polls and the Liberal-National Country Party coalition gained the largest majority it has ever had in the history of federal parliament.

The surviving members of the parliamentary Labor party quickly fell into the party's old habit of tearing itself apart publicly. Whitlam, who three days earlier had been hailed as a great leader, was now criticized for incompetence and tyranny. He was blamed for the Labor party's defeat (10.7, 10.8) and his leadership was challenged. But at the caucus meeting held on 27 January 1976 to decide on the leadership of the party Whitlam was easily re-elected. At this meeting it was also decided to reintroduce the practice of having leaders face regular election by caucus (10.9).

The Labor party, yet again, faces a long struggle out of the wilderness.

10.1   Fraser keeps options open
Age, 13 October 1975

"I think I'll never be involved in a more difficult decision."

FRASER KEEPS OPTIONS OPEN
A query still on early poll. From John Jost.

CANBERRA—The Federal Opposition Leader (Mr. Fraser) yesterday refused to close the option of denying the Government Supply and so forcing an early election.

Mr. Fraser told the Liberal Party's Federal Council that the decision now confronting the Opposition was of "enormous moment".

"I think I will never be involved in a more difficult or momentous decision," Mr. Fraser said.

Although he said that he still had an open mind on the question of rejection of Supply, he made it clear that he believed the Opposition had the right—and even a duty—to reject it.

Mr. Fraser quoted the Prime Minister (Mr. Whitlam) in support of the right of the Senate to reject a Federal Budget. He quoted from a speech Mr. Whitlam made in 1970.

Sources close to Mr. Fraser claimed to reporters after his speech that it was simply an attempt to state the alternatives and the reasoning behind them.

They told observers who felt Mr. Fraser's speech indicated a preference for "a grab for power" that such an interpretation would be wrong.

Disaster
Mr. Fraser said "We must avoid at any cost the situation which has arisen in other countries where governments rise and fall with monotonous regularity.

That is the real road to disaster. That is why the decision which now confronts the Opposition is of such enormous moment.

The decision is not one between expediency and principles. It is between two conflicting principles.

On the one hand there is the principle that a Government with a majority in the Lower House should in the ordinary course of events run its full term.

This is a sound and important principle of our constitutional practice. It is a principle on which I place very great weight.

Reasonable continuity of government depends on observance of the principle that, in the normal course of events, the Government supported by the Lower House is entitled to Supply. Our system of government would not work unless this were the case".

After outlining the importance of preserving conventions, Mr. Fraser said the constitution "quite deliberately gives the Senate the power to reject appropriation bills".

"The question of rejection of the appropriation bills should be suggested to the Senate only with the greatest possible reluctance," he said.

"It can only be considered at all because of the second principle to which I referred—the obligation of an Opposition, of any political party, to the people of Australia.

There is no question that this Government has done, and is doing, grave damage to Australia.

People who are retired, who thought they had adequate savings to look after themselves, after three years of Labor find they are utterly dependent on the Government. They are destroyed until they die unless the situation can be redressed.

Have not the small businessmen, thousands of whom are seeing their livelihoods wiped out at this moment, the right to ask us to act?

It is a major obligation on us as a political party to take these facts into account."

Mr. Fraser said "the incompetence, the damage, the failures of the worst government in our history cannot be ignored.

The conditions of Australia must be weighed in the balance against the principle of continuity of government," he said.

"Anyone who seeks to read into these statements a decision on either side would be wrong. I have merely tried to describe for you the nature of the immensely difficult decision that must be taken, and taken soon."

10.2   Connor sacked by Whitlam
Canberra Times, 15 October 1975

I WAS MISLED SAYS PRIME MINISTER
MR CONNOR RESIGNS

Mr Rex Connor stepped down from the Ministry and his portfolio of Minerals and Energy yesterday painlessly and without drama.

Mr Connor's resignation was required of him by the Prime Minister, Mr Whitlam, but the manner of his going was on his own terms.

Mr Connor offered no explanation or justification to Parliament, to caucus, or in his public statement for misleading the public over the part he has played in the overseas loans affair.

He went along to the caucus meeting yesterday morning with his letter of resignation, offering caucus the option of accepting it, and only when caucus did so he handed it to Mr Whitlam.

Sugar-Sweet

And caucus' acceptance was sugar-sweet party rhetoric. By 55 votes to 24 they moved that:

"Rex Connor's offer of resignation be accepted with regret, and we place on record the party's admiration for the assiduous and dedicated manner in which

Mr Connor has sought to implement Labor policy to preserve Australian ownership and control of its energy and mineral resources."

It was everybody's day for being kind.

The opposition sought no explanation from Mr Connor for his resignation, nor was there any motion of censure of lack of confidence in the Government.

They merely concentrated on trying to get some admission from Mr Whitlam that he was involved in some way with Mr Connor's dealings with international commodities dealer, Mr Tirath Khemlani.

There was no Opposition statement that Supply would be refused in the Senate, or any suggestion of a link between Mr Connor's resignation and refusal.

The Government was waiting for it, with a major speech ready for Mr Whitlam. It is now expected that Mr Fraser will state the Opposition's intentions today—if only because Opposition senators will need to know how to phrase their speeches on the Appropriation Bills.

Throughout Question Time in the House of Representatives Mr Connor sat on a far back bench, smiling gently.

A close friend, Mrs Joan Taggert, sat in the Speaker's Gallery watching him. Mrs Taggert said later that Mr Connor was still under doctor's orders to rest at home, but if he had not made an appearance he would have been called "a dingo."

In a press statement, last night, Mr Whitlam emphasised that it had been through his painful duty in preserving parliamentary convention and standards that "a great Minister and a close friend and colleague has fallen".

Assurances

He said he wanted to make the clearest possible distinction between Mr Connor's conduct as a Minister and the fundamental principle that the Parliament must be able to accept assurances given it by a Minister.

"There was I believe, a departure from the principle," Mr Whitlam said. He had been misled by Mr Connor, and in consequence had given a misleading answer to the Deputy Leader of the Opposition, Mr Lynch.

"It is not the content of those telex messages which constitutes any breach of propriety", he said. "It was his failure to tell me about them."

10.3   Fraser stops supply: Whitlam refuses to call election
Age, 16 October 1975

GO TO PEOPLE, SAYS FRASER
NO, SAYS PM
From John Jost, our Chief Political Correspondent

CANBERRA—An unprecedented constitutional crisis threatens to paralyse the Australian Government.

Opposition senators yesterday blocked a key loan bill by 29 votes to 28. Today they will block the 1975-76 Budget Supply bills.

The constitutional drama climaxed at 2.45 p.m. yesterday when the Opposition Leader (Mr. Fraser) called on the Government to resign and go to the people.

The Prime Minister (Mr. Whitlam) rejected Mr. Fraser's demand. He said he would not "be blackmailed or panicked."

Last night he won authority from Labor Caucus to call a half-Senate election at a time of his own choosing.

It might be some weeks before it is known whether a half-Senate or House of Representatives election will be held.

Yesterday's events in Canberra are unprecedented in Federal Political history. No Federal Government has ever been denied Supply.

With the funds blocked, it is a matter of weeks before the Government will be unable to pay its bills, including public servants' salaries, capital works and recurring costs.

Pensioners and people on social service payments are unlikely to be threatened by the blockage.

What they said

MR. WHITLAM: 'He (Mr. Fraser) has said that he intends to use the accidental numbers he thinks he controls in the Senate to delay passing the Budget until the money runs out.

In other words he intends to produce chaos in order to prevent the Government from being able to govern . . .

I state again the basic rule of our parliamentary system: Governments are made and unmade in the House of Representatives—in the people's house. The Senate cannot, does not, and must never determine who the Government shall be.'

MR. FRASER: 'The Labor Government 1972-1975 has been the most incompetent and disastrous Government in the history of Australia. Although Australia has one of the strongest and healthiest economies in the world, in three years this has been brought to the brink of disaster by incompetence of the worst kind . . .

From the Parliament and from the people I now call on the Prime Minister, if he has a shred of decency left, to put an end to this whole sorry episode and place himself and his Government before the ultimate tribunal of the people.

We will use all the constitutional opportunities available to us to ensure that this occurs.'

10.4   Governor-General Sacks P.M.

Age, 12 November 1975

KERR SACKS P.M.
From John Jost

CANBERRA—The Governor-General, Sir John Kerr, yesterday sacked the Prime Minister, Mr. Whitlam, and dissolved Parliament.

Sir John appointed the former Opposition Leader, Mr. Fraser, as Prime Minister.

He commissioned him to form an interim Government until elections for the House of Representatives and the Senate are held probably on December 13 or 20.

Mr. Fraser would not confirm the date late yesterday.

Sir John's unprecedented actions were taken without any warning to the Labor Government or Mr. Whitlam.

Late last night Mr. Whitlam met the ACTU and ALP president, Mr. Hawke, the Federal ALP secretary, Mr. David Combe, and other leading Labor men at John Curtin House, to begin planning Labor's campaign.

Mr. Fraser dined with some close colleagues.

He is expected today to have about 12 L-NCP frontbenchers sworn in as an interim Ministry, and later announced December 13 as polling day.

Mr. Whitlam was stunned by Sir John's action.

At a Caucus meeting earlier yesterday, he told Labor M.P.s that he proposed to call a half-Senate election for December 13.

He said that Sir John was "favorably disposed" to this course when he spoke with him by telephone just before the meeting.

Later in a Press conference, Mr. Whitlam said Sir John had never discussed the possibility of unilaterally sacking the Government and calling for a double dissolution.

Asked if Sir John gave him the impression that he believed a general election was the proper course, Mr. Whitlam said:

'Kerr's cur'

"On the contrary, he gave me the other impression. He knew that I had, and was likely to continue to have, the majority in the House of Representatives. And he also knew that the Opposition didn't have a majority in the Senate".

Speaking before a wildly cheering crowd at the steps of Parliament, Mr. Whitlam described Mr. Fraser as "Kerr's cur" for accepting the commission.

Earlier, tourists in Parliament's Kings Hall cheered Mr. Whitlam and jeered Mr. Fraser and the NCP leader Mr. Anthony.

Sir John also refused to take notice of a successful no-confidence motion against the interim Fraser Government, carried in the House of Representatives before it was dissolved.

His secretary Mr. David Smith, made an appointment for the Speaker of the House of Representatives, Mr. Scholes, to deliver the no-confidence resolution to Sir John at 4.45 p.m.

But at precisely this time parliamentary officials made the announcements proroguing the Parliament.

This action is also unprecedented. Australia has never had a Government which did not fall as a result of being defeated on a no-confidence motion in the House.

At a Press conference, Mr. Fraser said Sir John had commissioned him to form a Government "to permit the deadlock between the two Houses of Parliament to be resolved".

"It will be my sole purpose as head of the Government to restore responsible management to the nation's affairs and to ensure that Australia has the general election to which it is constitutionally entitled and which so far has been denied it," Mr. Fraser said.

"Until the judgment of the Australian people has been registered at this election, my Government will make no appointments or dismissals, nor initiate any of our policies.

"The Liberal and Country Parties took the action we did after three years of grossly incompetent and damaging economic mismanagement, and after the second man who had acted as Prime Minister had been dismissed for deceiving the Parliament.

The Australian people will have their say. The choice is theirs at the ballot box."

Mr. Fraser denied that he had any foreknowledge of Sir John Kerr's intentions.

He also refused to say whether he would bring down a new Budget if he won the election. He refused to comment on the maintenance of wage indexation—regarded as a critical element for economic recovery.

In his press conference Mr. Whitlam said: "Clearly, the great issue, almost the sole issue of this campaign, will be whether the Government which the people elect with a majority in the House of Representatives will be allowed to govern from now on.

The whole system is under challenge. Up until the very last division it was plain my government had a majority in the House of Representatives where we have always believed governments were meant to be made and unmade."

Mr. Whitlam said he did not know if Mr. Fraser had "made a deal" with Sir John Kerr—"at least I am making no allegations".

Supply

He pointed out that Supply had not run out when he spoke to Sir John Kerr at 1 p.m. yesterday.

"And as we all know the Senate passed the Budget Supply Bills at about a quarter past two this afternoon. And when Mr. Fraser read portions of Sir John Kerr's views to the House of Representatives, those views were no longer well-based because by that time Supply had been passed," he said.

Asked how he felt about being a Prime Minister sacked by the Crown, Mr. Whitlam laughed and said: "I'm the first for 200 years—since George the third sacked Lord North."

Mr. Whitlam said that in the future no other Prime Minister would have his commission withdrawn.

10.5   Statement by the Governor-General
Press release from the Governor-General

STATEMENT BY THE GOVERNOR-GENERAL
I have given careful consideration to the constitutional crisis and have made some decisions which I wish to explain.

Summary
It has been necessary for me to find a democratic and constitutional solution to the current crisis which will permit the people of Australia to decide as soon as possible what should be the outcome of the deadlock which developed over supply between the two Houses of Parliament and between the Government and the Opposition parties. The only solution consistent with the Constitution and with my oath of office and my responsibilities, authority and duty as Governor-General is to terminate the commission as Prime Minister of Mr. Whitlam and to arrange for a caretaker government able to secure supply and willing to let the issue go to the people.

I shall summarise the elements of the problem and the reasons for my decision which places the matter before the people of Australia for prompt determination.

Because of the federal nature of our Constitution and because of its provisions the Senate undoubtedly has constitutional power to refuse or defer supply to the Government. Because of the principles of responsible government a Prime Minister who cannot obtain supply, including money for carrying on the ordinary services of government, must either advise a general election or resign. If he refuses to do this I have the authority and indeed the duty under the Constitution to withdraw his Commission as Prime Minister. The position in Australia is quite different from the position in the United Kingdom. Here the confidence of both Houses on supply is necessary to ensure its provision. In the

United Kingdom the confidence of the House of Commons alone is necessary. But both here and in the United Kingdom the duty of the Prime Minister is the same in a most important respect—if he cannot get supply he must resign or advise an election.

If a Prime Minister refuses to resign or to advise an election, and this is the case with Mr. Whitlam, my constitutional authority and duty require me to do what I have now done—to withdraw his commission—and to invite the Leader of the Opposition to form a caretaker government—that is one that makes no appointments or dismissals and initiates no policies, until a general election is held. It is most desirable that he should guarantee supply. Mr. Fraser will be asked to give the necessary undertakings and advise whether he is prepared to recommend a double dissolution. He will also be asked to guarantee supply.

The decisions I have made were made after I was satisfied that Mr. Whitlam could not obtain supply. No other decision open to me would enable the Australian people to decide for themselves what should be done.

Once I had made up my mind, for my own part, what I must do if Mr. Whitlam persisted in his stated intentions I consulted the Chief Justice of Australia, Sir Garfield Barwick. I have his permission to say that I consulted him in this way.

The result is that there will be an early general election for both Houses and the people can do what, in a democracy such as ours, is their responsibility and duty and theirs alone. It is for the people now to decide the issue which the two leaders have failed to settle.

10.6 Labor Leaders Address Angry Demonstrators on Steps of Parliament House
Age, 12 November 1975

'SIR JOHN CUR' ANNOYS CROWD
From Ben Hills

CANBERRA—Parliament went to the streets yesterday—to the steps of Parliament House and the biggest gallery since federation.

About 2000 people jammed the car park and crowded the steps of Parliament House in what Liberal front-bencher Jim Killen described as the most extraordinary demonstration he had seen in 20 years in parliament.

. . .the crowd was given a two-hour bull-horn harangue by half the former Labor Cabinet.

Inside, flapping from the empty House of Representatives, was the official proclamation:

"Whereas by Section 57 of the Constitution it is provided that if the House of Representatives passes any proposed law and the Senate rejects or fails to pass it . . . therefore I, Sir John Kerr, Governor-General of Australia, by this, my proclamation, dissolve the Senate and the House of Representatives."

Labor leaders address rally

But outside on the steps the business of politics was in full cry. One by one the political heavies of the Labor party—Whitlam, Crean, Hayden, Uren, Hawke, said their piece to the cheers of the crowd.

They chanted "We want Gough", they sang and danced 'Australia Fair', they waved hastily painted banners with slogans like "Sir John Cur", "For Gods Sake Stop Raping Democracy", and "Suspend Fraser"—beside a drawing of a gibbet.

The crowd, mostly off duty civil servants and their families, started building up about 4.45 p.m., when the Governor-General's secretary, Mr. David Smith, arrived to dissolve Parliament.

Dressed in a formal black jacket, Mr. Smith stood impassively at a lectern at the top of the steps reading the proclamation. His monotone was inaudible because of the jeers and chanting.

Inside the building, the packing had already started. In the offices of most of the 27 Ministers, staff had begun filling cardboard boxes with documents and preparing to shift.

Mr. Whitlam stayed in the Prime Minister's suite "for the time being", according to his staff . . . but the rest of the Cabinet was moving out.

Outside the non-members' bar, sucking cans under the poplar trees, the corps of Press and Private secretaries, all of whom face the sack in about a fortnight, were planning to work on without pay during the election campaign.

The mood of the crowd was viciously anti-Liberal. When Mr. Fraser left for Government House to be commissioned as Prime Minister, his car was struck and a beer can was thrown.

Later, police had to rescue shadow Foreign Minister Andrew Peacock from a jeering, jostling mob.

10.7   Cairns Attacks Whitlam's Style of Leadership
Age, 15 December 1975

CAIRNS IN ATTACK ON 'CULT'
By Ian Day

The former Deputy Prime Minister, Dr. Cairns, on Saturday night attacked Mr. Whitlam's leadership of the Labor Party and called for more radical policies.

"Everyone knows I don't approve of Mr. Whitlam's form of leadership," Dr. Cairns said, at the Melbourne tally room.

"I don't believe in the cult of personality."

He accused the Labor Party of being "far too leader-conscious."

"It is not a question of Whitlam, or of John Smith."

But he said he would not challenge Mr. Whitlam for party leadership, and he did not know whether anybody else would.

He said it was time for a thorough reassessment of Labor's objectives.

"I think it is a tragedy for Australia that we are not more capable of accepting a party of change, that we are so timid and conservative, and so vulnerable to the influence of the media as we have proved to be," he said.

Asked whether he blamed the media for Labor's defeat, Dr. Cairns said: "Very much. It has given a completely unfair picture of the Labor government.

It sensationalizes and dramatizes, it doesn't inform.

"This is a capitalist society," he said. "The capitalist class is the ruling class and their ideas are ruling ideas. It is all tied up with money."

10.8   More Criticism of Whitlam: Leadership Challenge
Canberra Times, 16 December 1975

Cameron Critical on Leadership
WHITLAM TO BE CHALLENGED
By Tony O'Leary

Public criticism of the former Prime Minister, Mr Whitlam, from within his own party and considerable speculation about a likely successor points to a strong challenge to his position when the Labor Caucus meets in Canberra on Monday.

Saturday's disastrous results for the ALP are also believed to have influenced Mr Whitlam to reconsider an earlier undertaking that he would remain in Parliament as ALP leader for a further six years.

The ALP Federal President, Mr Hawke, who had discussions with Mr Whitlam in Canberra for most of Sunday, indicated yesterday that Mr Whitlam was considering an early retirement, at least from the leadership position.

The election defeat prompted the former Minister for Science and Consumer Affairs, Mr Cameron to state yesterday that the results showed the Australian electorate would not support a Labor Party led by Mr Whitlam.

'Based on Mistakes'

Mr Cameron, who was removed by the former Prime Minister from the sensitive portfolio of Labor and Immigration, said that the whole of the Liberal Party's campaign had been based on mistakes that had been made by Mr Whitlam without the approval of caucus.

Mr Cameron in a later interview said, "I've had many, many people come to me and say, 'Well, look, I can't stand Mr Whitlam. I could vote for the party but not while he is leader'. I think they are right."

Asked why the party should dismiss Mr Whitlam, Mr Cameron said in his opinion he was a liability as a leader.

Mr Hawke told a press conference in Melbourne yesterday that he had gained the impression from discussions with Mr Whitlam that he would not want to lead the party to another election.

Asked if he believed he himself would make a good leader, Mr Hawke said that he would but that the question was not relevant since the decision was a matter for caucus.

Questioned about whether he was considering contesting a seat to become eligible for the leadership, Mr Hawke said he would be available to move into parliament.

The press conference came after speculation yesterday that Mr Whitlam had decided on Sunday to hand over the leadership to Mr Hawke, if he could get a seat in parliament.

This speculation has caused some indignation on the part of former Labor ministers and is likely to improve the chances of challenge to Mr Whitlam on Monday.

The former Deputy Prime Minister, Mr Crean, when asked if he would contest the leadership position, said yesterday that this was a "possibility."

Mr Crean also has reason to challenge Mr Whitlam since he was demoted by the former Prime Minister from Treasurer to Minister for Overseas Trade.

Asked to comment about the possibility of Mr Hawke leading the party at some time in the future, Mr Crean said that caucus did not elect leaders conditionally and that Mr Hawke would not be available as a candidate on Monday.

There was no rule of succession in the ALP and there were many people whom he considered would make good leaders of the party, Mr Crean said.

The former Minister for the Capital Territory, Mr Bryant, who was not one of Mr Whitlam's close associates in government, said he believed there were plenty of people already in caucus who would make good leaders.

Mr Bryant indicated that there were moves to have the former Prime Minister re-elected.

The Premier of South Australia, Mr Dunstan, who is regularly tipped to move into the Federal arena, confirmed yesterday his previous attitude that he is not anxious to go into Federal politics.

Only if Requested

Responding to further speculation about such a move, Mr Dunstan said that he would only make a move if requested by both the ALP Federal Executive and caucus.

In an interview on the ABC yesterday, Mr Cameron said he believed both Mr Crean and the former Minister for Manufacturing Industry, Mr Bowen, "were candidates of excellent quality".

"They would please those people who were displeased with Mr Whitlam's style of leadership", he said.

The position of deputy leader of the party also is likely to develop into a contest with the former Minister for Education, Mr Beazley, announcing yesterday that he would stand for the position. There is also speculation that the former Minister for Labour and Immigration, Senator James McClelland, could stand for the deputy leadership.

10.9   Whitlam Re-elected: Temporarily
Canberra Times, 28 January 1976

Election Review in 18 Months
Uren Elected Deputy Leader
CLEAR WIN TO WHITLAM

The former Prime Minister, Mr Whitlam, was re-elected by a comfortable margin to the leadership of the Parliamentary Labor Party at a meeting in Canberra yesterday.

The caucus meeting decided, however, that fresh elections for executive positions including those of leader and deputy leader should be held in 18 months, providing the party an opportunity to review the performance of its new executive.

Mr Whitlam received 36 votes from the 63-member caucus, easily defeating the other two contenders, Mr Bowen, the former Minister for Manufacturing Industry, and Mr Crean, the former Deputy Prime Minister.

The only surprise in the leadership ballot was the fact that Mr Crean received only 13 votes, one fewer than Mr Bowen.

In the contest for the position of Deputy Leader Mr Uren, the former Minister for Urban and Regional Development, was narrowly successful in defeating seven other candidates.

After the final distribution of preferences Mr Uren received 33 votes, defeating Mr Keating, the former Minister for Northern Australia and a much younger contender, with 30 votes.

The former Government Leader in the Senate, Senator Wriedt, was successful in gaining the position of Senate Opposition Leader with 38 votes. The only other contender for the position, Senator James McClelland the former Minister for Labor received 25 votes.

Another surprise result from yesterday's meeting was the election of Senator Jim Keefe, of Queensland, to the position of Deputy Leader of the Opposition in the Senate. Senator Keefe defeated three former ALP ministers in the ballot for the position.

Unsuccessful nominees for the job were Senator James McClelland, Senator Doug McClelland, the former Special Minister for State, and Senator Wheeldon, the former Minister for Repatriation and Compensation.

Chronology of Main Events

1901	May	Federal Labor party formed
		Watson elected leader
1904	May—August	Watson government
	September	Alliance with Liberal Protectionists
1905	June	General support promised for Deakin
1907	October	Fisher elected leader
1908	October	Fisher forms government
1909	June	Fisher government resigns
1910	April	Labor wins majority in both Houses
		Fisher forms government
1911	October	Commonwealth Bank founded
1913	May	Labor defeated
		Fisher resigns
1914	June	Double dissolution called by Cook
	September	Labor wins election
		Fisher becomes prime minister again
1915	July	Members of caucus attack the government
	October	Fisher resigns
		Hughes elected leader
	November	Hughes postpones the referendum for increased federal powers
1916	August	Hughes is persuaded to hold a referendum to introduce conscription
	September	Hughes expelled by New South Wales Labor party
	November	After the conscription defeat, Hughes and his supporters walk out of caucus
		Labor goes into Opposition
		Tudor becomes leader
1917	January	Labor refuses to join a coalition
1920	November	Mahon expelled from parliament
1921	October	Conference adopts the socialization objective
1922	April	Charlton elected leader after Tudor's death
1923	April	Federal executive becomes involved in the disputes in New South Wales
1926	July—September	Labor party divided over referendum to increase

		the government's powers over trade and corporations
1928	April	Scullin elected leader
1929	September	Bruce government defeated in House of Representatives
	October	Labor wins election Scullin becomes prime minister
1930	August–September	Theodore resigns Scullin visits Britain Niemeyer visits Australia
	November	Caucus forces a new financial policy on ministers
1931	January	Theodore reinstated Lyons resigns
	March	'Lang Labor' splits off and New South Wales branch expelled
	June	Premiers' Plan adopted
	November	Scullin government defeated in the House Labor loses election
1935	October	Scullin resigns Curtin elected leader
1940	June–August	Curtin and federal conference refuse to accept proposal for national government
	October	Advisory war cabinet formed
1941	October	Government defeated in House of Representatives Curtin becomes prime minister
1942	October–January	Conscription for service in south-west Pacific adopted by conference
1943	March	Curtin threatens to resign
	June	Brisbane line allegations Curtin calls election
1945	July	Curtin dies Chifley elected leader
1947	September	Bank nationalization bill introduced
1949	December	Chifley government defeated
1951	April	Double dissolution called
1952	June	Chifley dies Evatt elected leader
	September	Referendum on communist dissolution bill defeated
1954	October	Evatt attacks the 'groupers'
1955	March	Labor party splits
1960	January–March	Evatt resigns Calwell elected leader

1963	March	The 'thirty-six faceless men' charge
1966	November	Conscription in Vietnam an electoral issue
		Labor badly defeated
1967	January	Whitlam elected leader
1968	April	Whitlam resigns over Harradine affair; narrowly secures re-election
1970	September	Federal executive disbands the Victorian branch
1972	December	Labor wins election
		Whitlam and Barnard become a two-man ministry until 21 December, when full ministry sworn in
1974	April	Gair appointed ambassador to Ireland
		Liberals use their Senate numbers to block supply
	May	Labor re-elected
1975	October	Liberals use Senate numbers to stop budget
	November	Whitlam dismissed by governor-general
		Double dissolution called
	December	Labor annihilated in election
1976	January	Whitlam re-elected leader

Further Reading

This list is by no means exhaustive. It gives only some indication of what other books are available and useful for studying the federal Labor party. These books will lead readers to a wide variety of other sources.

GENERAL

Childe, V. G. *How Labour Governs*. Melbourne: Melbourne University Press, 1923. 2nd ed., 1964.

Crisp, L. F. *The Australian Federal Labor Party 1901–1951*. London: Longmans, 1955.

McQueen, Humphrey, *A New Britannia*. Melbourne: Penguin, 1970.

Rawson, D. W. *Labor in Vain*. Melbourne: Longmans, 1966.

Weller, Patrick (ed.). *Caucus Minutes 1901–1949: minutes of the meetings of the federal parliamentary Labor party*. 3 vols. Melbourne: Melbourne University Press, 1975.

Several episodes in the history of the party are dealt with in the following books.

Denning, Warren. *Caucus Crisis: the rise and fall of the Scullin government*. Sydney: Cumberland Argus, 1937.

Lloyd, C. J. and Reid, G. S. *Out of the Wilderness: the return of Labor*. Melbourne: Cassell, 1974.

Murray, Robert. *The Split: Australian labor in the fifties*. Melbourne: Cheshire, 1970.

Oakes, Laurie and Solomon, David. *The Making of an Australian Prime Minister*. Melbourne: Cheshire, 1973.

Turner, Ian. *Sydney's Burning*. Sydney: Alpha Books, 1963.

BIOGRAPHIES

Crisp, L. F. *Ben Chifley: a political biography*. Melbourne: Longmans, 1961.

Fitzhardinge, L. F. *William Morris Hughes: a political biography,* vol 1. Sydney: Angus and Robertson, 1964.

Lang, J. T. *The Turbulent Years*. Sydney: Alpha Books, 1970. —— *The Great Bust*. Sydney: Angus and Robertson, 1962.

Oakes, Laurie. *Whitlam PM: a biography*. Sydney: Angus and Robertson, 1973.

Robertson, John. *J. H. Scullin: a political biography*. Perth: University of Western Australia Press, 1974.

Tennant, Kylie. *Evatt: politics and justice*. Sydney: Angus and Robertson, 1970.

Young, Irwin. *Theodore: his life and times*. Sydney: Alpha Books, 1971.

Index

Abyssinia, 101-3
Anstey, F., 75, 95
Arbitration, 14, 16, 117-18
Australian Constitution, 9, 13, 78-9, 143-4, 148-51; referendum on, 58-9, 71, 87, 93, 123-5

Bank nationalization, 3, 9, 101, 113-14
Barnard, L. H., 30, 32, 137, 143
Blackburn, M. M., 92
Bowen, L. F., 30-1, 152-3
Bretton Woods agreement, 101, 114-16

Cabinet, 18, 21, 23, 33-5; solidarity, 23, 25, 32, 33, 118
Cairns, J. F., 30-2, 39, 43-6, 49-50, 51-3, 119, 143, 151
Calwell, A. A., 3, 10, 45, 47, 102, 107-8, 110-11, 119, 131-3
Cameron, C. R., 30, 137, 151-3
Caucus: alliance with, 70, 73-5; attacks on, 17-18; attendance at, 12; committees of, 19; directions to, 7, 18, 56-7, 61-3, 122, 131-2, 133-5; election, (of leaders) 39-50, (of ministers) 7, 23-36; formation of, 12, 15; and national government, 101, 105-6; obedience to law, 104-5; powers of, 7-8, 39-41, 47-50, 70, 75-6, 85, 93-5, 145-6; relations with cabinet, 18, 21, 36-8, 53-5, 98-9, 114-16; rules of, 12, 16, 19; splits, 79-86, 96-8, 119; working methods of, 12, 16, 19, 21
Charlton, M., 60, 62, 75, 80-3
Chifley, J. B., 3, 8, 29, 36, 39, 42-3, 54, 101, 102, 113-18, 123, 127
Childe, V. G., 21
Communist Party, 2, 3, 87, 91-3, 101-2, 116-17, 135; attempts to ban, 119-25
Connor, R. F. X., 143, 145-6
Conscription, 2, 3, 10, 71, 79-86, 101, 106-13, 119, 132-3; referendum on, 71, 79
Crean, F., 30, 37, 43-6, 152-3
Curtin, J., 3, 8, 29, 36, 38-9, 42, 46-7, 50-1, 101-10, 118

Daly, F. M., 30, 43-6
Deakin, A., 24, 53, 70, 73-4
Dedman, J. J., 32-3, 116
Democratic Labor Party, 3, 119-20, 139-40
Double dissolution, 2, 4, 119, 140, 147-8

Election: of leaders, 39-50; of ministers, 24-36; of officials, 5, 7, 15
Evatt, H. V., 3, 29, 42-3, 102, 116, 119, 125-9

Federal Conference, 1, 5-7, 18, 80, 115; *1900*, 1, 12-13; *1902*, 12-14, 17, 20; *1905*, 25; *1908*, 22, 25-6; *1912*, 56, 58-9; *1915*, 56; *1916*, 56, 71, 84-6; *1919*, 33; *1921*, 89-91; *1924*, 91-3; *1931*, 97; *1940*, 101, 105-6; *1942*, 106-10; *1943*, 111-13; *1945*, 116-17; *1951*, 120-2; *1963*, 129-32; affiliation with communists, 91-3; powers of, 56-9, 61-2, 64, 87, 131-2; representation at, 64-6; 'thirty-six faceless men', 131-2
Federal Executive, 5, 7, 119, 127-9, 135-7; formation of, 56, 59-60; intervention in Victoria, 120, 127-9, 137-8; powers of, 60-1, 63, 97-8, 114-16; relations with New South Wales Branch, 7, 60-2, 88, 97-8, 122
Fenton, J. M., 60, 81, 95-6
Fisher, A., 2, 8, 10, 22, 26-8, 39, 41, 56, 58-9, 71, 77-8, 84
Forde, F.M., 42-3, 102-3
Foreign bases, 119, 129-32
Fraser, J. M., 4, 52, 143-54

Gair, V., 120, 139-40
George III, 149
Givens, T., 81, 83-4
Governor-general, 4, 143, 147-51

Harradine, B., 120, 135-7
Hawke, R. J., 152
Higgs, W. G., 32
Hughes, W. M., 2, 8, 10, 18, 28-9, 39, 41, 53-4, 56, 58-9, 71-2, 77, 79-86

Income tax, 9
Industrial groups, 119, 125-7, 129
Ireland, 87-9

Kennedy, J. F., 130, 133
Kerr, J., 147-51

Labor governments: performance of, 71, 75-8, 93-5, 100, 141-2, 145; sacking of, 147-51
Lang, J. T., 2, 88, 96-7

159